Reviews of National Policies for Education

Lifelong Learning in Norway

OECD

ORGANISATION FOR ECONOMIC CO-OPERATION AND DEVELOPMENT

ORGANISATION FOR ECONOMIC CO-OPERATION AND DEVELOPMENT

Pursuant to Article 1 of the Convention signed in Paris on 14th December 1960, and which came into force on 30th September 1961, the Organisation for Economic Co-operation and Development (OECD) shall promote policies designed:

- to achieve the highest sustainable economic growth and employment and a rising standard of living in Member countries, while maintaining financial stability, and thus to contribute to the development of the world economy;
- to contribute to sound economic expansion in Member as well as non-member countries in the process of economic development; and
- to contribute to the expansion of world trade on a multilateral, non-discriminatory basis in accordance with international obligations.

The original Member countries of the OECD are Austria, Belgium, Canada, Denmark, France, Germany, Greece, Iceland, Ireland, Italy, Luxembourg, the Netherlands, Norway, Portugal, Spain, Sweden, Switzerland, Turkey, the United Kingdom and the United States. The following countries became Members subsequently through accession at the dates indicated hereafter: Japan (28th April 1964), Finland (28th January 1969), Australia (7th June 1971), New Zealand (29th May 1973), Mexico (18th May 1994), the Czech Republic (21st December 1995), Hungary (7th May 1996), Poland (22nd November 1996), Korea (12th December 1996) and the Slovak Republic (14h December 2000). The Commission of the European Communities takes part in the work of the OECD (Article 13 of the OECD Convention).

Publié en français sous le titre :
Examens des politiques nationales d'éducation
La formation tout au long de la vie en Norvège

Foreword

In the spirit of "international co-operation and (...) the exchange of views" the Norwegian Ministry of Education, Research and Church Affairs (KUF) invited the OECD Secretariat to undertake an examination of lifelong learning in Norway that would permit sharing their experience and learning from others. The review was organised within the framework of the OECD's education policy reviews. In 2000 the Secretariat assembled a Review Team to assess the Norwegian efforts to make lifelong learning for all a reality. The team was chaired by Ingrid Moses, Vice-Chancellor, University of New England, Armidale, New South Wales, Australia. Other members were Ferdinand Mertens, Inspector General for Education, the Netherlands; Åsa Sohlman, Director, Ministry of Industry, Employment and Communications, Sweden; and Mark van Buren, Director of Research, American Society for Training and Development, Alexandria, Virginia, the United States. The team was supported by Gregory Wurzburg of the OECD Secretariat. The team visited Norway to carry out a number of interviews to gather further facts and solicit views on a range of issues related to lifelong learning in Norway. The Review Team also benefited from other background material provided by the Secretariat; this included the most recent *Economic Surveys* of Norway (OECD, 2000); a report on financing lifelong learning in Norway, and material from a number of "thematic reviews" of early childhood education and care policy, transition from initial education to working life, tertiary education and adult learning.

This report is the result of the inquiry. It is divided into two parts. The Background Report was prepared by the Norwegian authorities. It presents the Norwegian definition of lifelong learning and describes the national context in which lifelong learning is being implemented. It then provides an overview of the different arenas within which lifelong learning occurs and the challenges that must be met; presents evidence on demand for, participation in, and provision of learning opportunities; and summarises measures to facilitate lifelong learning.

The OECD Examiners' Report was prepared by the team; Chapter 2 which was contributed by Gregory Wurzburg reviews the social, economic, political, and institutional context within which Norway has articulated its vision of lifelong learning. Chapter 3 examines the goals and objectives of lifelong learning in Norway, who it is for, and who it involves. Chapter 4 examines unfinished aspects of the lifelong learning agenda in Norway, with a focus on integration of learning and working life. Chapter 5 addresses the issue of implementation of lifelong learning across multiple public policy areas and in co-operation with the social partners. Chapter 6 discusses overriding principles to guide formulation and implementation of further policies for lifelong learning. Annex II.A lists recommendations by chapter and section.

This volume is published on the responsibility of the Secretary-General of the OECD.

Table of Contents

Part I

Background Report

Part II
The Examiners' Report

List of Boxes

List of Tables

Part I

Part II

List of Figures

Part I

BACKGROUND REPORT

Chapter 1

Starting Point for the Inquiry

1.1. Chosen perspectives

The topic "lifelong learning" is broad. In order to make the review manageable, it has been necessary to limit the scope of the report and to choose some perspectives. One strategy has been to concentrate on information making it possible to answer questions related to OECD's four strategies for lifelong learning (OECD, 1996, p. 21). These can be formulated in four questions: what has Norway done to:

- strengthen the foundations for learning throughout life by improving access to early childhood education, revitalising schools and supporting the growth of other formal and non-formal learning organisations and situations? This question will be especially important in relation to early childhood education, primary and secondary school.

- promote coherent links between learning and work by establishing pathways and bridges that will facilitate more flexible movement between education and training and work? This is important dealing with secondary and tertiary education.

- rethink the roles and responsibilities of all partners – including the Government and the Ministry – who provide opportunities for learning?

- create incentives for individuals, employers and those who provide education and training to invest more in lifelong learning?

Competence development is the main task of the formal educational system, both public and private. However, private and public enterprises and services also contribute substantially to enhance the level of competence in their staff. Surveys indicate that the investment made by companies and services is at the same level as public allocations to formal educational. The intention is that the report shall reflect both learning arenas, as they are important elements related to lifelong learning. The formal education system is given much more space, however. This is due to the fact we have more or at least more easily available information about formal education.

The review poses several evaluative and normative questions. The purpose of the national report is to present information making it possible to answer these normative questions. The national report itself is, however, in its nature mainly descriptive. The report addresses the educational system as a whole and over the lifecycle of individuals. It focuses primarily on the system-wide and cross-cutting issues. The report refers to particular components of the educational system only to give facts and to illuminate important points and principles.

The report is firstly occupied with policy and political goals. This includes both short-term and long-term goals and goals of the school system and of other agents – both public and private – engaged in lifelong learning. The superior objectives for the whole educational system are presented initially. In addition to educational institutions, lifelong learning to a great extent is an ongoing activity integrated in working life, and the competence is the result of processes outside the school system. Attention has therefore been devoted to this activity.

Secondly, the intention is that the report shall contain some information about the effects and empirical status of lifelong learning in Norway. This covers such questions as:

- How do the *barnehager*[1] and the school system being part of lifelong learning prepare their ordinary pupils and students for further learning (knowledge – motivation – attitude) in a lifelong learning perspective?

- What possibilities are offered to persons who are over-aged compared to ordinary pupils to be enrolled in the school system?

- What opportunities do persons have to get new or to bring up to date their competence in the formal school system and on informal arenas?

- What is the situation for groups as handicapped, minority-groups, drop-outs and adults with poor qualifications?

- What agents are involved in lifelong learning, both public and private, what is the agents' responsibility and how are their efforts co-ordinated?

- What measures – statutory, economic and organisational – are at disposal to stimulate lifelong learning so that the political objectives are reached?

- Are the transitions from one part of the educational system to another smooth and do they function well? Are there well-defined paths through the system, and is it easy to change from work to education and back to work again several times in a lifetime?

- How is learning integrated in working life?

1.2. Definition of "lifelong learning"

Lifelong learning is more a kind of perspective than a new educational system. It can, however, involve new pedagogy and organisations. Lifelong learning should be regarded as the normal state in a modern society, and not as a possibility for the few who want or have to plot a new course in life.

In lifelong learning the individual is the focal point of policy. This implies that lifelong learning policies and programmes are to be judged primarily from the individual's point of view. In this perspective important questions are if learning opportunities are obvious and accessible and if the results are evident and useable. But it also needs to be evaluated from a societal perspective. This raises questions such as: Do lifelong learning in the public education, labour market programmes, education given by private institutions and working life complement each other? Do they compete with each other in an unfavourable way? And can the government take account of learning in different sectors and reallocate resources across formal sectors?

In addition to important features mentioned above, the following understanding is used as a basis for this report:[2]

- Lifelong learning is system-wide, it embraces education and training given at all levels in the formal school-system and on non-formal and informal arenas. It also comprises concepts as "further education", "continuing education", "distance education", and "adult education". Lifelong learning involves learning and training "from cradle to grave", and it focuses on the standards of knowledge and skills needed by all in all phases of a life span.

- The objectives of lifelong learning are to ensure that initial education and training provides a sound foundation for further learning, *i.e.* learn to learn, and that opportunities for learning during adulthood are available to everyone. Thus the learner and learning more than the teacher and teaching are put in the centre of attention. Lifelong learning presupposes that motivation to learn is instilled early in childhood in order to generate a capacity for self-directed learning.

- The purpose of lifelong learning is related to society at large, to different groups and interests and to individuals. It should map both economic objectives and objectives related to enhance social cohesion, democratic participation, equality, a second chance, etc. Since preparation for work cannot be regarded as a once-for-all process, it pays attention to the multiple transitions between learning, working and living throughout life.

- Lifelong learning for all requires a connection between the formal educational system, experience and learning in working and in every day life.

13

This definition is much in accordance with the official Norwegian concept. In the Report to the *Storting* No. 42 (1997-98), *The Competence Reform*, the Government states that "lifelong learning" covers all organised and unorganised learning throughout the whole life, including formal as well as informal education through work and other activities (p. 9). The same report emphasises that the Competence Reform must have two dimensions:

- Firstly, it must have a pragmatic objective in the sense that working life must be supplied with the competence necessary for a positive development. This involves working life itself, the authorities at all levels, educational institutions and certainly the individuals who must be in the centre.

- Secondly, the individual does not have value only as a wheel in a well-functional working life. Man is not the mean; man is the aim in itself. In addition to brain and hands, lifelong learning therefore must take into account emotions, values, mind and social contact (Report to the *Storting* No. 42, p. 3).

Notes

1. Direct translation of the German word "Kindergarten". This is a common term for different types of early childhood education and care institutions under the legislation of the Norwegian Day Care Institution Act, covering the age group 0-5 years.

2. This definition is mostly taken from OECD (1996), p. 15.

Chapter 2

The National Context

This chapter concentrates on the main characteristics of the Norwegian society. This includes important political objectives, administrative and industrial structure, the current economic and educational status and demography. The information is selected to give the background for the Norwegian efforts to facilitate and stimulate lifelong learning.

2.1. Political objectives for social and economic development

The objectives of the Government's economic policy (Report to the *Storting* No. 1, 1999-2000, N*asjonalbudsjettet*, p. 1) are to give everybody employment and to administer Norway's natural resources and milieu properly in a long-term perspective. The Norwegian oil-fortune should be administered to the benefit of future generations and in such a way that the country avoids a pressure on its economy. The Government is occupied with maintaining the scattered population-structure, and the economic policy is used to check the centralisation that has accelerated over the last years. The priorities of the country's regional policy are to develop the industry, to maintain and create new employment, stimulate establishment of new enterprises and to prevent migration from the districts.

The welfare state shall be developed further; it shall contribute to the security of both families and individuals, and make personal growth and development possible in all phases of life. The welfare state shall offer education, treatment and care in case of illness and economic security when the inhabitants become old, disabled and unemployed. This presupposes a public sector large enough where the services continuously are made more efficient and adjusted to the needs of the population.

A main target for the Government's trade and industrial policy is to strengthen the competitive powers of the Norwegian industry through innovation. An important element is to use any individual's knowledge, creativeness and ideas as a basis for establishing new business. As a consequence of industrial globalisation the enterprises operate to a greater extent on a market unrestricted by national boarders. In this situation, location, access to competent labour force, low costs of transportation and communication will be of great importance, according to the Government (Proposition to the *Storting* No. 1, 1999-2000, *Nærings- og handels-departementet*, p. 1).

2.2. Administrative structure

Norway is a constitutional, parliamentarian and democratic monarchy in the north-western part of Europe, the area is 324 000 km^2, and the population in 1999 was 4.445 million. The country is organised in three administrative levels:

- Important agents on *state level* are the Parliament (the *Storting*), the Government and several directorates. The State has an overall responsibility for the whole education sector and administers universities and university colleges directly. The State runs some hospitals and is responsible for parts of the communication systems. Labour market authorities are also part of the State system.

- The country is divided into 19 regional entities, *counties*, having from 75 000 to 480 000 inhabitants. The responsibilities of the counties are primarily upper secondary education, including both academic and vocational training, regional and cultural matters, hospitals, energy-supply, roads and other parts of the transportation system. Local taxes and national funding finance these assignments.

- Further the country is organised in 435 local units – *municipalities*. They are responsible for running day care institutions, public primary and lower secondary schools (compulsory schools), primary health and social care system, homes for the aged and nursing homes. Local taxes and national funding provide the economic basis for executing these assignments.

The *Storting* has implemented decentralisation of responsibility and political power, delegating considerable authority and financial freedom of action to the local level. Block grants are given, and county and municipal authorities determine their activities within the frames of existing legislation and regulations. In an international perspective, however, Norway is still characterised by a strong political centre, favourable attitudes towards the State and a relatively centrally regulated regime.

2.3. Industrial and business structure of Norway[1]

Norwegian industry and business consist predominantly of small- (fewer than 20 employees) and medium-sized (21-100 employees) enterprises. In 1997 about 149 000 enterprises were registered in private sector. Of these 92% had less than 20 employees, 81% had less than 5 employees and only 0.5% had more than 100 employees. When we look both at the total number of employment and their collective turnover, small- and medium-sized enterprises surpass the activity of the bigger companies. Small- and medium-sized business had more than 62% of employment and about 54% of the economic turnover. This type of enterprise structure makes investment in on-the-job training difficult when there are no co-operative arrangements or government support. Surveys indicate that small- and medium-sized enterprises therefore have a greater problem in maintaining the level of competence among leaders and staff members.

One important characteristic of Norwegian industrial structure is the strong element of rather big cornerstone enterprises in local communities. Many local communities are built around one – in many cases export-oriented enterprise – making the community vulnerable for international economic trends influencing the dominating enterprise.

2.4. Demography

2.4.1. Population development

Norway's population was 4.445 million by January 1st 1999. Statistics Norway has made alternative prognosis until 2050. Table 2.1 will only present the alternative "medium national growth" compared with the situation today.

According to this alternative the relative proportion of children and youths will probably diminish gradually, while the proportion of middle aged and old people will grow steadily in the coming decades. In 10-20 years the average age of the labour force will therefore increase. As a consequence, the proportion and number of employees with dated basic education will also increase. And smaller cohorts entering the labour market will lead to considerably less growth in the employable part of the population in absolute terms (NOU, 1997, p. 71).

Table 2.1. **Prognosis for population development in Norway (N = 1 000)**

Age group	1999		2005		2010		2030	
	N	%	N	%	N	%	N	%
All ages	4 445	100	4 592	100	4 692	100	5 085	100
1-5	362	8.1	348	7.6	335	7.1	354	7.0
6-19	785	17.7	844	18.4	859	18.3	817	16.1
20-44	1 609	36.2	1 582	34.5	1 565	33.4	1 590	31.3
45-66	1 069	24.0	1 218	26.5	1 324	28.2	1 381	27.2
67+	619	13.9	599	13.0	609	13.0	941	18.5

Source: Statistics Norway.

Seventy-four per cent of the population live in towns or built-up areas, but still many people live in areas with scattered population. The main areas of concentration are around the central eastern areas with Oslo as the focal point, the southern and western coastal regions with Kristiansand, Stavanger and Bergen as major cities, and further north the areas around Trondheim and Tromsø. The 1990s are characterised by centralisation of the population from more remote areas to the bigger cities and municipalities in their neighbourhood. This trend has been recently moderated, but Finnmark experienced the strongest net out-migration in 1998.

The Saami people form an ethnic and cultural minority in Norway, with a population of about 75 000, or 1.7% of the total population. The majority of the Saami live in the northern part of the country and in the capital, Oslo. The Saami Parliament was established in 1989. The Parliament is independent, elected by the Saami people and consists of 39 representatives. The Saami Parliament is consultative for the authorities in all questions concerning the Saami population.

2.4.2. A multicultural society

Until recently Norway was regarded as a homogeneous and mono-cultural society. In 1970, only 59 000 persons (1.5% of the total population) had parents born outside Norway. Gradually the number has increased and, in 1999, the number was 261 000 or 5.9% of the population.

The mixture of the background of the lingual minorities has also changed in the same period. In 1970 more than 84% had their roots in the Nordic countries, in Western Europe, North America or Oceania. In 1999 their proportion had dropped to 36%. In the same period the inhabitants originating from Eastern Europe and Turkey, Asia and Latin-America have grown from 16% to 64% (Statistics Norway, 1999).

Earlier, foreign cultural elements had time to be integrated in what was regarded as the "Norwegian" culture and in that respect contributed to a gradual change of the dominant culture. The rapid increase in the last decades has made other cultural expressions – values, ways of living, different appearance, religious expressions – much more visible in the Norwegian society. Handling this does not only require time; it also requires tolerance for cultural variety.

This has had impact on the educational system. In the end of 1998, 8 877 children in early child care and education institutions represented lingual minorities. This corresponds to 4.7% of the total number of children in early childhood education (Report to the Storting No. 27, 1999-2000, Barnehage til beste for barn og foreldre). In 1998-99, 36 000 pupils in compulsory school belonged to lingual minorities. This corresponds to 6% of the total number of pupils. The biggest minority groups speak Urdu, English, Vietnamese, Spanish and Arabic. In upper secondary education the number representing lingual minorities was 6 700 pupils (approximately 4%) speaking more than a hundred different languages. The most numerous groups are Urdu and Vietnamese.

2.5. Main economic development

In 1999, GDP was NOK 1 189 348 million (approximately $130 000 million). The most important export products are petroleum (including gas), foodstuffs (including fish and fish products), paper and wood-related products and metals. There has been a strong growth in Norwegian economy since the boom started in 1993. From 1993 to 1998 mainland GDP has increased with approximately 20% or 3.7% each year on an average. Including both industrial production and services the growth has been balanced. The curve has recently flattened, and the growth in the mainland economy in 1999 is estimated to 0.5% and scarcely 1% in 2000. When oil- and gas-production is included, however, the growth in GDP is estimated at 0.9% in 1999 and 2.9% in 2000, reflecting further expansion of oil prices and production. The trend is towards an economy divided into two parts: the demand from the protected part is still strong, while the demand from the petroleum-related part of the industry will probably be reduced for a period.

The yearly growth in productivity was in the 1960s and 1970s between 3.5 and 4.7%. In the two last decades of the last century this dropped to 2% per year on an average, which was very close to the productivity growth in the United States in the same period. When we look in more detail at the development in the 1990s the Norwegian productivity has dropped from 3.5% in the beginning of the decade to 1.3% in 1998.[2]

Public finances are strong by traditional measures. The surplus on the general government balance has been 6-7% in the past years, and was estimated to be approximately NOK 81 billion in the budget for 2000, which is nearly 15% of nominal GDP; this level is expected to continue in the medium term. The authorities have built up an oil-fund as a reserve and for future investments. The size of the fund was estimated in 2000 to close to NOK 400 billion. The dependency on the petroleum industry is high, and there would have been an estimated deficiency of NOK 13 billion if we disregard the petroleum revenue.

2.6. Education levels

The educational level in Norway is high relative to levels in other OECD countries (OECD, 2001). Table 2.2 provides details of the population broken down by highest level of educational attainment achieved, age and sex.

There are important nuances to note in the general pattern of high levels of educational attainment:

- There are considerable regional differences. In Hedmark 30.7% had secondary school as their highest level. In Oslo only 17.7% had left the educational

Table 2.2. **Highest completed education level of persons 16 years and over, by age and sex**

	Total	Primary and lower secondary level	Upper secondary level	Tertiary level (1-4 years)	Tertiary level (4 years >)
Both sexes by age	3 500 909	24	54	18	4
16-19	212 643	30	70	0	–
20-39	1 294 685	8	63	24	5
40-49	616 268	16	55	22	7
50-54	294 693	24	52	18	6
55-59	207 448	31	49	15	5
60-66	244 981	41	44	12	3
67 >	630 191	54	36	7	3
Males	1 714 314	22	56	16	6
16-19	108 723	30	70	0	–
20-39	660 354	9	66	20	5
40-49	314 790	16	55	20	9
50-54	150 284	22	51	18	9
55-59	103 640	28	48	16	8
60-66	118 944	36	45	13	6
67 >	257 579	47	40	8	5
Females	1 786 595	27	52	19	2
16-19	103 920	29	71	0	–
20-39	634 331	8	60	29	3
40-49	301 478	17	55	25	3
50-54	144 409	26	53	19	2
55-59	103 808	34	49	15	2
60-66	126 037	45	43	11	1
67 >	372 612	59	34	6	1

Source: Statistics Norway (1998), *Weekly Bulletin*, No. 50.

system at this point. On the opposite end of the scale 36% of Oslo's population had passed exams from universities or university colleges, while only 16.1% had exams on this level in Oppland and Hedmark.

- Regional disparities in education patterns are reinforced by the fact that persons with higher education are more likely to move from more remote districts than persons with less education. Though the number of employees with higher education increased nationally by 7.3% from 1987 to 1997, nearly a third of this growth was concentrated in Oslo.

- There is a considerable difference in educational level related to age and sex. A greater proportion of the cohorts born after 1955 has upper secondary and completed tertiary education than the generation born before that time. This is due to the restructuring and expansion of the lower secondary level in the 1960s. Older men are, on average, more highly-educated than older women; that pattern is less pronounced for 40-55-year-olds. Women in their 20s and 30s are somewhat better educated than men.

2.7. Employment

The expansion in Norwegian economy has been accompanied by a strong growth in employment. The employment increased by 238 000 persons from 1993 to 1998. This corresponds to approximately 10% of the total labour force. The employment rate has never been so high as in 1998 when 80.8% of people aged 16 to 64, and 73% of people in the age group 16 to 74 were engaged in working life.[3] Comparable figures for other OECD countries are 69.8% and for the EU the employment rate is 67.9%. The proportion of long-term unemployment is relatively low compared to most other countries. In 1998, 8% and in 1999 7% of the unemployed had been job seekers for more than 12 months. On average the job seekers were unemployed for approximately 16 weeks in 1999. The development of the labour market has also been more positive for women than for men and also more so for young job seekers than for the remaining labour force.

There are nuances in this positive picture. A greater proportion of employed women in Norway work part-time (48%) compared to 25% in OECD countries. Norwegian women do also make more traditional choices of occupation than women do in other OECD countries. In Norway 80% of women work in the ten occupations that are most female-dominated while the OECD average is 60%.

Persons with poor formal qualifications are over-represented among the unemployed. Figures from 1995 show that the unemployment rate among persons without upper secondary education was 6.5%, and 5% among those with upper secondary education. Only 2.7% of the persons with tertiary education were registered as unemployed at that time (NOU, 1997, p. 71). The same tendency can be observed in data from 1997 (Norges Forskningsråd, 1999). Other figures show that 84% of the population having higher education are working, compared to 79% of those having passed upper secondary education and 64% of those having only compulsory education (NOU, 1997, pp. 79-81). Also the percentage of unemployment among immigrants is considerably higher than in the labour force at large. Statistics from the Central Bureau of Statistics in November 1999 show that 6.6% of first generation immigrants were unemployed.

2.8. Education, qualifications requirements and economic outcomes

There is an ongoing restructuring of and mobility between different industries and branches. Compared to 1998 there is a clear decline in the number employed in industrial production, and some reduction in primary industry and transport and communication. The strongest growth has come in business-services, education and health and social services. The dynamics in the labour market is under-pinned by the fact that a considerable number of jobs are created and lost every year. A study of Norwegian manufacturing and service industries during the period 1976 to 1992 shows that the annual job creation and loss was equivalent to about 7-9% of the total number of positions (Salvanes, 1996).

The research also suggests that this re-structuring has consequences for qual-ifications requirements. In the long run the overall tendency is to replace jobs that require the least skills with jobs that demand more education and skills. This has contributed to higher unemployment among persons with poor qualifications. Thus, young people had more problems in getting into the labour market, because they had not finished higher education and lacked work experience. From 1993 to 1995 the relative proportion of jobs where secondary education was regarded as most productive increased from 35 to 44% (Larsen, 1996). But this does not necessarily imply an overall shift upwards in qualifications requirements. The number of jobs where higher education was regarded as most productive decreased from 59 to 50%. This has provided grounds for some to suggest that there may be a surplus in the supply of highly-educated labour in the future. While, if this were true, it would not necessarily argue against the need for compe-tence development in working life, it would suggest that competence develop-ment might take the form of something other than additional years of university studies and diplomas (NOU, 1997, p. 54).

There have been appreciable payoffs to education at both a macro-economic and micro-economic level. Research suggests that education contributed mod-estly to economic growth in the period 1972-1990. Changes in the educational level of the labour force were found to have contributed to 9% of the growth in productivity per working hour in Norwegian industry in this period. Higher educa-tion has in addition significance for local industrial development. Being rather big institutions, universities and university colleges bring substantial income to their regions and municipalities. Through higher educational institutions the regions have competence centres at their disposal that contribute to problem-solving, competence development and development of new enterprises. The multiplica-tion effect of higher education institutions is calculated to be from 1.7 to 2.5. This is considerably higher than corresponding figures for other kinds of activity where the factor normally varies from 1.2 to 1.5 (NOU, 2000a).

Norwegian studies on the impact of education on the individuals' income show a rather homogeneous picture. One survey covering the time-span from 1980 to 1995 indicates that there are positive economic returns from participation in continuing education and training. On average wages increased by 5 to 6% for an additional year of education; 6.5% for employees in the private sector and 4.5% in the public. There are small differences in the effect of education for women and men, though returns are slightly stronger for women. The return related to length of education however is lower in Norway than in most Western countries, but on the same level as in Denmark and Sweden.

Analyses indicate that the return has decreased in the 1980s and 1990s, more for those with a general education, less for those who chose a professional education. The effect depends upon educational level. The higher the level, the higher the return, and the return is higher if the additional year leads to a qualification. There are also great variations between the sectors. The general trait is that the return is higher in the private than in the public sector.

The effect of education has been relatively stabile in the 1990s, but some studies indicate that differences in income between groups with different educational level in private sector have increased in the 1990s. Other studies show that persons who participate in ordinary job market courses increase their possibilities of receiving a job compared to those who do not participate. A third article documents that persons attending labour market training in 1991-92 had an increase of about 6% of their yearly income compared to those who did not participate. There have also been attempts to estimate the total income over a life span for groups with or without tertiary education. The conclusion is that lawyers, doctors and masters in business economy earn more than the reference group, while teachers and nurses earn less.

2.9. The Scandinavian model[4]

To understand the Norwegian policy and efforts within lifelong learning, one should take into account what is often named "the Scandinavian or Nordic Model". The model has the following main characteristics:

- At national level the Nordic countries have a long democratic tradition, a rather strong centralised and regulated economic regime, a socially founded redistribution of benefits.

- They have a strong and relatively undivided union movement, a strong social-democratic party and centralised tripartite co-operation between authorities, labour unions and employers' federations.

- At enterprise level, the model is characterised by strong traditions for negotiations, a high percentage of the Norwegian employees are organised in one of the federations, a low conflict level (stability), flexible problem-solving through different forms of participation and co-operation.

- In educational policy they have been progressive and pupil centred underlining pupil activity in the tradition of John Dewey and the German concept Arbeitsschule.

Due to the highly-centralised and influential trade unions and employers' federations, collective agreements have a dominant position regarding labour regulation. The scope of the agreements is not only to fix wages; they also regulate employee participation in decision-making, consultation and co-operation and training and education. Collective agreements have, to some extent, acquired a law function, since they often extend statutory protection and legal rights.

As part of the model, it is customary in the Norwegian civil service that trade unions are consulted in a wide variety of contexts. The social partners of working life are regularly closely involved in social, educational and legislative reforms: as members of official public commissions, through consultations in the process and through hearings. In connection with educational reforms the authorities also involve bodies representing parents, students and pupils.

Many of these characteristics can be observed in the Competence Reform that has been given high priority in the Norwegian society recently. Social partners have taken important initiatives, and they have been involved in developing a national policy in this field. They have also accepted their share in and their responsibility for effectuating the reform. The authorities have on their side initiated a report, submitted the Report to the *Storting*, followed up the proposal by changing relevant laws and funding parts of the reform and through an action plan. This will be commented in more detail later.

Notes

1. The paragraph is mainly based upon Report to the *Storting* No. 41 (1997-98), *Næringspolitikk inn i det 21.århundre.*
2. Address given by Governor Svein Gjedrem, Norges Bank, Thursday 17th of February 2000 (see *http://www.norges-bank.no/english/*).
3. *Norwegian Labour Market Policies* 2000, Report to the Norwegian Parliament, Ministry of Labour and Government Administration, Oslo.
4. The information is obtained from the Norway Social Partners' Joint Action Programme for Enterprise Development.

Chapter 3

The Learning Arenas – An Overview[1]

The concept of lifelong learning has re-entered the political agenda in recent years, particularly following the "European year of lifelong learning" in 1996. In keeping to the principle of lifelong learning, Norway is implementing comprehensive revisions and reforms in the country's initial education and training systems.

According to the philosophy of lifelong learning, education is considered an entity, encompassing all ages and all types of learning environments, including occupational and social knowledge and skills acquired outside the formal educational system. The system shall not only prepare young people for entry into employment or tertiary study, but also provide them with a broad knowledge base and foundation for lifelong learning.

3.1. An intense reform period

The general objectives of the reforms are to increase the competence in the population, ensure quality and create a better integrated and co-ordinated and more coherent educational system and educational policy. Another general objective of the reforms is that education and training at all levels shall be the basis for a future system for lifelong learning (NOU, 1997, p. 98). Further, it has been a long-range policy to integrate theoretical and vocational education and training and give these two educational directions equal status and prestige. Other goals especially connected to Reform 94 and Reform 97 are to develop a more flexible system, to increase the range of options available and to provide a wide scope of competency that prepares young people for a society undergoing continuous change. A parallel objective is to retain a decentralised school structure.

The reforms are founded on several motives: there is a strong pragmatic motive in the sense that education shall serve the needs for competence in the labour market. Secondly, the ambition is to establish a caring educational system. Thirdly, there is a focus on imparting cultural values and strengthening the pupils' identity. Further, the reforms uphold the policy of equal educational rights and opportunities. And lastly, the reforms contain a liberation-motive in the form of progressive pupil-centrism.

3.1.1. Measures to operationalise lifelong learning in the heart of the public school system

The authorities have taken several didactical measures to support lifelong learning. This can be observed in both the social and educational objectives of the public school system, in the curriculum, the working methods, the assessment system and in the roles of pupils, students and teachers.

From knowledge to competence: The Government papers from the 1990s introduce the concept of competence. This is a broader and more dynamic concept than knowledge. The authorities state that tomorrow's competence must embrace intellectual, creative, manual and social skills. The basic academic foundation must still be present. It must be broad and lasting and form the basis for mobility between trades and occupations. Competence for the future must also include the Norwegian tradition of popular adult education. It is an important aspect of this tradition to develop the individual to become democratic, participating and engaged in democratic and social issues. In addition to knowledge and skills, competency includes having the will and ability to use the knowledge and to apply it in real life situations. Competency should be basis for action, creativity and intuition and for ethical judgement and discernment (Report to the *Storting* No. 42, 1997-98, *The Competence Reform*, p. 13-14).

In order to meet the requirements of working life, employees in manual labour and practical occupations need general and theoretical insight. On the other hand, theoretical and general education should be linked with practice and real world to give better understanding and enhanced ability to apply theoretical knowledge. This understanding of competency is very present in the common Core Curriculum introduced by the Government in 1993.

The aims of education: Norwegian authorities have explicitly integrated important elements of the concept of lifelong learning among the principal objectives of the educational system. The educational system shall serve both the society and the individual. The ambition is to maintain an educational system that is among the world's best concerning academic standard and breadth in recruitment. The Minister of Education underscores that "a just educational system is the key to a just society".

According to the Core Curriculum "the aim of education is to furnish children, young people and adults with the tools they need to face the tasks of life and surmount its challenges together with others". Further it states that education shall qualify people for productive participation in today's labour force, and supply the basis for later shifts to occupations as yet not envisaged. This shall be obtained by giving the pupils skills needed for specialised tasks and a general level broad enough for re-specialisation later in life. Education shall impart lasting attitudes and learning (Core Curriculum, p. 5).

The objective is that pupils shall be integrated in the common culture, but at the same time develop their individuality and own characteristics. The comprehensive school must be characterised by diversity and variation and by an embracing and open-minded internal community. Adaptation is therefore an integrated part of public education and training. This includes both adaptation to the local community and to the needs, capacity and interests of the individuals.

Curriculum: In primary and lower secondary education greater emphasis is put on common subject matter and on art and culture in the curriculum introduced in 1997. It is a basic principle that there should be made local and individual adjustments. The proportion of common subject matter increases up through the grades. The teaching shall, increasingly, be organised in cross-disciplinary themes and project work. The schools are encouraged to use the neighbourhood and local community to exemplify, concretise and supplement the common subject matter in the different disciplines and themes.

In upper secondary education the specialisation has been reduced, leaving specialisation to later stages and further training at work. Theory and practice shall be integrated in all areas and disciplines. In the future, vocational training is based on a common platform with greater elements of theoretical and general subject areas. Parallel to this, the intention has been to job-orient the common disciplines in all branches of study. As part of Reform 94 project work has become compulsory. The intention is to introduce a cross-disciplinary approach and to alter the teachers' and pupils' relationship and roles.

Educational methods and assessment: Play and social activities are regarded as important methods for learning and development for pre-school children. In primary and secondary school the methods applied shall give pupils opportunities to be active, acting, creative and autonomous. Pupils shall meet and solve practical and concrete tasks, tasks that develop their autonomy and that give them the opportunity to study a problem in depth and from different angles. The chosen methods shall strengthen the pupils' skills to collaborate. By doing this, they will learn from each other, they will acquire social and communicative abilities, skills to plan and assign tasks and responsibility, find answers to challenges and evaluate the result of their efforts and insight in democratic processes.

The educational reforms in the 1990s instructed the teacher to focus more upon informal assessment as a supplement to formal evaluation. At least at compulsory school level assessment is turned into a continuous activity similar to supervision. At primary and lower secondary levels there are no national exams all pupils have to pass. In grade 10, however, every pupil must pass one centrally given exam. The system in upper secondary education represents a combination of nation-wide and locally given exams.

27

Ideally, there should be consistence between educational aims, content, methods and the assessment system. To get a system in accord with itself the authorities have taken steps to develop a system that contributes to practical relevance of knowledge and that assesses the ability to apply knowledge in concrete and new contexts. The Government emphasises that pupils and apprentices shall actively participate in the evaluation process. In upper secondary education much is done to develop exams that are cross-disciplinary and are close to real life situations.

New roles for pupils and teachers: The Core Curriculum represents a shift of focus from teaching to learning. It is therefore expected that the learner – the pupil – show effort, strength of will and endurance. The pupils shall have the ability and will to manage their own learning and at the same time give their neighbour a helping hand when needed.

The teachers must be highly-qualified in their fields. They must have a sure grasp of their subject matter, and know how it should be conveyed to kindle curiosity, ignite interest and win respect for the subject adapted to the learners' abilities, needs and interests. These are requirements that teachers traditionally have met. The plan, however, also underscores the role of the teacher as a mediator, personal model, instructor and tutor. The teacher has become the leader of the pupils' community of work. This strengthens the teacher's role as an instructor and professional leader.

3.1.2. The Competence Reform

In the 1990s the accelerated changes in working life and society led to intense interest for competence renewal and development both for the sake of society, of the individual and the industry. The renewed interest for the perspective in the 1990s can be regarded as the terminal of a complete overhaul of the Norwegian educational system. The focus has been on adults and their competence needs to enter or to stay in working life. The Parliament initiated this phase of the reform wave in 1996 by asking the Government for a Report to the *Storting* on competence development. In answer to this the Government appointed the same year a commission (the *Buer Commission*) which discussed and reported on the following questions:

- the contribution of continuing education and training and the need for knowledge and skills in society, industry and public services and administration;

- the interaction and demarcation between the different public measures in the field of continuing education and training;

- impediments to and incentives for continuing education and training;

- the access to continuing education and training as a statutory right; and

- arrangements for the documentation and evaluation of skills.

The commission used international experiences and projects in its report, and evaluated the different models of continuing education and training. The social partners were well represented in the commission. In October 1997, the Buer Commission on adult education and the development of competence in working life and society delivered a report *New Competence. The Basis for a Comprehensive Policy for Continuing Education* (NOU, 1997). After a broad, public hearing the Government put a Report to the *Storting, The Competence Reform* (No. 42, 1997-98) for the Parliament in June 1998.

The Government states that the changes in society and labour market are now so rapid that lifelong learning must be systematic and integrated in the way the whole educational system is planned and organised. The dividing line between the educational system and working life must be reduced, and it is an ambition to establish a close co-operation between the social partners of working life, the individuals and the authorities to realise the reform.

According to the Government, the basis for the Competence Reform should be the need of the labour market, the society and the individual. The reform shall embrace all adults primarily both in and outside the labour market; it will have a broad, long-term perspective, and aim for broad, differentiated opportunities for adult education and continuing education and training provided by both public and private institutions and organisations.

The reform shall take into account several objectives:

- *Competence related to working life*: The reform must have a pragmatic aim in the sense that it must make arrangement providing Norwegian industry with the necessary competence to secure progress. The needs defined by working life must be given priority. By putting working life and the individual in focus the Competence Reform shall bring the Norwegian society forward and hopefully also benefit the international society.

- *Co-operation between working life and educational system*: The competence of the working force in general should be developed. The competence includes knowledge, skills and attitudes. Important attitudes are flexibility and ability to adapt to new job situations. The needs of the small- and medium-sized enterprises should be emphasised. The chosen measures must benefit and satisfy these enterprises' needs. It is therefore important to establish a closer collaboration between the educational system and the industry.

- *Maintaining social equality*: Education and competence have great importance for distribution of income and influence upon equality between the sexes, generations and social groups. It is important to avoid creating new class-divisions. The reform, therefore, cannot only include those in the labour market. It must also take into account those seeking jobs and those who represent a labour force reserve. Priority should be given to groups who have problems entering the labour market, *i.e.* women in part-time jobs, handicapped and unemployed.

- *Man as the ultimate aim*: The individual does not have value only as a highly competent wheel in a well-functioning working life. The Government states that man is not the mean, but the ultimate aim of the reform. The concept of knowledge must be broad and in addition to mind and hands, it must also comprise emotions, values, spirit and social abilities. A continuous competence development must have a long-term developmental perspective for the whole human being. It is therefore an objective to enhance the population's knowledge about political, social and cultural affairs.

The Report to the *Storting* focuses on a few important issues that can provide a better basis for developing and realising these plans. The reform is expected to:

- Continue the tradition of enlightenment where developing the individual to become active participants in the democracy and occupied with social affairs is emphasised. In this tradition knowledge and culture are united, carried by the vision that man is multidimensional.

- Secure adults an individual right to primary, lower and upper secondary education.

- Establish a system that documents and recognises adults' non-formal learning.

- Give employees statutory rights to study leave.

- Exempt employees from taxation of education paid by the employer.

- Reorganise the public educational system to meet the need of competence at the workplace.

An important objective is to develop educational opportunities that exploit the huge potential in the workplace as an arena of learning. One means will be to establish development programmes and funding schemes in order to encourage greater use of information and communications technology in teaching and the development of new flexible, user-adapted courses, adult teaching methods and media-based teaching. Other means will be joint projects between the workplace and the providers of competence in order to contribute to a systematic competence building. Other proposals are dependent on the social partners of working life. The Competence Reform has been one of the main issues in the annual wage negotiations and in other discussions about collective agreements.

The proposals in the Report to the *Storting* did not intend to meet all the challenges in basic and continuing education for adults. This will have to be a continuous task in the years to come, based on plans of action in the different sectors and branches of industry. The intention was that the Report to the *Storting* would be followed up by a national action plan for continuing education and adult education. This plan was published spring 2000.

The Government is planning a gradual implementation of the reform where the employers, the employees and the public must contribute. The Government is occupied with maintaining Norway's competitive powers in an international context. The implementation of the reform must therefore take into account the situation in the labour market and the development of interest, prices and wages in Norway compared to its competitors.

The authorities are occupied with another aspect of the reform: there is already an extensive further education activity in working life, and the industry spends great resources to secure relevant competence. The challenge for the reform, according to the authorities, will be to increase the quality and the return from these efforts, to enhance the activity and better the distribution.

The reform reinforces the policy shift in the 1960s. Social justice is still an important aspect, but education is mainly regarded as an investment and as a resource for the national economy and its competitiveness. The reform focuses on the needs of working life and the individual, on flexibility, mobility and economic return. It brings in some new aspects, however. On the one hand, the reform continues the Norwegian effort towards integration and uniform organisation by giving the formal school system an important role in adult education and lifelong learning. On the other hand, we can observe certain aspirations to de-institutionalise adult education. This implies that the market is given a stronger influence on the provisions, while the authorities' influence will be reduced.

3.2. Early childhood education and care

The national government has in recent years given high priority to safeguarding children and young people and their families, securing a healthy and stimulating environment during their growing up. A national programme to support parents in raising their children has been going on since 1994 and has now become a permanent offer to parents. The objective is to prevent psychosocial problems. An important goal is to strengthen parental function by using an approach that emphasised the parents' resources and their way of mastering their parental skills in raising their children. The programme is based on establishing a dialogue between parents and supporters representing different relevant services. A special effort is made to involve fathers in the daily routine of raising their children.

The main public provision for children from birth to compulsory school age, is the *barnehage*. The Day Care Institution Act of May 1995 regulates the activity and states that the purpose of the *barnehage* is to "provide children under school age with good opportunities for development and activity". The *barnehager* have a well-trained group of educated pre-school teachers.

The Ministry of Children and Family Affairs has the superior political responsibility. The administration and supervision of early childhood care institutions has increasingly been transferred to the municipalities. The municipalities or private non-profit organisations run most of the institutions. All *barnehager* receive a state subsidy from the Ministry of Children and Family Affairs through the municipality, all parents make payments for their children's attendance, and the municipality subsidises the public early childhood education that they own and run. The municipalities decide themselves whether they will subsidise private *barnehager* or not.

By 1999 attendance had reached 62% of the children aged one to five years which represents 189 000 children (Statistics Norway, 1999). Attendance in early childhood education increases with age. 27.8% of the one-year-olds, while more than 82% of the five-year-olds attended in 1999. Twenty-four per cent of the children attending *barnehage* in 1999 were less than 3 years of age and very few children were under twelve months. The reason for this may be a statutory right giving parents the choice between 52 weeks of leave at 80% of normal pay or 42 weeks at 100% in connection with the birth of a child. It is the goal of the Government that the system should have the capacity to accept every child who wants a place in a *barnehage* – full-time or part-time – by the year 2003.[2]

Anne Inger Borge has summed up Swedish and Norwegian studies on the impact of attending early childhood education (Søbstad, 2000 and Borge, 1998, pp. 152-153). She concludes that *barnehager* of high quality – and Norwegian institutions are regarded to have high quality – can have long-term positive effects on academic progress in school and on emotional and social aspects. The effects last until the persons are their 20s. Children having attended *barnehage* got better grades, they were more independent and showed higher ambitions than children who had been looked after at home. Children in early childhood education did also have less behaviour problems, and they were more confident. In particular boys showed a reduction in problem behaviour.

The cash benefit scheme (*kontantstøtten*), implemented in the end of the 1990s, has probably strengthened and maintained the distribution of age in the *barnehage*. This arrangement is aimed at families with one- and two-year-olds who do not use a fulltime programme in a *barnehage*. It is possible to combine part-time stay in *barnehage* and an abridged support. The support is approximately

NOK 3 000 per month for every child. The intention is that parents should spend more time together with their children.

The cash benefit scheme is under evaluation. So far statistics show that 75% of the families make use of the arrangement. Fathers with children in the actual age group are as active in working life as other males, and their employment rate is much higher than among mothers in the same situation. Some mothers receiving the cash support work or study less; very few fathers have changed their behaviour. The parents look after 62% of the children receiving support, but a considerable proportion has chosen other arrangements. So far the cash benefit scheme does not seem to have influenced dramatically what kind of arrangements parents prefer for their children.

3.3. The Norwegian public school system

The *Storting* sets the overall objectives for the educational system and passes the education acts. The Ministry of Education, Research and Church Affairs[3] has the overall responsibility for administering and for implementing the national educational policy. The Ministry determines standards and the general framework of teaching. This is done in form of syllabuses that state course objectives and national regulations for conducting examinations. Each county has a national education office that carries out central government functions.

Norway has still a rather centralised educational system in an international perspective. Norway has detailed curricula and syllabuses for primary and secondary school, and until recently a national approval system for textbooks.[4] The trend is towards greater flexibility, however, and there has been an ideological change in choice of political instruments. The ambition has been to substitute direct regulations and governing with governing by targets. So far this change is uncompleted and today both governing principle live side by side. In an evaluation of higher education this regime is described as "rule-oriented managing by objectives" (Kyvik, 1999, p. 224).

The State has delegated responsibility and decision-making power to municipalities and counties in questions related to education. The municipalities have responsibility for running and administering *barnehager*, primary and lower secondary school, while the counties have responsibility for the upper secondary education. The State, however, contributes substantially to cover the expenses through a block grant system that comprises all central government support to education, culture as well as health care. Higher education institutions are funded directly by the Ministry, and the university and university college boards report to the Ministry. The institutions have full academic freedom, and the universities do also have extensive autonomy in administrative affairs. The funding of higher education is

33

the result of framework allocations and allocations based upon results. The last element is increasing.

In a few fields, there are still earmarked grants: *i*) this goes for the teaching of mother tongue and Norwegian as a second language to migrant children and for the teaching of Norwegian as a second language to adult migrants; *ii*) further, extra state subsidies are given to avoid regional disparities, *e.g.* to schools or vocational courses where recruitment is so low that courses cannot be organised in each county and *iii*) to schools for pupils with special needs; *iv*) there are also special measures for the three northernmost counties; *v*) enterprises approved for training receive state grants through the county authorities to cover the cost of the training component in the apprenticeship period.

According to the Education Act, the State is responsible for developing adult education in general. The municipalities on their hand shall plan and develop the primary and lower secondary education for adults in their community, while the counties have the same responsibility and tasks concerning upper secondary education. If the need for teaching programmes cannot be covered by existing provisions, approved study associations can offer the courses.

3.3.1. *Primary and lower secondary education – compulsory education*

From July 1st 1997, the *Storting* lowered the school entrance age from seven to six years. At the same time compulsory education was extended from nine to ten years. The arguments were partly *economic*: by transposing six-year-old children to pupils the authorities could exploit the idle capacity in primary schools on the one hand and give a greater proportion of younger children access to *barnehage* on the other. Secondly, the Government underscored the *technical-cognitive competence requirements*: private and public working life required higher competence and new skills. Compulsory school from six would give the best prospects to secure continuity and to offer a coherent and co-ordinated educational programme. Thirdly, it was important that children were offered *an equal educational programme*. Including the 6-year-olds in school would in contrast to voluntary arrangements secure everybody equal opportunities (Telhaug, 1997, p. 195). This reform was also inspired by *international models* and was part of a strategy to establish an educational system more transparent with the system in other countries.

The ten-year compulsory education is structured in three stages: primary school including pre-school to grade four; middle stage from grade five to seven; and lower secondary school covering grades eight to ten. From 1 July 1998 all municipalities have to offer voluntary programmes in music and the arts for children and adolescents. 350 out of 435 municipalities have already established such programmes.

Norway is sparsely populated and many of the primary and lower secondary schools are small. It is not unusual for children belonging to different grades to be in the same group and share a classroom. Twenty-nine per cent of the primary and lower secondary schools belong to this category, but they teach only 12% of the pupils. Many primary and lower secondary schools are combined and include grades from primary, middle and lower secondary stages. The number of small and combined schools is decreasing, however.

3.3.2. Upper secondary education

In the late 1980s and beginning of the 1990s, some fundamental problems in upper secondary education were observed, giving the background for what is called Reform 94:

- The system did not have the necessary capacity. The result was a long queue of youngsters waiting for admittance and of adults lacking the educational foundation and opportunities of the young ones.

- The prestige of the vocational courses was sinking compared to courses preparing students for higher education.

- Too few pupils passed through the system, and many took several courses on the same level.

- The pupils had few possibilities to continue vocational training after passing the basic level, and pupils with completed vocational training had restricted possibilities of entering higher education.

- The possibility of getting apprenticeship after taking the foundation courses was limited.

- The course structure was complicated, overlapping and the courses highly-specialised.

- The syllabuses including the academic substance were not well adapted to the future needs of the individual, the society or to the labour market. The systematic contact with the labour market was not satisfactory.

- The school had limited possibility and abilities to adapt the education to the needs of different groups of pupils. Educational opportunities for adults in upper secondary education were declining.

- The responsibility for young people who neither attended upper secondary education nor were inside the labour market was unclear.

On this background were set some overall objectives of Reform 94. The reform should raise the general competence in the population, make the labour force more flexible, increase the participation in upper secondary education, postpone the choice of future occupation and reduce the number who had to restart their education because they had changed their minds. The reform should contribute to a good balance between width and specialisation, focus upon basic knowledge and basic skills that are more permanent, and create tighter connection between society, working life and secondary education (Report to the *Storting* No. 32, 1998-99, Vi*deregående opplæring*, p. 75-76). The reform should raise the status of vocational training and find solutions to the drop-out problem (Briseid, 1995).

Upper secondary education – being the responsibility of the counties – covers most of the education and training between lower secondary school and tertiary education.[5] In 1999 upper secondary education taught and trained approximately 169 000 pupils and about 31 000 apprentices. Since 1976 there has been a unified comprehensive system which provides both academic education and vocational training, often in the same institution, *i.e.* in comprehensive schools. Since August 1994 all young persons between the ages of 16 and 19 have a statutory right to three years upper secondary education. The premise is that everyone should either be eligible to higher education or have obtained a journeyman's certificate after three years attendance.

Today the programme is organised in 15 basic areas[6] of study – foundation courses – in the first year, a reduction from more than one hundred compared to the situation before Reform 94. Examples of such areas are: general and business studies; health and physical education; hotel, cooking, waiting and food processing trades; electrical trades; and engineering and mechanical trades. Specialisation starts in grades two and three in what is called advanced courses I and II and in apprenticeships. Admission to advanced course I is based on attending and passing the relevant foundation course. The enterprises approved to train apprentices are responsible for the practical training after advanced course I.

The young people are entitled to start in one of the three foundation courses to which they have given priority in their application. The reform has made it easier for pupils who choose vocational training to achieve university and university college eligibility. Three of the areas prepare pupils for direct entrance into university colleges and universities. Ten are vocational in character and are leading to a trade or journeyman's certificate. Students following these lines can, through an additional year, reach the qualification needed for academic studies. The counties have been given a distinct responsibility for following up youths in the actual age group who neither attend school nor have a job.

One of the most interesting traits in Reform 94 is the increased responsibility taken by the enterprises and institutions for training of apprentices. Apprentices get instruction through a combination of school attendance and work. In the two first years, instruction is given at school, while the specialisation – lasting up to two years – is given as on-the-job-training. This training is often combined with some teaching. The number of apprenticeship has increased considerably since 1994. In 1999, 16% of the cohort were apprentices. If it is impossible to establish an on-the-job-apprenticeship, the county's school authorities are obliged to offer an advanced course II at school as an alternative. The final exams will be the same whether the training takes place in an institution, an enterprise or at school.

In the general and business courses the majority of the written exams are country-wide. This includes all common subjects and the subjects related to the specific area. Oral exams are local. In the vocational areas locally given exams are predominant.

3.3.3. *Higher education*

In higher education lifelong learning is a meeting place for four policy fields: adult education, higher education, regional policy and labour market. Adult education and higher education are taken care of by separate departments in the Ministry of Education, Research and Church Affairs, while the Ministries of Municipal and Regional Affairs and Labour and Government Administration are responsible for the last area.

In 1999, the public sector of higher education in Norway encompasses 4 universities (75 000 students), 6 specialised university colleges (7 000 students), 26 state university colleges (75 000 students) and 2 colleges of arts and crafts. The public institutions receive a block grant directly from the Parliament through the Ministry, and they report to the Ministry. In addition, there are 30 private colleges, the majority with religious affiliations. Most of the students, however, study ICT and business administration in private colleges. The total number of students in 1998 was 175 000; 159 000 in the public sector and 16 000 enrolled at private colleges (Statistics Norway, Current educational statistics 4/99, p. 6). Military academies and Colleges for Police Education are not included.

According to the University and College Act their main tasks are teaching, research, develop-mental, artistic and aesthetic work on an advanced level and imparting their knowledge to the public. They are also obliged to offer or organise further education within their fields of study and research (University and College Act, paragraph 2.5). So far the extent of this activity is relatively small, and it is difficult to present precise figures.

The universities provide studies in liberal arts and science, medicine and dentistry, psychology, law, education and theology. The university colleges cover disciplines as agriculture, economics and business, veterinary medicine, physical education and sports, architecture and fine arts. Their functions are two-fold: research and teaching. They offer degrees at several levels, requiring combinations of studies lasting from 3.5 to 6.5 years. In addition they offer Ph.D. programmes, comprising a further three years of study.

37

In 1994, the most comprehensive reorganisation ever in the Norwegian higher education system was launched. A total of 98 colleges, many of them small and specialised, amalgamated into 26 larger and more multipurpose *state university colleges*. The reform encompassed the previous regional colleges (15), the colleges of education (25), engineering (15), health education (27), social work (3), and various other small and specialised colleges. The purpose of the reorganisation was to raise the academic standards of non-university higher education, to break down barriers between the various course-programmes, and to make better use of available resources in the various regions. The university colleges should establish a closer relationship with industry in their region, and the administrative burden on the Ministry and the academic staff should be eased.

The State university colleges offer 2-4 year vocationally-oriented study programmes, as well as a range of academic studies corresponding to university subjects for lower degrees. In addition they offer 18 autonomous higher degree studies (master and PhD) and 21 in co-operation with the universities. Teaching is the most important task of the staff members at the university colleges, but they also carry out research and development.

In order to promote co-operation and a more rational division of labour, a network (Network Norway) has been established linking all universities and university colleges. This shall enrich the various academic departments by enabling them to co-operate with regard to fields of specialisation and division of labour. The network should give students more options and make it easier to combine educational programmes from different institutions. Studies are fully interchangeable, and students can combine studies from different institutions without loss of progress into one degree/diploma.

In many areas, universities and university colleges have close relations to business and to society at large. The University of Tromsø for example and the State university colleges do also have tasks as competence centres in their region, tasks that are more emphasised in Norway than in comparable countries. Some study programmes at universities and university colleges include in-service training such as supervised practice *e.g.* in hospitals and schools. In addition, the universities have set up special offices responsible for establishing contact between the university and industry. The contact between higher education institutions and industry is also institutionalised through externally financed research projects at the institutions.

In May 2000 the Mjøs commission on higher education delivered its report. One chapter in the report deals explicitly with working life, higher education and lifelong learning (The Mjøs commission on higher education, Chapter 18). The commission emphasises the advantages and importance of learning as part of work. Working life gives competence that hardly can be obtained in the formal educational system. According to the commission the enterprises should therefore be given a more important position as an arena of learning. However, insofar as some jobs offer poor possibilities for competitive development, it may be appropriate to supplement practical learning in the enterprise with learning in a more formal educational setting. In these instances it is necessary that the theory is closely related to the practical working situation.

The commission suggests that the higher education institutions should more actively keep up their contact with former graduates by inviting them to seminars in order to maintain and develop their competences. The institutions should be given the freedom to be shareholders in or owners of enterprises providing further education. A permanent subsidy should be established to support application from partnerships between higher education institutions and organisations in working life aiming at educational programmes using the working place as an arena of learning.

In addition to the 175 000 students in Norwegian institutions, more than 12 000 study abroad receiving financial support from the State Education Loan Fund. More than 75% prefer to study in Europe, while 16.4% study at institutions in Northern America. The most popular fields are business administration, medicine, and art and handicraft (Statistics Norway, Current educational statistics, 3/99 and 4/99).

3.3.4. Saami education

The Saami people are the aboriginal population in the northern part of Norway. The Saami society is part of the Norwegian large society. However, having signed international treaties, Norway has special obligations towards the Saami people. Functional bilingual competence is regarded a necessary prerequisite for active participation of Saami people in society.

The main principle of Saami education is to give an education that is really equal to education of other pupils. The education of Saami pupils shall therefore take place within the framework of the comprehensive school system. This gives Saami pupils access to a common knowledge base. The objective is to develop multi-cultural understanding and contribute to positive attitude and knowledge that both will benefit the Saami local society and the Norwegian society.

Most educational arrangements targeted at the Saami population are run according to the ordinary legislation and as part of the ordinary educational and administrative system. It has been necessary, however, to take some special actions to meet needs in the Saami population. All pupils in primary and lower secondary education in Saami districts have a statutory right to learn Saami and to teaching in Saami in all subjects. Further, all Saami have an individual right to education in Saami wherever they live both in primary and secondary education.

39

There has also been established special arrangements for Saami pupils related to special education needs; these will be strengthened in the coming years.

Saami influence on the syllabus of the school is an important instrument to preserve and develop Saami language, culture and social life. The Saami Parliament is therefore responsible for the part education shall play in developing the Saami local community and Saami identity in Saami children and young persons. This applies for syllabuses for Saami language and specific Saami subjects as Saami handicraft and art (*doudji*) and learning how to keep reindeer. The Parliament does also prepare the curriculum guidelines in other subjects for Saami pupils, but these are finally authorised by the Ministry of Education.

3.4. Intermediate[7] and private educational institutions

There exist several educational provisions coming after upper secondary education[8] that neither are regulated by the Education Act, the University and College Act nor by the Act of Private Education. These are called education on an intermediate level. A recent survey indicates that in 1999 there exist more than 250 provisions of this kind with a length of more than 2 months. Altogether they had enrolled more than 13 000 students. Technical schools, being in this category, have *e.g.* enrolled approximately 3 500 pupils. Statistics covering the period mid-80s to mid-90s indicate that this level has been growing.

Categorised by type of education, 169 offer vocational education within different trades and occupations. In this category the most numerous group teach alternative medicine, ICT, economics and business administration. Other institutions supplement education within health and social work (6), 13 are within artistic education, 52 are bible schools, 5 offer education arranged by different industrial branches and 9 are educational programmes related to public services.

Education related to public services had the most students, primarily in officers' training schools. Other fields having registered many students are ICT and economics and business administration.

Private institutions and agents dominate this part of the educational system. Seventy-five per cent of the participants are enrolled in private institutions. Their provisions are with few exceptions open for everyone. Those institutions fulfilling some formal criteria receive state support based upon regulations in the Private Education Act. Pupils attending approved institutions are entitled to support from the State Education Loan Fund. The counties run technical schools and the State support is an integrated part of the block grant. Other public institutions at intermediate level are run by public services where the students have to be employed in the service or drafted in order to become a student.

A Government commission (the *Berg-Commission*) has considered these institutions. The commission concludes that this educational level is a necessary part of the total educational system. They argue that institutions meeting a set of criteria should be defined as an autonomous formal intermediate level organised and regulated by their own law. The Ministry should be given system-responsibility and responsibility for managing this level. Two boards should be appointed: one advisory board dealing with strategic questions and another board dealing with academic matters and quality. The commission proposes that the public authorities should have economic responsibility for the intermediate level (NOU, 2000b, p. 11).

Norway has a relatively small private school sector. About 98.5% of all children in Norway at primary and lower secondary level and 96% of those at upper secondary level attend public schools. Among the private institutions there are several international schools with about 2 000 pupils from grade one to thirteen. At tertiary level 8.7% or 16 000 students choose private institutions, the majority in the fields of economics and business administration, health sciences and teachers' education. The number of private schools are growing, however, making the system gradually more heterogeneous.

Private institutions are regarded primarily as a supplement and alternative to the public system rather than competitors. Most private schools are based on a particular religious, philosophical or educational platform or they offer training in fields where the capacity in the public sector is limited. Approved private institutions can award diplomas and as a rule they receive substantial grants from the State. Fees paid by the pupils, the students or their parents cover the remainder.

3.5. Adult education[9]

Adult education and lifelong learning should not be regarded as synonymous. Lifelong learning as a concept was however introduced in the 1970s in the preparation and implementation of the Adult Education Act of 1976. The interest and concern linked with lifelong learning has later been confirmed in reports from Government Commissions and in Reports to the *Storting*.

3.5.1. *Adult education*: A *brief overview of the past*

From the middle of the 19th century to 1950s, voluntary organisations and popular movements (religious, temperance, language, and labour unions) dominated adult education in Norway. In 1932, the various organisations established the Norwegian Association of Adult Education. The first private correspondence school was established in 1914 with vocational and general courses. In 1948, the Correspondence School Act was passed to regulate these activities. In the 1960s, new providers of adult education became active: local school authorities, manpower authorities and organisations in working life. Government policy was expressed in a Report to the *Storting* on "adult education" (1964-65). Adult education was defined as both vocational and general education, and it should be on

41

equal footing with basic education for children and young people. In 1966, a department of adult education was established in the Ministry of Education, Research and Church Affairs. In 1967, a State Council for Adult Education was appointed. State grants for adult education increased. In 1970, the Government appointed a commission to work out a proposal for a comprehensive act on adult education.

In 1976, the *Storting* passed the Adult Education Act. The Act applied to:

- study circles in voluntary organisations and institutions entitled to state grants;
- basic education at primary and secondary school level, organised especially for adults;
- alternatives to basic education for adults at all levels;
- further education and short courses (not part of basic education) in secondary schools and higher education institutions;
- vocational training for adults as part of the labour market policy;
- training given in or in connection with a firm; and
- other provisions for adults, assessed on individual basis.

The main objective of the Adult Education Act was to achieve a higher degree of equality (with regard to age, sex and region) in access to education and to promote democratisation of education. The Act did not, however, establish a statutory right for individuals to get adult education. Provisions of adult education were to be assessed and decided on locally in municipal boards, county boards, regional college boards and governing bodies of universities. The ILO-convention of 1974 on Paid Educational Leave was discussed in the Norwegian Parliament at this time, but no such right to leave was included in the Adult Education Act.

As a follow-up of the Adult Education Act and the discussion about educational leave, a government commission (the *Skard Commission*) on development of the right to lifelong learning for all delivered, in September 1986, their report "Lifelong Learning" (NOU, 1986). In the 1980s, cuts in state grants to adult education organisations led to larger fees and more vocational courses, like IT and business administration. In April 1989 the Ministry of Education presented a Report to the *Storting*, "More Knowledge to More People" (Report to the *Storting* No. 43, 1988-89), based on the work of earlier commissions on higher education, teacher education and lifelong learning.

In the late 1980s distance education become really "hot". In the latter report, distance education was considered important for several reasons: distance education should increase the percentage of young people choosing studies; it should broaden the recruitment to higher education (student in employment or with familial obligations); it should meet the needs for continuing education, and it should give educational institutions closer contact with working life and business. The Government encouraged and expected that the institutions took into to use available new technology.

Due to the costs, the Ministry gives grants to some institutions to finance partly or in total the development and provision of distance education course programmes. The Norwegian Executive Board for Distance Education at University and College Level (SOFF) evaluates project proposals and gives advice about priority. In a Report to the *Storting* in 1991, the Ministry stated that distance education should prioritise developing continuing education (Report to the *Storting* No. 40, 1990-91).

Originally, different forms of adult education had cultural and social objectives: the uneducated should acquire the established culture and knowledge; adult education and enlightenment were a means in the struggle of hegemony in and in the democratising of society; adult education was considered as *consumption*; adult education was not only regarded as an educational arrangement; it was also part of the country's cultural and social policy.

In the 1960s adult education was moved from cultural policy to educational policy in the party programmes. The aim was to obtain social justice and to reduce educational inequality. More importantly, adult education was connected to qualification requirements in working life. Adult education had to be understood as a means to improve the mobility of the working force and to solve unemployment in the regions. Adult education became *investment*. This gave less room for liberal education and preparing for leisure-time activities.

The shift in policy can be observed in a shift in the course types chosen by adults. They seemed gradually to prefer more job-oriented courses. Still the authorities wanted to be at the wheel and formal educational institutions were meant to play an important part. The *Storting* increased the grants by 500% from 1965 to 1971, and an additional 400% from 1976 to 1981. The public grants to traditional adult education reached their height in 1981. Senior researcher Sigvart Tøsse of NVI has asked if this year also represents a turning point in the adult education policy. The change can be characterised as a shift towards de-institutionalisation of training, a reduced state role in provision and financial support, and greater reliance on market forces for allocating financial resources (Tøsse, 1996, pp. 42-44).

3.5.2. *Providers of adult education*

Both the Adult Education Act and the new education act regulate adult education. Responsibility for this field is shared between public providers and adult and distance education associations representing non-governmental organisations with adult education as their main objective. The State subsidises adult education in accordance with the provisions of the Adult Education Act.

The Ministry of Education, Research and Church Affairs has an overall responsibility for administering the educational system and for implementing national educational policy also in this sector. Various other ministries are involved in continuing education and training, however. The Ministry of Labour and Government Administration is responsible for employment policy, the Ministry of Local and Regional Development for immigration policy, and the Ministry of Trade and Industry for the tools of industrial policy. The Ministry of Health and Social Services gives financial support to the employee who wants to run continuing education for and training of health personnel.

Different agents provide adult education. Here we shall only present them briefly. They are described in more detail in other chapters:

- *Upper secondary education*: Upper secondary education is an important provider of adult education.

- *Education resource centres*: The State runs one resource centre for adult education with more than 1 800 pupils. The counties have established about 250 resource centres in connection with upper secondary schools. Based on the schools' academic resources they provide competence development for both private and public demanders.

- *Study associations*: Study associations run adult education. These are volunteer, humanitarian, political and other non-governmental organisations whose main purpose is adult education and to promote the individual's personal development and to contribute to equal access to knowledge. Traditionally this is done on an idealistic basis. 22 study associations receive state support, among those *Folkeuniversitetet* and the Workers' Educational Association. These courses have about 800 000 participants.

- *Distant education*: It is fairly widespread. In 2000, 14 institutions receive state financial support. In 1998, 45 000 completed courses given by approved distant education agencies. Earlier they offered mostly correspondence courses, but today distance education possibilities are expanding as computers and video technology and national and international networks are utilised. The basic idea is the decentralisation of education programmes in order to meet needs of various groups for open and flexible learning.

- *Folk high schools*: There are about 80 folk high schools in Norway with 13 500 full-time equivalent students. Most of the institutions are boarding schools owned and run by religious organisations, independent foundations or county authorities. As independent residential schools, folk high schools in Norway focus on personal growth in a wide sense, developing the mind, spirit and body of students through teaching and social interaction.

By law (the Folk High School Act of 1984), folk high schools conduct no exams and issue no degrees; their mandate is to provide an all-round, liberal education that promotes lifelong learning. They are "schools for life". They provide general educational courses for young people and adults and offer courses in arts, crafts, music and several other areas.

- *In-service training and competency development*: In both the public and private sector, collective wage agreements require that employers document the need for continuing training and develop training plans. Estimates indicate that Norwegian enterprises set apart 11.5-18 billion NOK to competence development (NOU, 1997, p. 91 and NOU, 1999). In addition several of the organisations in working life offer alone or together with their counterpart job-oriented education on different levels. The provisions are primarily aimed at their members as individuals.

- *Labour market authorities*: There is a strong focus on active labour market policies to combat unemployment in Norway indicated by the fact that Norway in 1999 allocated 1.29% of GDP to labour market programmes, of which 0.82% was allocated to active measures.

- *The Public Employment Service* (PES): It is supervised by the Directorate of Labour and comes under the jurisdiction of the Ministry of Labour and Government Administration. In 1999 the PES consisted of 18 county employment offices and more than 150 local and specialised units.

- *Private providers*: Private providers are marketing provisions independent of laws, regulations and collective agreements. A survey indicates that there are approximately 1 000 companies with 10 000 employees in this field. They cover both public and private enterprises and most trades. Small, medium-sized and big companies are their customers.

3.6. Working life as an arena for learning

3.6.1. *Agreement between the social partners*

The labour unions and the employers' federations – both within public and private sector – have entered collective agreements regulating their co-operation. Most of these agreements have sections dealing with competence development and the possibility to get leave for this purpose. The partners acknowledge the great importance of more education for the individual, for the enterprise and for society at large. They therefore underline the value of stimulating the employees to heighten their competence and the enterprises to offer their staff systematic education and training through internal and external provisions. Surveys indicate that both employers and the shop stewards in the public sector are rather satisfied with the collective agreements on this point. The relationship is better characterised by co-operation than conflict, and regulations and collective agreements are seldom the problem.

The aim of education and training, according to the agreement, can both be to maintain necessary competence for a present job or for a new and more qualified task in the company. In the private sector competence development shall be based on the enterprises' needs at the moment and for the future and the objective is to keep up competitive powers. The partners in the public sector underscore that continuous competence development is decisive for the institutions' ability to solve their tasks effectively and to meet the needs for future readjustment and development of public services.

The expenses for further education based on the needs of the enterprise shall be covered by the enterprise itself. A government committee proposed that the partners of working life must give priority to arrangements stimulating participation in further education and that grant should be set aside in the yearly wage negotiations. Financing lifelong learning has therefore become an important issue in the wage negotiations the last years.

In 1998 an agreed action plan for competence between the partners was accepted as an appendix to the collective wage agreement this year. Mainly, the plan represents a follow-up of the proposals given in the government-report and the following Report to the *Storting* on the Competence Reform. It accentuates the authorities' responsibility for realising the reform. The action plan confirms the individual employee's right to leave for educational purposes on certain conditions. (This later became part of the Norwegian legislation.) It claims that the authorities take responsibility for developing, financing and running adapted provisions. Further the partners require that persons without upper secondary education should be given a statutory right and public support to cover living costs.

The partners accept that they have to contribute through the wage negotiations to the financing of a job-oriented further education system. In 1997, the employers federation and the labour unions have set aside 191 million NOK. In addition the different trades allot means to this purpose.

The Competence Reform was one of the issues in the collective wage negotiations in 1998 and 1999. The partners found that they could not set aside means on those occasions. In 1999 the partners agreed, however, that a proportion of the wage frame could be set aside for financing subsistence for employees participating in job-related education in future wage negotiations. In accordance with this the biggest labour union required financial allocations in the negotiations spring 2000. This became one of the hottest issues in the negotiations. After a strike and careful political intervention from the Prime Minister the partners have reached more committing statements than expressed earlier.

3.6.2. In-service training

The social partners of working life initiated a co-operation about competence development long before the Competence Reform. The partners acknowledge the great importance more education has for the individual, the development of the enterprises and the society. The partners therefore emphasise the value of stimulating employees to increase their competence and the value of systematic training of the employees. Further education is an important means in the enterprises' creation of value. The competence must be based upon the present and future needs of the enterprises. The responsibility for competence building at the workplace lies with the employers, employees and their organisations jointly. The collective agreements both in public and private sectors require that employers document the need for continuing training and that they establish competence development and training plans. Several of the organisations in working life offer alone or together with their counterpart job-oriented education at different levels. The provisions are primarily aimed at their members as individuals.

Being less institutionalised and less visible than the traditional system of initial education this resource development has been characterised as "the shadow system" (Nordhaug, 1991, p. 16). As a consequence this system has received scant attention from researchers, and it is difficult to find precise and reliable statistics about the enterprises' investment in competence development. There exist some information and estimates, however (Report to the *Storting* No. 42, 1997-98, pp. 15-17):

- A survey from 1996 shows that private enterprises rank immaterial investments highest in value creation. Among immaterial investments competence was ranked the most important factor to adding value. Ninety per cent of private enterprises state that they were engaged in further education in 1996.

- About one-third of workers attend courses organised by their employers each year. The length varies, but most employees have participated in courses that sum up to about one week. In a five-year span 75% report that they have participated in one or several courses.

- Estimates indicate that Norwegian working life set apart 11.5-18 billion NOK to competence development (NOU, 1997, p. 91 and NOU, 1999). In 1996 this added up to an annual expenditure of 6 000 to 9 000 NOK per employee, which makes Norway one of the countries in Western Europe that uses the least in this field. A study carried up recently concludes that enterprises invest about NOK 10 000 per employee per year to competence development.[10] Based on this figure working life's investment will amount to about NOK 20 billion.[11] If we take into consideration costs related to day-to-day guidance and knowledge transfer, the sum may add to NOK 50 billion. This corresponds to the total public expenditure on education.

47 |

- Surveys give ambiguous results concerning the private and public sector's investment in competence development. According to some research the private sector upholds a strong position using about 5% to this purpose. Another study of eleven private companies indicates that they use from 1.4 to 4.5% for educational purposes. The situation in the public sector is equally confusing. Some surveys present a more positive picture of the public sector. These indicate that the State sector sets apart more than 5% and municipal sector more than 7% of the wage budget to competence development. Teachers are not included in this number.

- In the OECD area an estimated 2 to 5% is spent on employer provided training (OECD, 1998, p. 12). A tentative conclusion will be that the Norwegian working life spends about 3 to 4% of the annual wage bill on competence related courses, ranking Norway in the middle among the OECD countries.

- Factors that favourably influence learning at work are: the employee's exposure to change in technology and working methods and requirements from customers, colleagues and superiors, leadership responsibility, extensive outside contact, support and stimulation from the superiors, and reward for high competence (Skule and Reichborn, 2000, p. 30).

The investment in competence development varies on variables as industrial branch, company size and the specific company policy. It seems especially difficult for small- and medium-sized enterprises to raise money to fund education and training.

In-service training is well established in part of the health sector where doctors, dentists and psychologists participate in specialist education run and administered by their professional union. This consists of in-service training organised in programmes lasting several years.

There are surveys indicating that about half (49%) of the courses are given by external providers. This is most widespread in small enterprises. In the private sector less than half of education and training is internal where the enterprises themselves are responsible. Surveys confirm a corresponding picture in the municipalities. The general tendency is towards more internally arranged courses and competence development.

The enterprises employ different types of external providers and some use several:

- branch organisations are used by 60% of the enterprises;

- customers/providers are employed by 36%;

- professional course providers and consults are used by 53%; and

- public and private educational institutions are employed by 41%.

The many trade associations within the employers' federation run today approximately 1 000 courses. The federation thinks that such courses are not cost effective. The federation has therefore taken into service modern technology by establishing a "Competence Net" for their members. The net shall help the enterprises to: *i*) get easy access to relevant high quality provisions, *ii*) exploit competence between enterprises, *iii*) administer competence development and *iv*) document competence. The net is a pedagogical and administrative system for Internet based learning adapted to the needs of the businesses and employees. The net connects different providers and pilot enterprises. The network was opened in Autumn 2000. The substance is provided by public and private education institutions. Today the network offers 200 courses. The network shall function as a market and provide competence on several levels adapted mainly to the needs of companies, but also individuals.

3.7. Culture and cultural activity as an arena for lifelong learning

To grasp the complexity of lifelong learning the perspective must be broadened to include the competence children and young people pick up being members of organisations, and participating in cultural projects and leisure time activities. It is also relevant to include the influence of media and information technology as an arena for learning and socialisation and the guidance given to young parents.

Outdoor recreation provides a sound foundation for better health and a better quality of life. There are reports from day care facilities that increasing numbers of children have poor motor development, probably due to lack of outdoor play and physical activity. Experts hold that playing in natural surroundings will benefit the motor, intellectual and social development of the child.

The proportion of people who take part in outdoor recreation in Norway is high in all age groups, and outdoor recreation is still an important family activity on weekends and holidays. Later surveys, however, show changes in young peoples' attitudes and a reduced activity level.

The authorities have taken different actions to promote outdoor activities. The Planning and Building Act and the national guidelines pursuant to this act and state funds are important measures for safeguarding green areas, trees, lakes and rivers in the neighbourhood as playground and activity sites for young people and adults. Organisations, families, schools and *barnehager* are important target groups for this work. The interests of children and youths have had a relatively strong impact on specific objectives and strategies in municipality and county planning. A national programme for outdoor recreation pays special attentions to children and adolescents and various measures and activities are being implemented or planned to improve the conditions for participation in traditional outdoor recreation activities.

Children and adolescents are the most active participants in almost all cultural activities. More than 65% of all children between 9 and 13 years of age, and almost 50% of adolescents between 14 and 19, take part in one or more organised cultural activities. Sports is the most popular, followed by choir and musical activities. Girls are more active than boys in all fields except sports. Three out of four in the age group 9 to 19 years of age use the public or school library. School is the most important cultural institution for children and adolescents, and it plays a major role in diminishing the social differences in the use of cultural facilities.

Also in this field the authorities use a set of measures to stimulate cultural activity and to avoid harmful influence on young children. There are rules regulating radio and television commercials in relation to children and adolescents, and there are minimum age limits set for the public showing of films and videos. There are grants available for stimulating production and distribution of worthwhile children's and adolescents' films, books, magazines, theatre performances and concerts. More than one third of the grants from the most important state sources – the Norwegian Culture Fund and the Foundation for Audio-Visual Productions – are given in support of cultural activities for children. In 1995 two thirds of all the concerts were arranged or supported by the Norwegian Concert Institute, and more than 60% of the performances of the State Touring Theatre and about half of the exhibitions shown by the National Touring Exhibitions were specially intended for children and adolescents. The Ministry of Children and Family Affairs has increased the support for schemes for improving conditions for children and youths from 10-12 years up to 25 years of age growing up in the nine biggest cities. Almost all the municipalities have recreation clubs for children and youths from 10-12 years up to 18 years.

Participation and democracy is another important area. Participation in the decision process is thought to improve the accuracy and quality of the measures directed at children and adolescents. In addition it can contribute to develop knowledge about how democratic society functions and about democratic attitudes and practices. A Nordic network has been established for youths taking part in various participation projects. The Government has also for several years supported local development projects that encourage participation by children and adolescents in municipal and local planning. The Ministry of Children and Family Affairs has supported a project entitled "Children's influence on the cultural activities of organisations". Models of ways in which children and young people can take part in decision-making have been tested. A recent survey of children's and adolescents' participation in local decision-making and planning has shown increasing activity, particularly from 1991 onwards.

3.8. Resources and responsibility

The public expenditure on education in Norway amounts to 6.8% of the GDP while the OECD average is 4.9% (1997). Public and private costs related to higher education amounted to 1.3% of GDP. If we take into account the size of the Norwegian GDP and the rather low teacher wages, the absolute differences are even bigger. On the other hand, private investment in education is low in Norway compared to many other OECD countries.

3.8.1. *Investment in education and competence development*

Investment in knowledge capital comprises at least 10% of GDP in most OECD countries when we include public and private expenditure on education at all levels and enterprises' and individuals' costs related to further and continuing education. The total dimensions poses important political questions related to the total activity within the educational sector, how resources should be allotted to different kind and levels of education and between individuals, enterprises and public authorities.

It is difficult to give a precise picture of all costs related to education and competence development in Norway. Table 3.1 contains information about public expenditure related to educational level and some estimates related to in-service training. The figures are collected from different sources, apply to different years and there are some overlap in the column containing student numbers. The conclusion is that approximately NOK 120 billion is used for educational and competence purposes in Norway every year.

3.8.2. *Reallocation of resources*

The public allotments to different sectors are decided by the Parliament. The parliamentary budget decisions are comprehensive and rather detailed. Before the budget is put before the Parliament there are several rounds within the Government. The Government prioritises the sectors, the total frame of the State budget and the allotment to each ministry. In the internal preparation the general patterns is that different ministries defend their sector, while the Ministry of Finance co-ordinates the process taking care of the balance in the economy and the total frame of the budget. Usually the process ends up in small and incremental changes in the budget from one year to the other.

There are, however, examples of reallocation of resources related to education. In the late 1980s and the beginning of the 1990s Norway experienced substantial growth in unemployment, and many young people were affected. As a counter-measure, the authorities financed a massive expansion in higher educa-

Table 3.1. **Key figures in the Norwegian educational system, late 1990s**

Educational level	Number of institutions	Number of teachers[1]	Number of students	Expenditure (millions NOK)
Public expenditure				
Early childhood education	6 178[2]		187 100[3]	7 000[4]
Primary and lower secondary level[5]	3 278	49 717	569 044	28 436
Upper secondary level[5]	515	24 551	168 587	16 297
Higher education level[5]	68	11 981	167 757	16 560
Adult education			915 000[6]	1 192[7]
Labour market programmes[8]			35 889[9]	4 163[10]
Expenditure in working life[11]				
Direct cost related to competence development				11 500-18 000
Direct and indirect cost related to competence development				50 000

1. Man-labour year.
2. Report to the Storting No. 27 (1999-2000), Barnehagene i dag – ansvar, rammevilkår, utbygging og behov. The figure applies for 1998.
3. Statistics Norway (1999), Barnehager Foreløpige tall. The figure applies for 1999.
4. This figure is an estimate of the grants made by the State and the municipalities. Proposition to the Storting No. 1 (1999-2000), Ministry of Children and Family Affairs, p. 21. The figure applies for 2000.
5. Statistics Norway, Current educational statistics 3/99, p. 3. The figures apply for 1998.
6. Statistics Norway, Current educational statistics 6/99. The figure applies for 1998. It shows number of persons involved in adult education independent of length of the arrangements. Persons who have taken several courses may be counted several times and the figure may overlap with other figures in the same column.
7. Proposition to the Storting No. 1 (1999-2000), Ministry of Education, Research and Church Affairs, p. 21. The figures apply for 2000.
8. Proposition to the Storting No. 1 (1999-2000), Ministry of Labour and Government Administration. The figures apply for 1998.
9. This figure is the average number of labour market programme slots through the year 1998. Places in ordinary education and workplace training for persons with restricted choice of employment under the Social Security Scheme are not included.
10. Expenditure for labour market programmes in 1998. The expenditure includes living costs for the participants. The figure does not include expenditure for daily cash benefits and extra costs for participating in programmes financed under the Social Security Scheme.
11. These are very imprecise estimates indicating the total size of the expenditure.

tion by means of resources set aside for unemployment purposes. From 1986 to 1994 the capacity in higher education was increased from 101 000 to 169 000 places. Many of these new places were financed over the chapter for preparedness measures in the State budget. In first half of the 1990s more than two-thirds of the new places were financed this way (NIFU, 2000, pp. 9-10).

The State has, through law and other regulations, set requirements with which local authorities have to comply. These concern e.g. the size of classes at different levels, number of pedagogical staff in a class, the teachers' workload and qualifications, and minimum number of lessons at different levels and in different subjects. Fulfilling such requirements, the municipalities and counties can reallocate resources from one level of the educational system for which they are responsible to another. In reality, however, their freedom is rather restricted:

- Most local authorities do not have any economic surplus at their disposal. They therefore strive to comply with the minimum requirements.

- Even if equal educational opportunities and provision are the main objective, there are substantial differences in the municipalities' and counties' investment in education. In 1998 the investment varied between NOK 38 000 and NOK 63 000 in primary and lower secondary education and between NOK 49 000 and NOK 73 000 in upper secondary education (Statistics Norway). The Government concludes, however, that equal opportunities in compulsory education are not threatened so far (Report to the Storting No. 28, 1998-99, Mot rikare mål, p. 9 and pp. 28-29).

- The municipalities run early childhood education and compulsory education. This may open up for reallocation between the two sectors. Upper secondary education is run by the counties. Tertiary education, however, is run by the State under the control of the Ministry of Education, Research and Church Affairs. Labour market courses are under the control of the Ministry of Labour and Government Administration. Their activities are regulated by different laws; they have their own budgets and own budget processes.

3.8.3. Responsibility for the formal educational system

The educational reforms have not led to any important changes in the responsibility for initial education for adults. The Government has a superior responsibility for basic education, for student financing, taxation system and for legislation. The Ministry of Education is responsible for administering the statutory educational provisions of the Education Act as well as developing curriculum guidelines. Further the Ministry is, according to the Act,[12] responsible for the general development of adult education and for higher education. The Ministry of Education co-operates with other ministries, however, when deciding the guidelines for and capacity of educational programmes related to these ministries' fields of responsibility. The Ministry of Health and Social Affairs is, for example, involved in fixing guidelines for education of nurses and social workers.

National Education Offices, one in each county, were established in 1992. They have a quality control function and shall ensure that children and adolescents are given an appropriate education in accordance with statutory regulations. However, the emphasis is on consultation with each school, municipality and county. They give advice and stimulate the work in each municipality with regards determining the needs of primary and secondary education and making plans for the education in the individual municipality. Their responsibilities cover all levels of education – primary and lower and upper secondary education, adult education of the primary/lower secondary level, special education for adults, and education for adults with Norwegian as a second language. The exception is higher education, where their responsibility is limited to co-ordinating activities of relevance for the primary and secondary school, notably further education and teacher training. The offices have a responsibility for the co-ordination and co-operation between different actors of adult education in their respective regions. They are responsible for reporting, evaluation and following up results; supervision and control; management training and refresher courses and centrally managed R&D. Communication between the national authorities, teachers' unions, parents' associations, and pupils' and students' associations is also one of the tasks of the National Education Offices.

At county level we find *Educational Boards and Vocational Training Boards*. Their main purpose is to ensure that the terms of the Education Act concerning education and vocational training are observed, approve apprenticeship establishments, administer apprenticeship contracts, inspect apprenticeship establishments, *i.e.* approved enterprises, assess private candidates' practical experience and administer trade and journeymen's examinations. They appoint and train examining boards. The vocational training boards are the main link between the county education authorities on the one hand and the training establishments and representatives of the industry on the other.

The *local authorities* being responsible for the respective levels of initial educational do also carry the responsibility for planning and running adult education at the same level. This implies that the municipalities are responsible for adult education at primary and lower secondary level, and the counties at upper secondary level. The universities and university colleges have a delegated responsibility for courses on this level adapted to the users' needs. This pattern concurs with the Adult Education Act from 1976.

The municipal and county educational authorities cover the cost of primary and secondary education for the pupils including adults as part of their obligation following the block grant from the State. Adult participants must meet the cost of textbooks in upper secondary education, and there is a fee for both lower and upper secondary examinations. The educational authorities also meet the cost of the education of lingual minorities.

Adult education programmes outside primary and secondary education are financed by earmarked grants or subsidised by the Government. Grants are given to study associations and distance education institutions in accordance with the requirements of the Adult Education Act. These contributions are given on the basis of implemented hours of adult education activity, and according to special applications for pedagogical development work, etc. The main source of financing for the study associations is, however, the participants' fees.

3.8.4. The Competence Reform: responsibility and co-ordination

Different ministries, employers' federations, labour unions and private and public educational institutions and private enterprises and public services are all involved in implementing the Competence Reform. At present no authority co-ordinate and control the complete field.

In a reply to the social partners of working life in spring 1999, the Prime Minister confirmed the Government's strong commitment to the Competence Reform, but that resource development in working life must to a great extent be taken care of by working life itself. The Government underscores, however, that the public educational system shall play an important role in offering education and training to meet the need for competence in working life. To obtain this the public educational system must adjust to society's wishes and needs, and it must be able to develop and offer further education which is competitive. The present Government continues this policy stating that the Government will emphasise the close co-operation between the social partners of working life. "They know where the greatest needs are. They must be the important actors in directing the Competence Reform."[13]

The Prime Minister also stated that the Government's contribution to increased efforts in this field would be focused on making the necessary arrangements for stimulating educational provisions and on making lifelong learning a reality for the individuals through loan and grants offered by the State Education Loan Fund. Further he stated that the Government was prepared to grant additionally 400 million NOK in the State budget for the coming two to three years to finance parts of a competence development programme. The promise was followed up in the State budget for 2000.

The Ministry of Education, Research and Church Affairs and the Ministry of Labour and Government Administration with the Directorate of Labour and Public Employment Services (PES) play important roles in co-ordinating the policy in this field. So far, the dominating strategy has been to establish a clear-cut division of responsibility between the two ministries and consequently between ordinary education and labour market programmes.

The Ministry of Education, Research and Church Affairs is responsible for the co-ordination of the Competence Reform and as such also for lifelong learning. One of the Ministry's instruments for this purpose is an action plan summing up the objectives and action to be taken by the Government in the period until 2003.

The Ministry will stimulate the development of more flexible provisions and a better information system. This comprises an information plan summing up arrangements aiming at different groups and an information portal giving interested persons information about courses and other provisions. The information plan will be based upon the action plan. The planning of the competence development programme started in autumn 1999 as a joint project between the authorities and the social partners.

The *labour market authorities* will play limited direct part in implementing the Competence Reform. As part of their general services the Public Employment Service (PES) will give information and guidance to individuals about occupations and education. Secondly, as part of a labour market reform of July 2000 the Ministry of Labour and Government Administration has opened for the PES to offer commercial services to enterprises concerning enterprises training, among others services. This could include assessment of individuals' needs for competence development as well as for planning and implementation of training. Thirdly, it is expected that the demand for substitutes to replace people engaged in competence development may increase as a result of the Competence Reform. In this case the PES will assist enterprises in obtaining substitutes. This service is part of the general services of the PES when used on a more *ad hoc* basis. It may be offered on a more systematic and extended basis as a commercial service.

The responsibility and role of the political authorities and the social partners of working life in financing the Competence Reform are not finally decided. They all, however, accept that they must take a share. The *social partners of working life* have the responsibility for negotiating collective agreements and competence development according to the needs of the enterprise. The authorities expect that the enterprises develop organisations where learning processes permeate the activity and are an integrated part of being at work. The employer should stimulate the working staff to involve themselves in competence development; they should make competence development plans for their enterprise also having the employees needs and career in mind. Competence development covering the need of the enterprise is the enterprise's own economic responsibility.

The Government established in May 1999 a *Forum for Competence Development* and a contact group for the Competence Reform. The Minister of Education, Research and Church Affairs, being responsible for following up the Competence Reform, chairs the Forum, but there are members on political level from 8 other ministries. In addition there are members representing the social partners and higher education, study associations and distance education institutions.

The forum and the contact group are instruments to realise the Competence Reform and shall be an arena where the political authorities, the social partners and providers of educational courses and programmes discuss professional and political issues related to the reform. The forum shall meet twice a year with the Minister of Education as head. Both groups have participated in writing the action programme mentioned above.

Notes

1. The main sources for this chapter are: "Education in Norway", by Årang (2000); "Thematic Review of the Transition from Initial Education to Working Life – Norway, Country Note", by OECD (1998); *Faktablad on Videregående opplæring*, Report to the *Storting* No. 32 (1998-99); *The Competence Reform*, Report to the *Storting* No. 42 (1997-98), Chapter 3; and "Background Paper from the Ministry of Education, Research and Church Affairs to Nordic Transition Conference 1st–2nd November 1999", by Lysklætt (1999).

2. Press release No. 99117 from the Ministry of Children and Family Affairs, dated 21.12.99.

3. For short the Ministry of Education, Research and Church Affairs will be called the Ministry of Education in most connections in this report.

4. According to Circular f-42-00 the quality of textbooks is the responsibility of publishers, authors and academia from autumn 2000.

5. There are a few institutions falling between these two levels, see paragraph 3.4.

6. Two of the fifteen foundation courses are new and have started for the first time in Autumn 2000.

7. The information in the paragraphs is collected from NOU (2000b), pp. 13-15.

8. Not all of these provisions build upon completed upper secondary education, neither is the intermediate level a requirement for entering tertiary education.

9. More information about adult education can be found in OECD (2000).

10. This covers cost related to the courses, travel expenditure, lodging and wage related to absence from work.

11. This figure was used by the President of the Employers Confederation at the opening of Competence Network, Autumn 2000.

12. The Educational and Training Act regulates primary and secondary school and adult education.

13. Statement from the Minister of Education to the Parliament, May 4th 2000, p. 9.

Chapter 4

Challenges to the Learning Arenas[1]

The authorities, both the Government and the Parliament, have in Reports to the *Storting* and parliamentary recommendations related to educational policy presented what they regard as important challenges for Norwegian society and consequently for the educational system. These challenges are also relevant to lifelong learning. In this chapter the challenges are summarised from two angles: what social and economic changes do the Norwegian society undergo that ask for lifelong learning?; and what challenges do providers of competence have to meet in order to succeed? The chapter also contains some information about the situation in upper secondary school after Reform 94 and mechanisms for reallocating resources.

4.1. Social and economic challenges

The Government has drawn attention to several social and economic challenges that require greater knowledge and continuous competence development in the working force:

- *Globalisation and internationalisation of the economy*: The reduction of trade barriers and deregulation of markets have contributed to globalisation, a restructuring of industry and more intense competition both at home and abroad. Staff mobility over national boarders will increase parallel to globalisation. Maintaining competitive powers is decisive for the industry's survival and for national economic growth and full employment. It is necessary to get more out of everyone's talent and potential and to increase their ability to orient themselves in the flow of information.

- *Rapid technological change*: The spread of ICT happened faster than anticipated in the beginning of the 1990s. Technology has lead to and will necessitate readjustment of production and organisation; job-content and processes will change, jobs and occupations will disappear due to automation, and new occupations will emerge. Neither should one forget that the rapid development is not only related to working life. New technology transforms all sectors of society and thus also the life of individual outside work.

Important consequences of globalisation and technological change will be new organisational forms requiring staff members with more independence and stronger co-operative and language skills.

- *Migration to central parts of Norway*: It has been and is still an important political objective in Norway to maintain a decentralised settlement pattern. Recently the migration from the more remote districts to the larger cities and the municipalities bordering on these cities has again accelerated. The Government wants to turn this trend, through the Competence Reform, among other measures, and by extending the possibility to study close to the citizens' residence.

- *Need for competent workforce*: It is a recurrent discussion if and how Norway shall have a competent and big enough workforce to keep up the country's productivity and welfare society. One issue is if Norway should allow more immigrants to enter the country. Another is how to maintain and develop the competence in the population. It is regarded unrealistic to take 10% of the workforce out of work and bring them back to educational institutions to obtain competence development. Other more adapted and flexible organisational solutions must be found.

- *The skills gap*: The policy of the Government intends to prevent the trends mentioned above from leading to a skills gap.

Since nearly all the younger population completes upper secondary education, it is expected that many adults will experience a growing need to educate themselves up to the same level as the young generation. Even if participation in upper secondary education among the young is very high, research has discovered that as many as 25% of the total population or 1 million persons have not completed upper secondary education while many countries regard this level a necessary foundation for lifelong learning.

The problem is reinforced by the following facts: persons with the poorest qualifications have the highest unemployment rate and participate the least in competence development. Only one third of the employees participated in such initiatives the last year. Young people who drop out of school have difficulties re-entering the educational system, and many of them end up in the unemployment queue.

- *Effectiveness and re-allocation in public sector*: To keep up the welfare society, it is important that as many people as possible are involved in value creation. This requires a competent and flexible labour force not only in the private sector. There are political expectations that the public sector shall be more effective, be able to reallocate resources because of changes in the population structure and to render better service to the inhabitants.

- *Employees with other values*: So far loyalty has been a cherished quality in working life. The employees entering the labour market now, also called generation X, seem to a greater extent to value flexibility, variety, personal benefit and the opportunity to continuous development. The employer who offers these qualities will have an advantage competing for the highly-qualified employees. One way to gain this advantage is to use the enterprise as an arena for continuous learning and development.

- *Ethics and democracy*: There are conflicting tendencies in the Norwegian society. Norway has become a multicultural and more pluralistic society as a consequence of globalisation, internationalisation and rapid transformation of the society. In this situation the Government has given ethical, democratic and political values some attention. They are worried about increasing violence found in some young groups, a higher level of conflict between different groups and individuals and the decreasing participation in democratic elections and processes. In a local election in 1999 less than 60% of the voters participated.

Systematic and continuous competence development and lifelong learning are regarded as an important answer to these challenges. It is a national understanding that competence is the key to positive development for the individual, the enterprises, for working life in general and for the welfare society. Especially, measures targeted at the adult population must be initiated. Additionally, there is a belief in the socialising and stabilising effect of education. These expectations represent challenges to the providers of competence.

4.2. Educational challenges

The development described above is so fast that knowledge is easily outdated and new knowledge added with exponential speed. The Government underscores that the permanent and unchangeable knowledge and skills acquired while young are important elements in a changing world.

Knowledge and skills acquired in primary and secondary school will not give enough competence for a lifetime, however. New skills will be required continuously. An important basic skill will be the ability to obtain new competence and to possess the ability to adapt flexibly to new situations. This being the situation, one important challenge is to stimulate and motivate the labour force to participate actively and positively in long-term and comprehensive competence development. Another challenge is to decide how the competence needs in the private and public sectors should be defined and who should define the needs. At the moment the public needs for competence seem to be more precisely defined than the needs in the private sector.

The Government has formulated a set of criteria and requirements that the Competence Reform has to meet in order to succeed. This set deals both with the concept of knowledge, content, educational methods, localisation and co-operation:

- *Early childhood care as part of educational system*: Today's early childhood education and care institutions have both an educational and caring role. The *barnehage* Act states that the main purpose of the early childhood education is to "provide children under school age with good opportunities for development and activity". When all families who wish so may have a place in *barnehage* for their children, probably in a few years, the early childhood education and care institutions will become a more integrated part of the educational policy.

- *Role of basic education*: Systematic and continuous lifelong learning has substantial implications for basic education. Basic education must be broad and comprise content and working methods of long lasting value. One objective of Reform 94 and Reform 97 was to introduce a holistic view on learning and teaching. Learning shall be aimed both at head and hands, and there should be an interaction between cognitive, social, emotional and often motor activities. The intention is that upper secondary education shall introduce cross-disciplinary and project-oriented methods and integrate practice, theory and application in a fruitful whole. The constantly shifting specialisation should be taken care of by continuous further education at work or in a more formal setting.

- *Knowledge and competence*: There is a need for another competence in the labour market, a competence that includes both knowledge *about* (*theory*) and knowledge *how* (*skills*). It has become important to have a broad concept of competence and to strengthen multi-competence. General basic qualifications should include the ability to organise, accomplish, analyse and evaluate a work process. Competence must comprise socio-cultural skills as the ability to co-operate and the ability to function with others and as a part of a totality. In addition a competent labour force is expected to take initiative, to have ideas, communication skills and to be creative. These requirements have made the difference between knowledge and competence distinct. Competence has been emphasised since competence is a more dynamic concept than knowledge. It comprises the will and the ability to use and apply knowledge in a given situation and to take action based on this knowledge. Competence includes creativity, intuition, and the ability to exercise sound ethic judgement and discernment.

- *Balance between supply and demand of skilled workers*: There is a lack of pupils and apprentices to crucial trades in working life. This is most obvious in health and social services, but also in crafts related to construction and food industry.

- *Scope of lifelong learning*: Lifelong learning must have a broad perspective. The Government states that it is important to involve all groups of adults, not only those employed. This includes women in part-time work, minority groups and unemployed and handicapped so they can participate as actively as possible. The system must operate in a way that does not create losers. This must be done without lowering the general educational level, but by giving an education in accordance with the pupils' qualifications. Pupils should experience mastering through education. At the same time they should be motivated to achieve competence demanded by the labour market.

- *Supply of competence development*: To raise the level of competence in the adult population is a challenge for the competence providers both qualitatively and quantitatively. The Government thinks it is necessary to have more providers and a greater diversity in supply (Report to the *Storting* No. 42, 1997-98, *The Competence Reform*, p. 12). The supply must be well adjusted to individuals and enterprises needs in respect of content, organisation and pedagogy. And the supply must comply with more pragmatic, but still decisive, questions such as provisions independent of time and place. One important mechanism is that both basic and further education shall, to a greater extent, be developed and given on demand and as in-service training and in connection with the working place. The Minister of Education states that "Educational institutions must adapt to people's needs, not the other way around".[2]

- *Methods of teaching*: Pedagogy and evaluation systems must be reconsidered. Evaluation shows that teaching methods and teachers and pupils' role concept are lagging behind the objectives of the educational reforms. In lifelong learning perspective adults should be given the opportunity to gain new competence based on the knowledge they already possess. The opportunities embedded in information and communication technology should be exploited. ICT opens for flexibility and learning independent of time and space and making it possible to introduce adapted and customised education. The education must be better adapted to the adult part of the population when it comes to pedagogy, organisation, time and place.

- *The regional perspective*: Important objectives in Norwegian policy are to develop industry in the districts, to maintain and create new working places, stimulate residence in and hinder migration from the districts. Due to this, foundation courses and specialised courses at upper secondary level should be designed to enable adults and the young people to carry out most of their education near their residence. The chosen solutions must benefit and satisfy the needs of small- and medium-sized enterprises.

63

- *Co-operation between the educational system and the enterprises*: Divisions between the educational system and business must be reduced. The Competence Reform aims at broad, differentiated opportunities for adult education and continuing education and for training provided both by public and private institutions, by organisations and the enterprises themselves. In this connection it is important to establish a closer collaboration between the educational system and the business in order to develop entrepreneurship.

4.3. Recent developments in upper secondary education that bear on lifelong learning

The reforms in the 1990s have expanded people's statutory rights and resulted in an educational system with capacity to accept most of the applicants both to upper secondary and higher education. Still, it is important to examine if the new structures and privileges give equal opportunities to obtain competence for further studies and work, or if there still are barriers which influence pupils progression within an educational level and when they move from one level to another.

Reform 94 has been extensively assessed through an evaluation carried out by several research institutes. We know that the great majority of pupils from lower secondary education enter upper secondary education. There exist, however, structural barriers both for pupils with and without statutory rights. Pupils with statutory rights have met problems getting an apprenticeship. The statutory right does not guarantee access to advanced courses in accordance with the pupils' wishes for future profession. And young people have limited opportunities to get a job.

Some groups such as pupils with non-Norwegian background and adults without statutory rights have additional problems:

- *The situation among youths from linguistic minorities*: Over time we can trace a development where their recruitment pattern to upper secondary education has become more alike the pattern we find among youths with majority background. Among the pupils leaving compulsory school in 1995 there are small differences between majority pupils and pupils from linguistic minority groups. However, the general tendencies are that a greater proportion of youths from linguistic minorities becomes drop-outs or uses more than three years to reach the third level than among ethnic Norwegians. One factor explaining this is that they have more problems getting apprenticeship than ethnic Norwegians does (NIFU, 1998, pp. 1-3).

- *The situation for adults without statutory rights* became initially more difficult when Reform 94 was introduced. The number of adult applicants has dropped, strongest in the last class in upper secondary school. The number of adult applicants has become manageable for the counties and fewer are rejected. From one point of view this is a positive trend. When we regard the causes for this drop the picture is more negative. Adults were prioritised behind young persons with statutory rights applying for secondary education. They therefore got problems completing their education. This group has shown a stronger preference for vocational lines than the youths, but they have had fewer problems being admitted in the general foundation courses. They are more pointed in their applications and a greater proportion rejects an offer that differs from their prioritised choice.

The proportion of drop-outs among adults is higher and their progression is slower than among the young people. This is due to barriers in and outside the educational system: the courses are not well adapted to grown-ups. Norway lacks measures strong enough to neutralise the de-motivating forces outside school. And until Spring 2000 they did not have a guaranteed right to complete upper secondary education (NVI, 1998, p. 1). From August 2000 this is amended through a revision of the Education Act.

Other aspects of Reform 94 have also been evaluated. We refer some conclusions related to lifelong learning below:

- Most of the teachers share the aims of the reform and the values embedded in the Core Curriculum Plan. However, they use little time to discuss the possible impact of these values and how they should be applied in their teaching.

- Most teachers regard the Core Curriculum Plan and the syllabuses as flexible. The plans give good opportunities to choose methods and to adapt the teaching to the individual and to the local context and to job-orient the teaching programme.

- It is still a challenge to job-orient and integrate the common and general subjects in the vocational courses and to offer the pupils learning situations that integrate practice, theory and application and that require a combination of cognitive, social, emotional and in many cases motor activities and skills. Still, theory is taught in the classroom at the desk while practical skills are learnt in the workshop too much disconnected from theoretical knowledge and understanding.

- A major target of Reform 94 was to integrate vocational training in the public educational system as a means both to increase competence and recruitment into upper secondary education. In the evaluation of the reform the enterprises were asked about their experiences with this element of the reform. The overall impression is that the enterprises are satisfied with the effect of the reform. The training has become more systematic and the apprentices are better prepared for their practical training. The proportion who passes the final apprentice exam is higher than before the reform. In 1998, 92% succeeded which is 6% more than in 1997.[3] Some criticism is also raised, however, especially from the construction industry. The apprentice system has become more bureaucratic and the broad foundation courses make the apprentices less familiar with and less motivated for the different crafts (Michelsen, Høst and Gitlesen, 1999, pp. 53-54 and pp. 73-75).

- Two-thirds of the teachers identify themselves with the new teacher role, but the same proportion regards the role unrealistic related to the pupils they are teaching. The teachers think that the pupils are not mature enough. The pupils on their side seem to be reluctant to accept a role with so much commitment, and they have hardly been engaged in operationalising the aims of the teaching. They have started processes, however, indicating a greater involvement from pupils in planning, carrying out and evaluation of the teaching when they see the relevance and benefit of their involvement. The overall impression is therefore that the roles are pretty much the same after the reform.

- One issue is the element of common, general subjects (maths, English and natural science) in the vocational courses. The teachers with responsibility for these classes and their pupils are more critical than teachers and pupils in other foundation courses. It seems to be a problem to adjust the learning situation to the individual pupil, and the ambitions of the plans are said to be far ahead of the pupils' capacity.

- Another issue is the number of basic and advanced courses that upper secondary school should offer. On the one hand, specialisation in many courses makes it possible to establish and maintain upper secondary schools in the scarcely populated regions; but it also may force pupils to make vocational choices before they are prepared.

- The upper secondary school system still has a long way until ICT is a natural and integrated part of the education and training.

- The different courses are modularised to make it feasible for adults to participate and, in time, complete the full course. This solution seems suitable, but so far adults have only to a small degree made use of the opportunity.

In the Report to the *Storting* No. 32 (1998-99), the Ministry comments on the more critical remarks regarding the heavy element of theory in the vocational courses. In light of the challenges employees in the crafts also will meet in the future, the Ministry does not regard reduction of common general subjects to be a solution to the problem described. Instead more energy and pressure should be put into making the common subjects vocationally-oriented and adapted to the individual pupil's needs.

To achieve this the Ministry has initiated a programme where the objective is to develop and implement methods that contribute to give the pupils an education and training adapted to his or her qualifications and needs. This programme corresponds to a similar step taken in compulsory education, and will be carried out in the period 1999 to 2003. The counties will be responsible for the different actions taken within the frames of the programme. The Ministry will give financial support to the counties, establish a reference group and a research programme to evaluate the projects and their results.

4.4. Private sector views and expectations

Business life is less occupied with the educational system as such than with the individuals' need for and provision of new and relevant competence. The main question from their point of view is how to develop the employees' competence as part of their work, in a situation where they are motivated to learn.

The employers' confederation estimates that their members every year buy competence development from external providers for more than 5 billion NOK. This only includes their direct cost. We can observe some important trends in the businesses' policy. Firstly, looking upon the enterprises' choices in practice, it appears that internal teaching is the most widespread form for stimulating competence development in working life. Internal teaching is arranged by the employer using the enterprise's own competence or through a combination of internal and external expertise. The most common topics are professional training and leadership development. Experts expect that this form will expand in the future. Contrary to many European countries, Norwegian leaders do not expect any increase in the use of external providers of competence development in the coming four to five years. Secondly, reports from the public sector show that public services prefer to co-operate with public educational institutions in fields where they earlier had their own internal educational programmes. The advantage is publicly recognised exams and studies.

The enterprises have absorbed the growing number of apprentices, and the number who have to finish their training at school is strongly reduced. The enterprises that are approved to train apprentices report that the main reason for seeking approval is the possibility this gives to recruit qualified employees. Working life also regards higher education as an important means to develop competence for part of their employees.

What the enterprises ask for is more flexible and user adapted arrangements, more use of information technology and distance education, more flexible entrance requirements and greater ability to meet the needs of working life. There seems to be scepticism in working life today as to whether or not the public educational system has the necessary ability and willingness to meet these criteria.

The enterprises, on their side, should preferably have more knowledge about their existing and future needs for competence. Enterprises seldom have evaluated their competence needs or related them to investment thinking. Education and training are more an adaptation to immediate and running needs. The enterprises' knowledge about their needs is mainly intuitive. The employees define very often their own needs, and the employers accept these relying on the employees' discernment and loyalty. Neither are they sufficiently able to communicate their needs to the educational institutions. This problem seems to be most obvious and acute in small- and medium-sized companies – both public and private. They should preferably be more able to analyse and define their needs, and they should have more knowledge about what provision public institutions can deliver.

It will be a challenge to educational institutions to co-operate with businesses to give provisions tailored for the enterprise and to the employees. In doing this the institutions will need the enterprises' assistance and commitment. We have seen a tendency towards establishing new arenas where educational institutions co-operate with ministries and enterprises. In these settings demanders and supplier meet. They give the public services and enterprises the opportunity to become better and more demanding buyers. The effort to establish such arenas should be strengthened, according to the Government.

4.5. Public providers

Due to the network of upper secondary schools and about 130 adult education centres, the local authorities have every possibility to offer relevant courses close to the individuals' domicile. According to the Report to the *Storting* on the Competence Reform, however, the co-operation between the public educational system and working life does not function well enough. The public institutions are characterised by being too rigid and closed, and they lack enough insight into the needs of working life and the ability to adjust to the enterprises' needs. Therefore they do not deliver courses that are sufficiently adjusted and relevant in form, content and methods (Report to the *Storting* No. 42, 1997-98, *The Competence Reform*, pp. 11-12).

Reports from the National Education Offices document that most municipalities and counties lack complete education plans for adults and that provisions of lower secondary education have low priority. Further, the reports indicate that the provisions at primary and secondary level are hardly adapted to adults. The dominant form of open and flexible education for adults at this level is correspondence education.

The number of adults applying for lower secondary education is low. However, a significant connection between supply and demand is documented. In municipalities with an offensive approach the participation is higher than in communities with more sporadic provisions.

The public institutions have up to recently argued that they lack the necessary incentives and framework to be offensive operators in this market. Institutions in higher education lack the flexibility needed due to centrally given regulations and restricted economic freedom. They emphasise the following issues: admittance to charge fees; opportunities to develop and offer study programmes without the ministry's consent; and possibility to pay their own staff additional wage. A survey among university lecturers supports the view that public institutions still do not compete on equal terms with private enterprises: "This is the case not only for the question of fees, but also for the approval of new study programmes – where one would expect that the institutions was a guarantor of quality" (Brandt, 1999, p. 26).

Models are being developed to improve co-ordination between school and working life. The standard model for vocational training demands closer contact with industry, and this is encouraged by the implementation of comprehensive syllabuses covering the whole period of training, both in school and in the training enterprise. Contact between schools and local companies and organisations has grown recently, with more schools establishing market- and community-related resource centres. Many schools report having close and constructive links with local commerce and industry.

The Government has also taken steps to make the public system more pliable. The Ministry is authorised by the *Storting* to accept pedagogical and organisational experiments in higher education. To increase the flexibility and the opportunity to offer courses adapted to the market's needs, public institutions in higher education are now allowed to establish or to abolish courses lasting three semesters or less. They can offer decentralised studies of maximum thirty credits (*i.e.* one and half-years of full-time study). The Ministry held this authority earlier. At the same time some restrictions in the opportunity to take tuition fees for further education courses have been removed. The institutions are now allowed to charge fees for courses lasting up to three semesters.[4] A collective agreement has given the institutions the possibility to reward extra employees who engage in market-related courses.

69

Notes

1. This chapter is mostly based upon the Report to the Storting No. 32 (1998-99), *Videregående opplæring*, p. 75-79, and the Report to the Storting No. 42 (1997-98), *The Competence Reform*, pp. 10-14. The views presented are in accordance with the views presented by the new Minister of Education in a statement to the Parliament, May 4th 2000, pp. 3-5.

2. Statement from the Minister of Education to the Parliament, May 4th 2000, p. 10.

3. Press release 01-02-99 from the Ministry of Education.

4. Circular from the Ministry of Education, Research and Church Affairs F-086/99, pp. 1-2.

Chapter 5

Evidence to Date on Demand, Participation and Provision

5.1. Demand for competence development

Labour market surveys show that employers prefer persons with higher education in 37% of their positions while they prefer 63% having primary and secondary education even if they could recruit persons with higher education. The prognosis is for a possible surplus of highly-educated labour force, and a deficit of employees with upper secondary education (NOU, 1997, pp. 53-54). This indicates that Norway does not face a general competence problem in the sense that the educational level will be too low. However, this analysis cannot be used as an argument against a competence development in working life. In working life there is a consistent need for keeping qualifications up to date. This is different, however, from a general rise in educational level measured in university degrees and years of study.

Globalisation, international mobility, new industrial structures and introduction of ICT will result in more frequent job shifts in the future and in great changes in job content and performance. The anticipated and announced readjustment in the public sector will create needs for competence that can contribute to flexible change and effectiveness. The age and competence structure in the Norwegian population asks for competence development in the existing working staff. The number of young persons recently educated is not high enough to meet the needs for competence in society and working life. Given today's structure and participation in education, the average age of working staff will increase by approximately 10 years in the coming 30 years.

Due to these elements Norwegian authorities expect a far greater demand for competence development in the coming decades. This includes both increased participation in basic education, increased investment in further and continuing education (second bite students) and greater activity in adult education (second chance students). The motivation may both be related to job career and a general interest in knowledge and personal development.

Even if the educational level in Norway is high and a big proportion of the younger population continues on to upper secondary (97%) and to higher education (more than 40%), macro statistics indicate that approximately 1 million inhabitants lack upper secondary education. Statistics based on self-reporting give a number that is lower but still high. Anyhow, Reform 94 will probably lead to a situation where many adults will feel a growing need for further education up to the same level as the younger population leaving school today.

In a study more than 87% report that they regard more learning as very or rather important, and about 70% of the working staff wished to have further education in 1999. The reasons for this interest are mostly related to working life, their present job and career (Mjøs Commission on higher education, Chapter 18). Twenty-five per cent consider formal education as very or rather important, while 75% do not express need for formal education. A majority regard daily work as the main source of professional knowledge. People prefer three channels for learning: through work, in form of shorter job-related courses and further education leading to formal competence (Skule and Reichborn, 2000, p. 42).

The following paragraphs give more detailed information about the demand for competence development:

- In 1999 about 70% of the age group 25 to 67 expressed a wish to attend courses at a higher level of education.[1] There were small differences between men and women. A majority preferred shorter courses, but 15% expressed an interest for ordinary studies.

- Surveys show that ⅔ of the inhabitants, who themselves report an educational level below upper secondary education, have thought of taking or wish they had taken education at this level.

- This taken for granted, close to 300 000 persons could be potential future pupils. This exceeds today's number of pupils in upper secondary education by about 100 000.

- 75% express great or some need for professional updating. 65% need more skills in ICT. About 25% say they need formal education. Primarily the needs are job-oriented.

- Prognosis calculating the demand expects that approximately 30% will prefer general subjects, while more than 60% will choose occupational courses.

- The older the person is, the less interested he or she will be in taking courses at the level of secondary education. But even in the age group above 60 more than half wished they had education at this level.

- A majority of adults (70%) prefer that competence development take place in a social setting as opposed to individualised distance education.

- The majority of those who had concrete plans for further education wished to take higher education. The increasing proportion with upper secondary education will also influence the demand for higher education. Even 30 to 40% of the pupils in vocational courses plan to enter higher education after having received their certificates.

5.2. Participation in competence development in general

Competence development will become more closely related to the needs of the labour market. This change in policy and attitude can already be observed in the choices adults make. In 1978, 24% of the adult population had participated in courses altogether. 11.3% had participated in job-oriented courses. In 1996, nearly 40% had attended adult education courses, 30% in job-related courses. This shows both an enormous growth in total participation and a shift towards economically-founded courses. At the same time most of the provisions lead to formal competence.

Seventy-five per cent of the employees have attended one or several formal courses in the last five years. Most of participants report that their objective was to meet new competence requirements in their existing job (NOU, 1997, p. 91). There are considerable differences in attendance, however. The following pattern can be observed:

- Unskilled workers have a considerably lower attendance rate than other employees.
- Participation increases parallel with the employees' rank and general educational level. In ten institutions within the public sector staff members with higher education use on an average 133 hours (7-8%), while those without higher education use 69 hours (4%). There are, however, great differences between the institutions.
- There are great differences related to age. In a study in ten public services, the youngest staff members, aged 18 to 30 years, participated in competence development approximately 190 hours per year or 10-11% of their working hours. The age group 51-60 used less than 60 hours per year or about 3% to this purpose. The explanation can be that the older staff members are more selective and that the number of relevant choices is less. There were great differences between the services. In military service the staff used 287 hours on average, teachers 62 hours, while staff members in high court used 39 hours a year to competence development.
- The statistics contain scarcely any information about the attendance of the retired and unemployed in competence development and adult education. One study shows that 9.5% of the retired attended courses the last three years. ⅔ of these courses are related to leisure time activities. Even in this

73

group some prefer job-related courses. Women in this group are twice as active as men. The main reasons for attending are interest in the topic (33%), personal development (20%) and the wish to meet new persons (10%). The main barriers seem to be health problems (24%), lack of interest or no need for new competence (45%).[2]

- One study documents that 12% of persons over 60 years had participated in labour-related courses in 1996, and that 16% had attended other types of courses. The proportion had tripled since 1978 (Skaalvik and Engesbak, 1996, p. 104). We know that less than 1% of the participants in distance education courses and approximately 10% of the participants in courses run by study associations are older than 60 years. Further, we know that about 13% of participants in labour market courses are 41 years or older.

- In the public sector we have some information about barriers hindering employees from participating in competence development. A failure on the part of the employer to reorganise work while employees participate in activities is a factor that demotivates employees' from participation in such activities. The main barriers are intense work pressure, lack of economic support to cover costs of living, family obligations and problems to find a substitute. One result is that tasks are piling up while the participant is absent. Regulations and collective agreements are seldom reported to represent any problem.

- Generally speaking there are small differences between men and women, a result that differs from several international studies.

5.3. Competence providers and participation

OECD expects a development towards more flexible and customised provisions: the provisions will be shorter, more will be modularised and they will be given as distance education, education at job, and different combinations of self-studies and group discussions and meetings. To a greater extent further education will utterly be related to occupation and profession. Important elements will be to exploit the opportunities using ICT and the working place as an arena for learning.

Public educational authorities are responsible for adult education courses corresponding to various levels of formal education. The State subsidises adult education in accordance with the provisions of the Adult Education Act. The public school system will have no monopoly for providing the demanded education and training. In further education and lifelong learning, the working life itself and private providers are expected to play an important part. The public system is, however, expected to be an important provider. The Competence Reform can from one angle be considered as the authority's strategy to consolidate the public educational system as an important provider of competence in a lifelong learning perspective. One reason is that by increasing the public commitment in this area it may increase the quality and relevance of both the public basic education and public provision of further and continuing education. Another reason is that public provision is supposed to take better care of the principle of equal access to competence development.

On all educational levels the aim is to stimulate further flexibility in order to answer the needs of adults. For instance, public educational institutions are expected to develop more flexible learning methods and to offer courses that are more flexible with regards to time, place and duration. As already mentioned, the study programmes in upper secondary education are modularised. In this line we can also categorise the intention to develop further network services and technology for institutions in higher education.

5.3.1. Participation in adult education: an overview

Statistics on the adult education area are rather incomplete and fragmentary. At present, no statistics give the full picture of the total investments in competence development. Table 5.1, however, gives some information about the activity in the field.

5.3.2. Primary and lower secondary education

The municipalities are responsible for organising and running primary and lower secondary school including arrangements for those with special needs. The responsibility also comprises planning, developing and organising adult education in their area and offering adult basic education. With about 3 300 primary and lower secondary schools throughout the country and about 130 adult education centres, the municipalities may provide ample learning opportunities for adults in the vicinity of their homes. Provisions at this level can also be organised by adult education and distance education associations. The minimum age for participation in these programmes is 16 years. The *Storting* has given adults an individual right to lower secondary education, and extra costs are covered by the State. This decision will become effective in August 2002.

Publicly authorised primary and lower secondary education for adults are organised in separate courses. The education usually covers 9th and 10th class levels depending to a large extent on the participants' skills and knowledge. Curricula for respectively Norwegians and foreign language users are developed. Both are based on the primary and lower secondary schools' curricula. They are, however, more flexible in meeting adults choices and learning assumptions, and they underline the pedagogical principles of adult education. On this basis revised examinations have been established in five subjects: Norwegian, mathematics, English (written), and two of the following three subjects: social, religious and nat-

Table 5.1. **Participation in adult education, by topic/provider, 1996-98**

Topic/provider	Description	1996	1997	1998
Study associations (*Studieforbundene*)	Courses of different duration	743 808	711 351	681 359
Folk high schools	Main courses and shorter courses	27 878	29 474	28 236
Distance education institutions	Individual enrolment	58 000	52 207	44 731
Labour market courses[1]	Training towards job requirements	44 346	34 059	32 869
Adult immigration education	Courses of different duration	52 260	39 787	28 957
Primary and lower secondary education for adults under municipal responsibility	Offering examination	2 868	1 426	1 877
Special needs education at primary and lower secondary level for adults	Offering examination	6 043	5 287	7 310
Other adult education at primary and lower secondary level	Courses of different duration	..	..	1 297
Upper secondary education for adults under the responsibility of the county	In ordinary classes and part-time pupils	31 615	34 826	26 942
Further and continuing education at university and university college level	Further and continuing education	85 570	85 570	94 078

1. The Directorate of Labour, *Annual Report* 1997, 1998 and 1999.
Source: Statistics Norway, Current educational statistics 6/99. The table includes courses that vary substantially in size. Some are very short, others are full-time courses for one year. Further, persons who attend many courses, are counted many times. The table should therefore be interpreted with care.

ural studies. Having completed these exams, adults are granted the same rights and formal competence as pupils having an ordinary diploma.

The extent of this activity is relatively small. Recent reports from the municipal education offices show some expansion when we include lingual minorities. In 1998, 1 877 adults participated in courses related to primary and lower secondary school. 23 Norwegians in the age group "20 years and below", and 571 Norwegians in the age group "21 years and older" were registered in such studies. At the same time, the total number of persons from lingual minorities (immigrants and refugees) in the age group "21 years and older" was 1 094 (Statistics Norway, Current educational statistics 6/99).

In addition there are courses regarded as non credit-giving education or as special needs education. Such activity can only be documented in the statistics from 1998.

5.3.3. Upper secondary education

The counties have the foremost responsibility for planning and organising upper secondary education and for administrating apprenticeships for adults. Upper secondary education for adults is conducted according to the regulations covering upper secondary education and the subject syllabuses. Reform 94 has introduced didactical guidelines for adult educational programmes. Distance education methods are frequently used.

Adult education at upper secondary level is given at one of the 535 upper secondary schools, at one of the about 250 county-based adult education centres and at the State Adult Education Centre. The provisions can be ordinary courses, compressed part-time or full-time courses, and distributed courses or evening courses. Reports from the National Education Offices, however, give the impression that the counties put little energy into adapting the provision to adults.

In addition, some study associations, distance education institutions and labour market authorities offer courses that qualify as components in a full secondary education programme. To stimulate this activity the State's support to study associations and distance education institutions was increased with 10 million NOK in 2000. This amount is earmarked for courses at upper secondary level and shall be used to reduce the participants' own financial share.

Adults can sit nearly all exams as private candidates. They can also be enlisted as ordinary students and keep every right even if they are absent from up to ⅓ of the lessons. Adults wishing to follow vocational courses have to fulfil additional requirements regarding age (over 21) and qualifications.

The number of adult pupils in the public school system was reduced from 21% in 1994 to approximately 10% in 1998. This trend was most visible in advanced course II in upper secondary education. Still, nearly 22 000 full-time pupils and nearly 10 000 part-time pupils were older than 19 years of age in public schools in 1998. In addition study associations had registered 22 000 participants – most of them part-time – and distance education institutions 1 600 full-time equivalents in their courses.

Table 5.2 shows the total numbers of applicants to upper secondary education distributed by age in the period 1994-99. The share of adult applicants – 20 years and older – is diminishing. Their share was 24% in 1994 and only 9% in 1999.

Table 5.2. **Applicants to upper secondary education, by age, 1994-99**

Age	1994	1995	1996	1997	1998	1999
< 17	56 030	50 006	50 725	50 701	51 141	49 810
17	34 627	44 138	46 751	47 581	46 999	47 192
18	24 442	21 361	20 979	29 861	30 661	32 208
19	14 202	10 933	7 188	8 422	8 235	8 142
20	9 658	6 277	3 787	3 927	3 619	3 516
21-25	18 991	12 599	8 305	8 005	6 551	5 225
26 >	12 046	7 568	5 942	7 047	6 162	5 161
Total	169 996	152 882	143 677	155 544	153 368	151 254
Share of 20 >	24%	17%	13%	12%	11%	9%

Source: Statistics Norway, Current educational statistics 7/99. The table contains only applicants to available school places in the main applicant round (*fellesinntaket*). This includes applicants to foundation courses, advanced courses I and II. There has been changes in the definition of an "applicant" in this period. The figures are therefore not comparable between years.

Statistics for courses specially organised for adults[3] do not exist. Table 5.3 presents some information about adults' proportion of the total number of pupils at different levels in upper secondary school. The table shows that the share of adults has dropped by more than 6 percentage points since 1994. We find the decline at all levels in the upper secondary education, the largest in advanced courses I. Here the numbers of adults were almost 9 percentage points lower in 1998 than in 1994, a drop of more than half.

Adults can register for the final apprentice's exam as "practice candidates" without being registered as a pupil or having formally been an apprentice (see Section 6.2. below). Table 5.4 shows a large increase in the number of practice candidates from 1994 to 1998 and then especially from 1996 to 1998. More

Table 5.3. **Full-time pupils and the share of adults in upper secondary education, by level, 1994-98**

	Pupils				Share of adults			
	Total	Foundation course	Advanced course I	Advanced course II	Total	Foundation course	Advanced course I	Advanced course II
1994	191 427	71 178	62 798	57 451	16.6	8.5	16.5	26.9
1995	177 868	65 494	57 430	54 944	13.3	6.3	9.8	25.2
1996	171 120	65 498	56 404	49 218	12.8	7.7	10.1	22.5
1997	167 091	64 542	55 197	47 370	12.1	6.7	8.9	23.0
1998	160 371	63 170	53 108	44 093	10.6	5.6	7.2	21.8

Source: Statistics Norway, Current educational statistics 3/99.

Table 5.4. **"Practice candidates", 1993-98**

	Number of practice candidates	Percentage of total number of candidates
1993	6 906	50
1994	6 710	46
1995	7 088	46
1996	9 193	47
1997	16 817	59
1998	23 263	61

Source: Statistics Norway, Current educational statistics 3/99.

than 23 000 passed apprentice's final exam as practice candidates in 1998. This is more than 60% of the total number.

5.3.4. *Higher education for adults at universities and university colleges*

Further and continuing education for adults at higher education level can be taken at universities and university colleges. In addition it is possible to study through different adult and distance education associations having official approval from the universities and university colleges. Study associations or distance education associations have enlisted approximately 50 000 part-time or full-time students in their provisions at tertiary level.

It is difficult to distinguish between ordinary students and students seeking further education in higher education. Many of the students attending ordinary full-time programmes are adults returning to education for a shorter or longer period. The University of Oslo maintains that approximately 25 to 30% of its students are in this category.

Flexible learning may be obtained through part-time studies. Providing life-long learning for part-time students was rhetorically important from the 1970s to the 1990s. Part-time students are considered to contribute positively to the learning situation, and they bring increased competence back to the world of work. On the other hand, the authorities have argued that more should complete their studies on time as full-time students. The structure and provisions have been aimed at "normal" young full-time students – even if they have become a minority. This ambiguity is reflected in the educational policies: institutions are encouraged to cater better for part-timers, but governmental instruments do not motivate for strong actions. Part-time students may, however, receive state loans and grants provided that they study a minimum 50% of specified courses. The support is related to the students' income.

As mentioned earlier, universities and university colleges are obliged to give further education within their field of research and basic education. Higher education institutions offer courses mainly to former candidates who want to maintain and broaden their competence. It is a distinction between further education and continuing education. "Further education" comprises shorter courses without formal competence (non-credit-giving courses). The main goal is refreshing and updating of basic education. "Continuing education", on the other hand, is credit-giving courses that result in formal competence and can be part of a degree. These courses will often represent a specialisation or continuation of a basic education. In doing so, they co-operate closely with the participants' employers and unions. The courses can be free of charge, be financed through tuition fees or through contracts with business enterprises or organisations. Form and adaptation vary from on-campus-courses to ICT-based distance education courses.

If the numbers from the University of Oslo are representative, approximately 25 000 of the Norwegian university students in ordinary full-time programmes can be regarded as "lifelong learning" students. In addition 94 000 participate in further and continuing education courses run by universities and university colleges (see Table 5.5).

Since the 1980s the authorities have supported distance education initiatives with higher education by making the provisions more flexible. Pilot projects in distance education are the only field in lifelong learning at universities and university colleges that have received extra governmental money, even if the amount is small. Long-term provision of distance education must, however, be financed by the institutional budget.

Universities and university colleges have been in the front regarding development and implementation of ICT in lifelong learning in Norway. All campuses have access to Internet and to Uninett, the Norwegian Academic and Research Data network. Uninett and Nordic co-operation through Nordunett have contributed to a well-developed technical infrastructure. Now most institutions offer distance education course programmes using electronic technologies.

Table 5.5. **Further and continuing education at universities and colleges, 1998**

	Further education (credit-giving)	Continuing education (non-credit-giving)
Universities	5 855	16 212
Specialised university colleges	2 499	3 009
State university colleges	21 046	45 457
Total	**29 400**	**64 678**

Source: Statistics Norway, Current educational statistics, 3/99.

A co-ordinating body, the Norwegian Executive Board for Distance Education at University and College level (SOFF), was established in 1990 at the University of Tromsø. The body should advise on the distribution of the grant between institutions and stimulate and register pilot programmes. SOFF organises annual conferences and has initiated several reports on educational, technical and legal issues in distance education provided by universities and university colleges.

Recently, several initiatives have been taken in order to bring the provisions of higher educational institutions out of the campus to be in closer contact with new student groups and the labour market. Here we will present a few of them to demonstrate the public sector's attempt to adapt to the market:

- *The Network University* (NVU): The Network University is initiated by two universities and six state university college spread over the country. The aim of the network is to make higher education available, independent of geography and the participants' life situation and promote lifelong learning in the workplace. Their main distribution channel will be through ICT. The NVU collaborates with resource centres at upper secondary schools and study associations. The network underlines its district profile.

- *Norwegian University Network for Lifelong Learning* (*Norgesuniversitetet*): The Norwegian Council of Universities and University Colleges, the Employers Confederation and the bigger labour unions have appointed a board in order to establish a marketplace, database and network for working life related to higher education and competence development. In June 2000 they launched a database which includes information about further education courses open for enterprises and suppliers. The network does not intend to have any operational functions, however, and will emphasise practical information about provision. The State has allocated earmarked money to cover the expenses.

- *BedriftsUniversitetet* (BU): The University of Oslo, the Norwegian University of Science and Technology and the SINTEF Group have established *BedriftsUniversitetet*. The ambition is that BU shall become a provider of enterprise adapted and integrated competence within information and communication technology.

Others examples of initiative involving university and university colleges are: the Science University (*Realfagsuniversitet*), the ICT University (*DataUniversitetet*), Scandinavian Net University (*Skandinavisk Nettuniversitet*), the ODEL Net Work (*Odelnettverket*), Virtue and Nordic Net College (*Nordisk netthøgskole*). Some of them have international co-partners.

5.4. Providers outside the public educational system

In the paragraphs above we have given some key information about competence provisions offered by formal educational institutions at different levels. To supplement the picture, the next paragraphs will give some additional information about important providers outside the formal and public educational system.

5.4.1. Labour market authorities

Operating within the broad policy objectives of the Ministry of Labour and Government Administration,[4] the Public Employment Service (PES) offers job-oriented training to the unemployed. The prioritised group is first and foremost the long-term unemployed with low educational attainment. The training is aimed at bringing the unemployed into ordinary jobs and filling vacant positions as fast as possible. For this reason the training is of limited duration, and the training participants have to be at disposal for job placement.

Labour market training courses (LMT courses) (AMO-*kurs*) are part of the Government's labour market strategy and are fully financed by the State with no fees. LMT courses are a means for preparing the unemployed for work and for motivating them for participation in further education. The education authorities are responsible for the content and pedagogical aspects of the courses. The Ministry of Labour and Government Administration is responsible for the financing, the numbers, and the localisation of the courses as well as determining the level of demand and making decisions regarding who should attend. The activity varies and is closely related to the unemployment rate. The objective is to reduce the gap between the demands of the labour market and the qualifications of the unemployed.

The PES arranges courses for the unemployed and disabled job seekers, and focuses especially on the long-term unemployed with weak educational attainment. To be accepted in a LMT course, the unemployed young adults and adults must be over 19 years old. The age groups under 40 years of age are over-represented in the programmes, relative to their share of the registered unemployed. This applies particularly to the group 20 to 24 years of age. This reflects the attention being paid to the young unemployed in order to prevent marginalisation in early age.

LMT courses are mostly job-oriented and short. The upper limit is ten months. Vocational training is emphasised. The courses can also cover general subjects and lead to apprentice's final exams. There has been some criticism that the courses did not lead to formal competence. Therefore, the strategy now is that the participants should reach formal competence in so many cases as possible. The courses quite often cover the subjects and levels offered by upper secondary education. Upper secondary courses have been given a modular structure after Reform 1994. For this reason, it is possible to combine courses from upper secondary education with labour market courses to document competence towards a full diploma.

Table 5.6. **Participants and grants in labour market training, 1989-97**

	Courses	Participants	Grants (1 000 NOK)
1989	3 700	50 460	2 071
1990	4 195	58 200	2 190
1992	4 729	58 233	2 321
1993	4 959	62 390	2 389
1994	4 850	63 081	2 284
1995	5 000	61 200	1 887
1996	3 300	52 260	1 666
1997	2 645	39 787	1 342
1998	2 445	32 869	1 023

Source: Statistics Norway, Current educational statistics 3/99.

Long-term unemployed can also attend "job clubs" run by the PES for up to a month. The purpose of the job clubs is to assist the attendants in job searching and seeking both through theory and practical exercise. Counselling and assessment of the participants' qualifications are also part of the different programmes. This is taken care of by teachers at the course and by visiting civil servants from the local labour market authorities.

LMT courses take place in separate resource centres associated with upper secondary schools, or are organised as separate enterprises, or with private suppliers/organisations. They are run by school authorities, study associations or, to a marginal extent, by the PES (job clubs). The provider is selected after a tender. In order to offer provisions that match the needs and conditions of the individual and the labour market, the Ministry has established a set of requirements with which the providers have to comply.

Table 5.6 shows the participation in LMT courses and the grant to such courses in the period 1989-97. Up to 1994 there was an increase in both the numbers of participants and in the grants. Due to the positive development on the labour market, the efforts have gradually been reduced since 1995.

Though participants have to be at the disposal for the labour market while attending training, there are few examples where course participants have had to quit a course due to a job offer.

5.4.2. *Study associations*

Twenty-two study associations receive public subsidies for running educational work. Examples are the Folk University (FU) and the Workers' Educational Association (AOF). They are dependent on course fees, but such fees are not very high since one of objectives of the associations is to encourage democratic participation.

Study associations offer courses to support the individual adult's personal development and increase equality of opportunity. The associations are responsible for the content of the courses. National curricula and examination systems do not bind most of the courses. Everyone being 14 years old or more can, in principle, take part; the participants are supposed to influence the content and methods used in the courses. Most courses are organised and taught by a teacher, but in some instances the participants run the courses based on equal involvement without any teacher.

The courses cover, for instance, areas such as languages, the use of computers, topics related to different aspects of the society, cultural activities, arts and crafts, and organisational topics and activities. Some associations offer courses qualifying for lower and upper secondary education and higher education. The respective national guidelines and statutes regulate these courses. Study associations do also provide courses in development work within schools and educational institutions and labour market courses. In 1998 a course had in average 10 pupils or students and an average duration of 38 hours. (The minimum level for receiving public support for such courses is 5 participants and 12 hours.)

Table 5.7 gives an overview of the adult education through study associations in the period 1996-98 by age distribution. For 1998 the table also contains information about subject. One striking finding is that there has been a relatively large decline regarding the numbers of pupils/students from 1996 to 1998, a drop from almost 744 000 to 681 000 persons – or more than 8 percentage points.

In total 1 950 000 study hours were carried out. An increasing proportion of the courses is aimed at the labour market and the industry. The associations therefore co-operate closely with the industry and public education authorities. The most popular subject in 1998 was art and craft with approximately 275 000 pupils and students, almost 40% of the total number participating in the study associations courses.

A relatively large share of the study associations' credit-giving courses have their parallels in the public education sector. Table 5.8 gives an overview of such provisions in the period 1995-98. It seems to be an increase in courses at all levels, and especially in higher education and in the courses preparing private candidates for exam (paragraph 3-5 in the Education Act). Further, the numbers of students in higher education have increased by almost 44% from 1995 to 1998.

5.4.3. Distance education institutions

Distance education is fairly widespread. In 2000, 14 institutions receive financial support from the public authorities. They also charge fees to cover their

Table 5.7. **Pupils and students in study associations, by age and subject, 1996-98**

	Pupils	Age			
	Total	14-29 years	30-49 years	50 years <	Unknown
Total 1996	**743 808**	**194 056**	**194 783**	**111 810**	**243 159**
Total 1997	**711 531**	**206 587**	**233 957**	**139 766**	**131 221**
Total 1998	**681 359**	**187 893**	**234 112**	**147 823**	**111 531**
Languages	29 011	5 477	9 452	7 177	6 905
Art and craft studies	275 392	91 830	92 096	77 300	14 166
Humanities, religious studies	48 982	17 628	13 738	14 159	3 457
Social studies	29 396	6 730	8 555	3 623	10 488
Organisational and management studies	118 833	31 531	44 143	19 514	23 645
Economics and computer based studies	40 755	5 082	18 077	7 341	10 325
Health and social studies	61 282	7 465	18 084	7 968	27 765
Transport and communication studies	16 759	6 326	5 440	1 839	3 154
Natural sciences, engineering/ technology studies	18 691	3 417	5 481	954	8 839
Use of nature, ecology and environment studies	35 609	11 537	16 041	6 740	1 291
Services and service studies	6 487	862	3 007	1 133	1 485
Not available	162	8	68	75	11

Source: Statistics Norway, Current educational statistics 6/99.

expenses. The fees are higher than the fees charged by the study associations. In 1998, 45 000 students completed courses given by approved distance education agencies. Earlier they offered mostly correspondence courses, but today distance education possibilities are expanding as computers and video technology

Table 5.8. **Study associations' courses with parallels in the public education sector, 1995-98**

	Compulsory education	Upper secondary education	Higher education	§ 3-5 courses[1]
1995	461	13 658	33 229	3 275
1996	...	16 965	33 198	5 394
1997	734	18 099	...	5 514
1998	...	...	47 829	

1. Courses preparing candidates for examinations; these are provided for under paragraphs 3-5 of the Education Act.
Source: Statistics Norway, Current educational statistics 3/99. The table includes courses that vary substantially in size. Some are very short, others are full-time courses in one year. Further, persons who attended many courses, are counted many times.

Table 5.9. **Study activity (completed study hours) in distance education institutions, 1994-98**

Converted into whole-year-students

Type of institution	1994	1995	1996	1997	1998
Total	6 104	6 202	5 937	5 243	...
Upper secondary education		1 269	1 553	1 631	1 588
College/university	1 841	1 645	1 761	1 583	...
Independent courses	2 994	3 004	2 545	2 072	...

Source: Statistics Norway, Current educational statistics 3/99.

and national and international networks are utilised. The basic idea is to decentralise education programmes to meet the needs of various groups for open and flexible learning. Some of the courses are at upper secondary or higher education level. In 1996, 57% of the students prepared for exams in the public school system. Most distance education courses covered by the Adult Education Act lead to work-related qualifications. More than half of the courses cover subjects related to social and health care, management and economics and technical subjects.

Table 5.9 gives an overview of adult education in distance education institutions, measured by the study activity (completed study hours) converted into student equivalents in the period 1994-98. There seems to be a small decrease in the activity from 1994 to 1997.

5.4.4. Folk high schools

There are 82 folk high schools in Norway. The institutions offer two strands of learning. The first strand is a residential annual course, typically lasting 33 weeks from August to May, primarily geared to young adults and offering a wide variety of courses, some of them unique to this kind of school. Adult learning, the second strand, is implemented as short courses for adults lasting anywhere from three days up to sixteen weeks, often reflecting the same subjects or other subjects more relevant to the interests of people at a different stage in life. What joins together both strands and all courses is the centrality of interpersonal and intra-personal growth, a hallmark of folk high schools.

There are no exams or standardised curricula. Students can expand their own abilities, explore new options and gain new motivation for further schooling. This is done in two ways. First, even though the teaching is subject-oriented, it is also focused on social, creative and communicative abilities. The most popular subject areas among today's students are music, outdoor life and creative subjects, such as crafts, visual art and performing art. Second, by living in an educational and

Table 5.10. **Pupils registered in "folk high schools", 1990-98**

	1990	1992	1994	1995	1996	1997	1998
Total	31 255	31 498	30 843	30 961	27 878	29 474	28 236
One-year courses	12 965	12 863	12 360	11 808	10 914	12 259	13 496
Shorter courses	18 290	19 422	18 483	19 153	16 964	17 215	14 740
Converted into full-time equivalents	7 742	7 750	7 352	7 075	6 476	7 097	7 578
Full-time equivalents Main courses	6 899	6 878	6 558	6 248	5 726	6 354	6 967
Full-time equivalents Shorter courses	843	872	794	827	750	743	611

Source: Statistics Norway, Current educational statistics 3/99.

social community setting with 80-90 fellow students and staff, students gain inter-personal skills and learn to function in team settings.

The age limit for admittance to folk high schools is 17 years, but the schools can accept 16-year-old pupils. The average age of folk high school students is 19-20. Two of Norway's folk high schools have pensioners and senior citizens as their audience. Several ordinary folk high schools will also occasionally conduct similar courses, or other kinds of courses, for this particular audience.

Any given year, the number of students attending the annual courses corresponds to over 10% of all 19-year-olds in Norway that year. In 1998 the institutions had enrolled 13 200 students in the main course lasting 33 weeks, and 14 700 students attending shorter courses. This amounts to 7 600 student equivalents a year. On the average, schools have about 75 students and about 70% are girls.

At folk high schools tuition is free. National funding covers about 50% of the costs, $5/6$ being funded by the Government and $1/6$ by the counties. The boarding costs at folk high schools are covered by a fee paid by the pupils (approximately 35 000 NOK a year) and by state grants. The Norwegian students receive a substantial portion of the cost of room and board in the form of a scholarship from the State Education Loan Fund.

Table 5.10 gives an overview of the numbers of pupils at "folk high schools" from 1990 to 1998. There has been a small decrease in the numbers of pupils, especially in the shorter courses.

5.4.5. Resource centres

In the 1950s the PES administered and ran its own resource centres. Their main task was to re-educate and qualify persons in primary industries for the secondary industry. Over time, the concept proved to be too rigid, and the centres did not match the needs of society. They have therefore been shut down as part of a strategic change. Instead the PES has opened close co-operation with educational providers, both public and private.

The Ministry of Education runs one resource centre for adult education (SRV). The centre offers free upper secondary education to adults (over 20 years of age) in general, economic and administrative subjects. The centre has more than 1 800 pupils. As of the beginning of 2001, the centre was made part of a new centre of adult education. In addition to SRV the new institution will consist of the Norwegian Institute of Adult Education Research (NVI) and the Norwegian State Institute for Distance Education (NFU).

The counties have organised resource centres either connected to an upper secondary school or as autonomous institution. The number of establishments grew fast in the late 1980s. In 1996, 232 centres were established, most of them small. Half of them had a turnover less than NOK 100 000. The total turnover was estimated to about 350 to 400 million NOK. Being decentralised, they are situated close to small- and medium-sized enterprises and local public services.

The intention of the Ministries of Education and of Local Government and Regional Development is that the centres shall contribute to developing forms of co-operation between upper secondary school and local industry and working life that enhance the competence and better the use of resources in society. Their activity is not aimed at the ordinary pupils. They offer courses to working life in a region and to teachers, they participate in projects and product development, and they offer consultancy services. Establishing the centres has lead to a more systematic and professional provision of courses, the provision becoming more market oriented and more based on commercial principles. An indicator of customer satisfaction is the fact that most enterprises usually buy new courses (NOU, 1997, p. 100).

With access to the schools' broad competence and distributed structure, the centres can assist the local industry, especially small- and medium-sized enterprises. The provisions are used both by private and public demanders. About 30% of the turnover is related to courses given to local enterprises, while the PES, which is the biggest buyer of their services, finances about 70% of the turnover.

5.4.6. *Private providers*

Private providers are independent of public educational regulations and collective agreements. A survey indicates that there are approximately 1 000 companies with 10 000 employees in this field (NOU, 1997). They offer their services both to public and private enterprises and most trades. Small-, medium-sized and big companies are customers.

The private providers are flexible concerning content and form, responding to customers' needs and market conditions. Surveys show that private consultancy firms are an important source to competence development in private enterprises, while public educational institutions play a more modest part. This preference seems to be influenced more by the flexibility and professional customer relationship acquired than by differences in customers' satisfaction with the quality of the competence.

Notes

1. The Mjøs-commission on higher education, Chapter 18.
2. Information given by professor Einar Skaalvik, June 19th 2000.
3. The definition of an adult is 20 year and older.
4. The task of the Directorate of Labour is to realise the objectives laid down in the legislation and policies related to the labour market. It shall monitor trends and provide information and advice to the Ministry and external agencies on labour market issues. The county offices' job is to register the needs of job seekers and employers for services. Their function is to plan, develop and co-ordinate measures to reduce imbalances in the labour market.

Chapter 6

Additional Steps Taken To Facilitate Lifelong Learning

In the lifelong learning perspective it is important that the different parts of the system are looked upon as interrelated elements. To facilitate lifelong learning the authorities have taken into use a combination of measures involving several ministries, public and private educational institutions, enterprises and the social partners of working life.

We have already presented some of the most important measures to facilitate lifelong learning. Among these are the Core Curriculum and the accompanying guidelines and syllabuses. These documents, mainly concerned with the formal school system's inner life, show that Norway has a formal school system intending to give the youths knowledge, skills and attitudes which will prepare them for social life and working life, for participation in a democratic society and for personal development and growth. One objective is to give the pupils the basis for and the ability to learn to learn. These objectives support a lifelong learning perspective.

This chapter will deal with measures related mostly to statutory rights and different kinds of legislative and economic instruments used by the authorities to promote and facilitate lifelong learning in general and to compensate for the barriers experienced by poorly- educated groups. In this connection it is important to remember that both formal education system and working life are important contributors to lifelong learning.

6.1. Entrance requirements and priorities

6.1.1. *Day care institutions*

Today 188 000 children attend *barnehage*. This corresponds to 61% of the target group. In order to cover the demand, official calculations show that the capacity has to be expanded by 25 000. According to the Day Care Education Act, children with disabilities shall be given priority for a place at day care institutions provided that an expert panel concludes that the child would benefit from being present.

In 1997, nearly 2% of the children in *barnehage* were disabled, and 3% received additional support.

Children from linguistic, ethnic and cultural minorities have no statutory rights of access. The State allots earmarked grants, however, to local authorities to provide places in *barnehage* for these groups, which enables the employment of bilingual assistants. The State also finances attendance of 15 hours per week at *barnehage* during eight months for children of newly arrived refugees. Attendance by minority ethnic children at *barnehage* appears still to be low. According to a recent report only 39% have a place in the largest towns.

6.1.2. Compulsory and upper secondary education

Being compulsory, there are no entrance requirements to primary and lower secondary school. School is free of charge and the basic principle is that school materials are free. This also applies for adults. There are exceptions from this principle, and pupils and their parents have gradually been asked to pay for special events as excursions, and partly for textbooks.

As of Autumn 2002 adults who have not completed compulsory school or who wish to refresh their competence at this level, will be given a statutory right to lower secondary education. From the same date, this will also apply for special education.

As mentioned earlier, upper secondary education is available to all pupils who have completed compulsory education. Reform 94 gives all young people between the ages of 16 and 19 a statutory right to three years of upper secondary education. The applicants have the right to be admitted to one of three foundation courses that they have chosen. Admission to specific courses can be affected by factors such as the applicant's marks and the counties' course provision. If the number of applicants exceeds the number of places in the county, the pupils are assigned, depending on their marks from lower secondary school. However, more than 90% are accepted in their first choice course. A pupil with a handicap requiring special education has the right to be accepted on his or her preferred foundation course at the request of the pupil, his or her parents and teacher.

There has been a substantial reduction in the number of adults applying for courses in upper secondary education. In 1995, 55 000 applicants were 19 years old or above. In 1999, the number was reduced to 22 000. This may be due to the fact that adults have stronger preferences for their first choice. Also the low unemployment rate and the strong growth in employment can explain this trend, however. In the same period the number of refused applicants in this age group has been reduced from approximately 7 000 to 1 600 (Statistics Norway, Current educational statistics 7/99).

It is a generally accepted political objective to give adults with poor formal qualifications a statutory right to enter and complete upper secondary education. The Ministry put an amendment to the Education Act before the *Storting* in spring 2000 instituting these statutory rights from August 1st 2000. The regulations say that the provisions shall be flexible and adapted to the individual adults' needs (Circular F-42-00, O*m endringer i opplæringsloven og privateskoleloven*, pp. 1-2).

6.1.3. *Higher education*

It is a superior objective to open universities and university colleges to as many applicants as possible both to meet individual demands and to satisfy working life's need for highly-educated personnel. The argument has been that tertiary education gives a strong basis for adaptation to change and for occupational shifts. Knowledge makes good conditions for all-round personal development, for entrepreneurship and industrial innovation. As part of this strategy the authorities have improved the possibilities to study abroad for students who wish to do so.

In the Report to the *Storting* No. 36 (1998-99), *Principle for Dimensioning Higher Education*, the Government confirms this objective. In the same Report to the *Storting*, the Government says that the capacity makes it possible to admit more than 50% of the actual cohorts into tertiary education. This is in accordance with the view expressed by the Parliamentary Committee on Education in 1996 (Innst. St. No. 260, 1996-97). The committee regards the high proportion in tertiary education as a national advantage and strength. The challenge is to maintain the high number of students.

Because of smaller cohorts and less unemployment among young people, everyone who fulfils the formal requirements has been admitted to the university studies in liberal arts and sciences during the two to three last years. The decline in the number of applicants and changes in student behaviour have resulted in a situation where some of the institutions do not reach their expected student number. Most of the longer professional studies, *e.g.* medicine, are still regulated.

The normal entrance requirements are a diploma from three of the more theoretical lines in upper secondary education or one of the vocational lines supplemented with exams in common, general subjects.

Applicants can be admitted to higher education, however, without having passed the normal upper secondary final examinations. Such students must fulfil the specific minimum subject requirements in Norwegian, English, history and social studies, mathematics and natural science, be 23 years of age or older, and have at least five years of work experience or a combination of work experience, education and training.

Since autumn 1999 projects have been initiated whereby students are admitted to certain studies at a few higher education institutions on the basis of non-formal learning. Admission is based on either written or oral tests and age, combined with guidance or self-evaluation or relevant work experience.

A commission, appointed by the Government, has proposed that this right should be extended so that students can also be admitted on the basis of work experience. The same commission has launched the idea that students can be exempt from parts of the academic programme due to their real competence. These proposals are mainly in accordance with views held by a majority of the Parliament expressed in connection with the Competence Reform (Innst. St. No. 78, pp. 16-18). The Government put forth in spring 2000 a proposal for the Parliament giving persons over 25 years of age without a diploma from upper secondary education admittance to higher education based on their non-formal education.

Admission to some areas of professional studies is highly competitive, since demand exceeds the number of places available. Entry to higher education is thus regulated quantitatively and determined by the capacity of the individual institution. The basic principle for ranking students for these programmes is based on their marks from upper secondary education.

6.2. Private and practice candidates

An adult has the right to sit an exam in secondary school as a *private candidate*. Adults have the same legally secured right with regard to universities and university colleges. This implies that they can register as candidates in most fields without being enrolled at the institution. The exceptions are related to lacking laboratory capacity or similar problems. Also private candidates can be supported by the State Education Loan Fund. Due to the total capacity in the higher education system, most students are enrolled as ordinary students. The number of private candidates with support from the State Education Loan Fund is therefore very little.

Section 3.5 in the Education Act allows adults who wish to document their qualifications to register for a craft or journeyman's final examination without formal education in the field. They are called "practice candidates". There are some requirements, however: the applicant must document 25% longer relevant and varied experience than the ordinary apprentice period. This period can be shortened after special evaluation made by the county authorities. The number of adults using this possibility has increased considerably and in 1998 nearly 19 000 passed the apprentice's final examinations as private candidates. This is more than 60% of the total number who passed this exam this year.

This arrangement is well known in the labour market both among the employees and the employers. In an evaluation the enterprises supported statements in favour of the arrangement. It enhanced the competence in the company, stimulated further learning and contributed to higher quality of the work. The employees' motivation was a wish to document formally their competence and to strengthen their position in the labour market. Most of them had experienced positive support from their employers, they found the requirements – both in theory and practice – to be relevant and useful and at a manageable level (Pape, 2000, pp. 12-13).

So far vocational training in working life has been reserved for pupils who aim for a final apprentice exam. This has excluded pupils with weak qualifications. From autumn 2000 this group is given the opportunity to sign a contract with the aim of reaching a level lower than apprentice exam. The training can partly or in total take place in a business. These pupils shall have an individual programme, and the programme shall be concluded with a competence test. This right also applies to adults (Ministry of Education, Research and Church Affairs, Rundskriv F-42-00).

6.3. Documentation of non-formal learning

The Adult Education Act from 1976 gave the individual the right to get one's non-formal learning assessed or tested. Non-formal learning includes in-service training and courses and experience from different arenas. There was hardly a system developed to handle these evaluations and the right was never implemented.

One of the most important elements of the Competence Reform is to implement this right. The Education Act states that it is the responsibility of the State to provide the opportunity for adults to document their knowledge and skills at any level and in any field related to the public educational system irrespective of how they have acquired these qualifications. This right shall make it possible for the individual to enter the formal school system at a level corresponding to his/her competence and shorten his/her road towards an exam or a diploma. The intention is that this shall motivate adults to increase their competence by entering the formal educational system, if necessary repeatedly. A project has been started to establish a system for documentation and recognition of non-formal learning related to upper secondary education. The plans are worked out in close co-operation with the social partners and various providers of education.

6.4. Right to educational leave

In the collective agreements both in the private and public sectors, there are paragraphs giving employees the right to educational leave within certain conditions. If the leave is founded in the employee's personal wishes and needs, leave *can* be given, most probably without salary. In cases where the education is part of the enterprise's competence development plan, leave can be given with salary.

95

In November 1999, the *Storting* passed an act to take effect from 1 January 2001 giving the individual a statutory right to leave from work for educational purposes. This is primarily a codification of earlier collective agreements between the social partners of working life. The law states that persons having been in working life for more than three years and in the same enterprise the last two years have the right to full- or part-time leave up to three years to join an organised educational programme. The act does not regulate the question of salary and living cost in connection with leave.

6.5. Teacher training

As a consequence of the educational reforms the national framework curricula for teacher training was revised and put into force in 1998/99. The training shall lay a foundation for the challenges teachers will meet in primary, secondary and adult education. Therefore the training must be related to working life. The teacher training takes into account the principle of lifelong learning both with regards to comprehensiveness and coherency in basic education, as well as in further and continuing education. Problem-based, self-directed and team-based methods and project-work are included in all study-programmes. Adult teaching methods are included, and the students shall be able to use computer technology in their teaching.

There has also been developed a plan for competency development and further training of teaching personnel in compulsory school, and *Norgesnettrådet* are instructed by the Ministry of Education to give priority to further education of teachers. A new programme for the education of vocational teachers in upper secondary school will be carried out in the period from 2000 to 2006. Phase 1 has started in four regions where they offer education of teachers in five vocational lines.

6.6. Economic measures

6.6.1. *State investment to implement the Competence Reform*

As already mentioned, the Prime Minister stated the Government's commitment to follow up the Competence Reform in Spring 1999. Among the preferred means the Government would propose an additional grant of approximately 400 million NOK over a period of two to three years. In the State budget for 2000 the Government follows up the authorities' efforts and contribution to realise lifelong learning through several substantial grants. The grants to adult education sum up to 1.2 billion NOK representing an 8.9% growth compared to 1999. 180 million NOK extra are allotted to measures in connection with the reform as a follow-up of the Prime Minister's promises. Half of this amount is earmarked for the following purposes:

- An important element of the reform is the development of education opportunities, which exploit the huge potential lying in the workplace as an arena for learning. 50 million NOK will be used to competence development projects where providers for further education and demanders are invited to participate and co-operate. The programme will support projects that aim at developing new pedagogy and educational methods in further education, projects that contribute to a situation where further education to a greater extent is arranged within the enterprises and institutions. This also includes project where the aim is to develop new methods for spreading competence that are cost and learning effective by using ICT and multimedia.

- 10 million NOK are granted to map the need for lower secondary education for adults and to test educational methods for this group in some selected municipals. Another 10 million NOK are allotted to develop educational models in upper secondary education adapted to adults' demands and life situations. The aim is to make it easier for adults to attend lower and upper secondary education.

- 10 million NOK will be used to continue a project with the objective of developing and implementing a well-functioning documentation and assessment system at secondary level. This is added to 10 million NOK that was allocated to this purpose in 1999.

- The State's support to study associations and distance education institutions is increased with 10 million NOK. The amount is earmarked for courses at upper secondary level and shall be used to reduce the participants' own financial share.

In addition earmarked grants are set aside to finance competence development for teachers in fields like content and organisation of lower secondary schools, developing ICT as a pedagogical tool, and differentiation and adaptation of teaching. The Ministry will contribute to arrangements that give teachers the opportunity to study in-depth where the school asks for higher competence.

6.6.2. Loans and grants

As mentioned, the Storting passed a law in 1999 giving employees the statutory right to leave work in order to engage in competence development if this can be done without creating difficulties for planning and running the business effectively. So far this leave will be without pay. To compensate for the loss of income, the interested employees are entitled to use the State Education Loan Fund. The regulation of the fund will be changed in order to give adults better arrangements.

The students can have a monthly income of 5 000 NOK without deduction in loan and grant, and the allowance will normally not be counted against the income of the employee's spouse. The Government has expanded the grant to the State Education Loan Fund by 90 million NOK in 2000 to cover costs coming out of these regulations.

6.6.3. Tax exemption

Until 1999 enterprises' financial support to employees' competence development was registered as a benefit the employee had to report as income. This was therefore taxed. In order to stimulate employees to engage in competence development, the Taxation Law has been amended. As long as the education programme the employee attends has relevance for his and her present job, the benefit will not be taxed in the future.

6.6.4. The Norwegian Industrial and Regional Development Fund (SND)

In Reports to the *Storting* in the 1990s the Government has emphasised the need for stronger efforts to stimulate competence development in industry and business. The Norwegian Industrial and Regional Development Fund (SND) is an important agent in this endeavour. SND shall promote innovation, business development and turnaround operations in Norway; the fund is involved in more than 15 000 Norwegian companies.

The objective of SND's engagement is to increase the profitability and competitiveness of the enterprises by improving their ability to carry out continuous readjustment and innovation. SND has a special responsibility for stimulating competence development in small- and medium-sized companies. SND emphasises developing innovation and market competence and strategic ICT competence.

SND has at its disposal a set of instruments and contact with both industry and competence milieu that contribute to competence development: subsidies to individual companies, support to projects covering industrial branches and broader programmes. SND's financial tools are equity capital, low risk loans, venture capital loans, grants and guarantees. In 1999 SND allocated NOK 320 million for competence development.

Examples of programmes are:

- FRAM, a leadership and strategy development programme for small- and medium-sized companies. About 500 enterprises participated in the programme in 1999. This year the focus was on the companies' competence related resources and on developing their intellectual capital.

- BIT contributes to developing and implementing integrated ICT solutions for industrial branches. The pilot companies co-operate with their branch federation and ICT companies in developing solutions that make their business processes more efficient and improve their market communication.

6.7. Information and counselling system

6.7.1. Educational guidance related to working life

It is the school's responsibility to give the pupils the means they need to make their education and occupational choices. School shall also contribute to the pupils' ability to make fruitful use of these means. Vocational guidance and information about working life are integrated elements in the study programmes. In lower secondary school this is concentrated to social studies in grades nine and ten. The pupils shall work with the characteristics of Norwegian industrial and occupational structure, examine different educational lines, and gain a realistic attitude to a varied and changing labour market.

At upper secondary level there is a service at every school that has the task of providing information about different branches of study, the choice of subjects, apprenticeship training possibilities, and of giving individual advice on the choices faced by the pupils. The service will also have information about working life, employment opportunities in addition to opportunities for further and higher education. The service is mainly taken care of by a counsellor or learning co-ordinator. This field is given priority and will be followed with new actions.

The labour market authorities are responsible for the general guidance related to choice of education and vocation. The educational system has a responsibility for their students. Based upon an evaluation of Reform 94, the Ministry advocates a closer co-operation between the counsellor, the labour market authorities and the partners of working life, among others, in order to develop a system underscoring lifelong learning.

It is an objective of educational policy to promote the recruitment to vocational training. Steps to boost recruitment include strengthening vocational guidance, increasing the number of apprenticeship places, implementing economic stimulation, easing transfer between areas of study, and making sections of general subjects common for vocational and general areas of study. Internet-based vocational guidance tools and a paper-based guide for teachers and career counsellors are being developed.

Recruitment to vocational training in defiance of traditional, gender-bound choices is a principal goal. Work on the project "Conscious educational choice" focuses on the strategies needed to achieve this aim.

There is often a contradiction between the expectations placed upon career's staff in schools and the means, time and resources available to them. In addition, school counsellors tend to know more about the general educational programmes, than the vocational programmes. To give the learners and apprentices satisfactory guidance, further efforts will be taken to strengthen the counselling service in the immediate future. Among those efforts a three-year project is being implemented, involving splitting the counselling service into a socio-pedagogic component and a career-guidance component.

6.7.2. Follow-up service*

Before Reform 94 no institution had specific responsibility for young people without a job or place in the educational system. As part of the reform each county is now required by law to establish a follow-up service for young people at risk aged 16 to 19 years. This mainly applies to young people who have no permanent job, have not applied for or accepted a place in upper secondary education or an apprenticeship. There are several reasons for drop out. Some pupils have academic problems in school, others are in opposition to school and pursue other interests.

The object of the follow-up service is to provide training options for all young people leading, in so far is possible, to an approved qualification. The follow-up procedure is carried out in close co-operation with the various municipalities, counties and national authorities that share responsibility for this group. An important partner is the PES. This field is also prioritised by upper secondary schools. 50% of school counsellors regard the follow-up service as an important motivator in their work.

The service has a good overview of their potential clients. Twelve to 13% of the pupils have been in contact with the follow-up service in the first two years after leaving compulsory education. In 1998 12 546 pupils were registered. Only 10% refused the service's assistance. 30% got a temporary job on their own. More than half of the rest are successfully assisted by the follow-up service in finding some kind of education or training.

Still, the conclusion in an evaluation covering the period 1994 to 1998 is rather reserved:

"If we sum up what the follow-up service has achieved the first four years of the reform, we have to conclude that the service to a limited extent has been able to re-integrate the whole target group in education and work. Nearly half of the teenagers wishing an offer of education or work were unemployed in 1997/98" (Grøgaard and Midtsundstad, 1999, p. 250).

* Ministry of Education, Research and Church Affairs (1999).

Evaluations document great differences from one county to another in the service's ability to assist young persons. Low success rate is related to lack of suitable provision of work or training. The follow-up service not being responsible for these provisions is dependent upon municipal services or the PES. The co-operation is mainly constructive, but there exist problems. Budget for some of the PES is to some extent unpredictable, and the existing regulations of upper secondary education limit the possibility to develop new suitable provisions. Some civil servants in the follow-up service have interpreted their role as being a kind of pupils' *ombud*. Bringing success initially, this may cause problems in the long run.

Research shows the importance of well-functioning co-operation between the involved agents. The Ministry of Education will strengthen the cross-departmental co-operation in order to elaborate special educational programmes for students who need an alternative to the ordinary programmes.

6.8. Assistance to pupils with special needs

The Government states that a good basic education is an important requisite for lifelong learning. Persons lacking this foundation participate the least in further education, and they are over-represented among the long-term unemployed. In the following paragraph we will describe some specific actions taken to the benefit of some exposed and vulnerable groups.

6.8.1. Handicapped pupils and students

The right to special needs education is authorised in the Education Act. The kind of assistance depends on professional assessment related to the actual education. The statutory right also applies for adults who need education and training due to illness or injury. This group is entitled to renewed education supported by special needs education. Further, adults with insufficient compulsory education have a statutory right to special needs education. The education should be equal to ordinary primary and lower secondary education. The main purpose is to give the adults possibilities to improve their quality of life, to be more self-supporting, and to manage basic skills required in the labour market.

Handicapped pupils are given priority in the choice of upper secondary courses. Those who need special assistance due to disabilities or learning difficulties are entitled to special education programmes. As a matter of policy, these pupils are enrolled in ordinary schools whenever possible and hence are a part of the integrated school environment, but they sometimes receive their education in separate classes. The support offered depends on the nature of the disability. Those with learning disabilities will often get help in smaller groups and may be given more time to complete a course. Schools are also equipped to help those with physical handicaps so they can fully participate in the educational and social life of the school. Subject teachers are responsible for their education in co-operation with the parents, specially qualified teachers, the school administration and if necessary a resource centre.

Handicapped pupils may be granted the right to more than three years' education. When basic education in the school is combined with the completion of vocational training at an approved enterprise, education and training may last up to 4 years by combining the in-company training with productive work over 2 years.

Within higher education there are no legal obligations to lead an offensive policy favouring disabled students. Recently, the authorities have required that the institutions develop an action plan taking care of this group's needs. Each institution is responsible for their provision of advice and assistance. In practice most institutions provide special services for this group of students. At the University of Oslo, for example, there is a Section for Disabled Students with the purpose of giving service to students with special needs, and there is a net of contact persons at all faculties. Other universities have similar arrangements. The University of Science and Technology has initiated a programme taking into consideration many relevant aspects concerning these students: housing and physical environment, social integration, teaching methods and assistance, alternative examination forms. The common denominator is adaptation to the students needs. Disabled persons on rehabilitation schemes may attend higher education while receiving rehabilitation support.

Study associations also provide courses aimed at specific groups. This education is based on the Adult Education Act with the intention of giving disabled groups equal educational opportunities. 90% of this group is handicapped or functionally disabled. The study associations receive extra funding for this training and education. Table 6.1 gives an overview of this activity in the period 1995-98. The figures give us a rather unclear picture. There has been a decline regarding study

Table 6.1. **Courses run by study associations for specific groups, by study hours and pupils, 1995-98**

	Study hours	Pupils	
		Total	% women
1995	88 676	21 996	61
1996	91 625	22 464	62
1997	78 999	20 464	64
1998	74 788	23 397	63

Source: Statistics Norway, Current educational statistics 3/99.

hours used to this purpose, but it seems at the same time to be a small increase in the number of pupils.

6.8.2. Lingual minorities

As the unemployment has been reduced according to the general positive development in the labour market, the employment of persons from lingual minorities has increased and unemployment decreased. Still, these groups have a more difficult situation on the labour market than the rest of the labour force. In November 1999, 6.6% of the first generation immigrants were unemployed. This is twice that of the labour force at large.

According to the political objectives of the Labour Market Authorities for 2000 it will still be important to improve the opportunities of lingual minorities to get access to the labour market. Also the social partners of working life have observed that minorities have a higher unemployment rate than the rest of the population. This is regarded a waste of human resources and a source to social problems and inequality in society. The action plan negotiated by the social partners of working life therefore stresses increased effort to help immigrants, refugees and asylum seekers.

The number of courses in Norwegian as a second language has grown as a result of the increasing number of persons with non-Norwegian background. Language skills and familiarity with Norwegian society are considered important for social integration, for participating in further education and to get a job. This perspective largely determines the content of these courses. Education of adults in Norwegian as a second language is extended from 1998 so that the immigrants are given enough lessons to reach a minimum level of competence. The courses are limited to a 3 000 hours course for persons with little or no schooling from their home country, and to an 850-hour course for persons with better educational background. The courses are offered to all inhabitants with Norwegian as their second language with exception of those who have Swedish, Danish or Saami as their first language. An agreement between the partners specifies the employers' obligation to give immigrants leave to participate in Norwegian courses.

From 1998 immigrants between aged 16 to 20 years who have not completed lower secondary school have been offered courses to pass the examination at this level. Responsibility lies with the municipalities. To encourage the municipalities to organise courses at this level, they receive national grants.

Despite the increasing number of lingual minorities entering Norway in recent years, there was a decline for some time in the numbers (included refugees) that took courses in Norwegian as a second language. Numbers from 1998 indicate a change in this trend (see Table 6.2).

Table 6.2. **Courses for adults in Norwegian as a second language, 1994-98**

	1994	1995	1996	1997	1998
Teaching hours	547 235	613 368	572 715	556 776	673 653
Participants	27 525	25 565	22 268	22 040	28 957
Persons	13 179	13 909	13 598	11 252	17 345
Costs (1 000 NOK)	276 259	296 565	275 593	251 120	310 736
Accredited-courses compulsory levels, 16-20-year-olds					613

Source: Statistics Norway, Current educational statistics 3/99.

The Ministry of Local Government and Regional Development, in co-opera-tion with several other ministries, launched in 1998 a revised plan against racism and ethnic discrimination. The plan focuses on discrimination in the labour market and in the educational system and on the need to increase the expertise of public sector employees by providing services to a multicultural population.

6.8.3. Unemployed

The great majority of youths (95%) use their statutory right to upper secondary education. The "Youth Guarantee" ensures that persons under the age of 20 neither in school nor in work are offered a job or a place in a labour market pro-gramme. Even though the registered unemployment among youths has declined during the 1990s, the proportion of job seekers in this group compared to job seekers in general is relatively constant. In 1999 the average number of registered unemployed under the age of 20 was 2 486. This amounts to 1.5% of the popula-tion in the age group. In the same year the average number of participants in labour market programmes in the age group was 1 340.

Unemployed persons receive daily allowance from the PES. Ordinary educa-tion including individual living costs is taken care of by other public arrangements. Therefore, unemployed receiving daily allowance should, usually, not study on an ordinary basis. If they choose to study, they should use the ordinary arrange-ments. This policy has been criticised especially in times with relatively high unemployment, and there are today a few exceptions to this policy. Unemployed can attend education and training taking place outside ordinary working hours or in shorter courses.

6.8.4. Persons with restricted choice of employment

In 1999 the Directorate of Labour registered on an average 54 700 persons with handicaps limiting their choice of employment. This represents an increase of

3% from spring 1998. The authorities state that the heavy priority of those who are restricted in choice of occupation, will continue. A special attention will be paid to those who have complex problems and therefore need much assistance. As part of their rehabilitation, approximately 18 000 attended ordinary educational programmes and another 700 labour market training courses initiated by the labour market authorities in 1999.

Annex I.A

Overview of Earlier Assessments and Evidence

This annex presents some information about existing statistics and existing and ongoing research and evaluation related to the educational system and to lifelong learning. The information should make it possible to look at what we know about the educational system in general, and lifelong learning in particular, in the short- and in the long-term and from a qualitative and quantitative perspective.

The main intention with statistics, evaluation, research and policy analysis is to give public planning and social management the best possible factual basis and knowledge.

Former OECD reviews of Norwegian education

OECD has evaluated different aspects of the Norwegian educational system several times. Here we summarise some of the recommendations given or questions posed by former expert groups in the 1980s and 1990s, starting with the newest one. In general, the evaluations have been positive to the Norwegian educational system and the steps and actions taken by the authorities.

Early childhood education and care policy (1998)

In 1998 early childhood education and care policy was reviewed. The expert group was positive in its conclusive remarks. In their report from 1999 ("Thematic Review of Early Childhood Education and Care – Country Note on Norway"), the group drew special attention to the qualifications of the pedagogical staff in *barnehager*, the authorities' effort to get males into the staff and the parental leave system. The panel also underscored positive features such as the non-instrumental view upon childhood, the will to preserve childhood as an important life stage, the recognition of children's rights and the time reserved to outdoor activities.

The group stated that Norway was no longer homogeneous in its population and beliefs. According to the group this raised a discussion on how children should be cared for, about gender roles and the role of the State. They also pointed at the political discussion about the benefit scheme (*kontantstøtten*).

Some areas required further consideration, according to the expert group:

- There were issues of equity and cost. There remained major inequalities in the system, both with respect to access (provision varying between areas) and funding (parent fees vary dependent on private or public ownership of *barnehager*). This might affect the attendance of children from less advantaged backgrounds. This could also affect the increasing minority ethnic population in Norway.

- There were issues of structure. At a local level most authorities had moved to integrate responsibility for children's services bringing early childhood care, schooling and

SFOs within the same framework. Nationally, responsibility continued to be split between the Ministry of Children and Family Affairs and the Ministry of Education. The panel suggested that Norway review these arrangements.

- Most staff working in *barnehager* and SFOs had no training or a relatively low level of training. Trained early childhood teachers formed a minority. This situation should be considered in light of a wider review of staffing, and issues of recruitment, retention and gender of staff.

- Though SFOs played a major role in the lives of many children from 6 years upwards, they were not subject to any national regulations.

- Due to major policy changes in recent years, there were a number of important areas where further research and evaluation were called for. The expert group asked for better statistics with respect to government transfers and public and private cash flows to institutions, private family day-care and the extent of unmet or latent demand for places in pre-school institutions.

The transition from initial education to working life (1998)

In 1998 Reform 94 and the steps taken to ease transition from education and training to working life were evaluated. The conclusions were very supportive of Norwegian policy in this field. The group advocated fine-tuning rather than any fundamental realignment of goals or basic policy instruments. The panel pointed at several issues however:

- Norwegian research suggested that the problem of repeated spells of unemployment might be concentrated in certain groups of youths, particularly those from working class families with low levels of education and those working in retail and construction industries in which employment tended to be highly seasonal.

- It was debatable if the width of the pathways was an advantage or disadvantage. Narrower pathways could produce graduates who were more immediately useful to employers. The number of Advanced I courses led to a situation where factors other than student interest and local labour market demand became decisive for the individual pupil. Fewer but broader courses could make sense in this situation.

- Many of those who failed to obtain an apprenticeship and who were offered an alternative school-based Advanced II course in the same vocational field carried fairly high risks. Failure rates in many courses had been high. It was therefore important to improve the connections between this track and work.

- For similar reasons, the general education track was risky for many of those who failed to find an apprenticeship and who took a general education course rather than a school-based vocational course.

- The mismatch problem – the imbalance between supply and demand in some apprenticeship classifications – brought many issues to the fore. The signalling system should be improved. Among the more important actions were career education and guidance prior to the selection of a Foundation course and when choosing Advanced I and II courses.

- There appeared to be no common mechanisms in Norway for tracking destinations, particularly from upper secondary education into work, and for feeding the results back to colleges, schools, students and parents.

- Little attention had been paid to the connection between the general education track and work. For those who left upper secondary education without vocational qualification and higher education, the labour market was likely to pose particular problems.

- Reform 94 had posed particular challenges for teachers of general subjects within vocational tracks. The subjects should be relevant to the vocational area without compromising academic standards. The reform had also raised issues of student motivation and interest. Among employers, students and many teachers there was a feeling that the practical content of the first two years should be increased and theoretical content decreased and spread over a longer period to reduce the separation from working life.

Based on this the expert group put forward four suggestions:

- More attention needed to be paid to the ways in which the general education track led on to working life.

- The attention that had been paid to improve the quality of the apprenticeship track needed to be complemented by equal attention to the quality of the school-based vocational track.

- Greater flexibility should be introduced to the apprenticeship track in order to increase its links to working life.

- The excellent relationships that existed among the key institutional stakeholders at the national and regional levels could be complemented by an equal effort being devoted to a strengthening of the links between the key actors at the local level – the students, their teachers and employers.

Thematic review of the first years of tertiary education (1997)

The expert group who reviewed the first years of higher education in 1997 found much satisfaction at the level of the individual course, programme or institution. Standards of provision were generally high, teachers and students interacted often in small groups, and there was very often, especially in the regional institutions, a close working relationship with the community and employers. There were, however, a number of problems calling for attention:

- There was a queuing problem and the apparent lack of concern in a situation where many young people had to wait for years before they got access to their chosen course.

- Relations between tertiary education and the labour market were not as close as they might be.

- The traditional orientation towards passing exams rather than good teaching and rich learning experience and the lack of a clear profile in many degree programmes were all matters of concern. There was a tendency that the universities continued teaching as in days of low numbers, keeping much the same degree structure. It seemed that too little resources went into teaching. There could be too much measuring and not enough development of knowledge, especially knowledge that came from the field, the community, the workplace and other practical settings. The purpose and value of programmes should be reviewed, and the curricula, organisation and teaching revised, with an emphasis on addressing and meeting the well-defined needs of the students and the society.

- Evaluations at institutional and department level were occurring, but evaluation could be extended very usefully, made more systematic and given a national character. The panel therefore suggested that consideration be given to establishing a national agency, independent from, but closely related to the Ministry and the Parliament.

- There were considerable challenges to institutional management in both the university and the university college sectors. There was a need to strengthen the education, training and support services for people occupying demanding and responsible positions of management and leadership in higher education institutions.

- The panel did not recommend fees, but indicated that there were cost issues that could be addressed and efficiency gains made by taking an open-minded attitude towards the principle of new ways of sharing the increasing costs of tertiary education.

- Given the uncertainty, not to say scepticism over the reality of "Network Norway", the panel welcomed the initiatives taken to give the concept more substance and to provide a direction through the establishment of a national agency.

- The panel pointed to the devolution of central Ministry power. This was consistent with the strengthening of the university college sector that had occurred, but also with the recognition of the value of a more entrepreneurial role and more self-management in the universities. Decentralisation of power implied, on the other hand, a strengthening of the strategic, steering role of the Ministry and other central bodies.

The recommendations in this report have influenced the work of the Mjøs commission dealing with higher education. In chapters related to the quality and efficiency in the learning environment, the commission refers to the OECD report and some of the commission's suggestions are in accordance with the recommendations of the panel. There has been direct contact between OECD representatives and the commission.

Reviews of national policies for education (1988)

The panel reviewing Norwegian educational policy in 1988 was occupied with the different aspects of steering and decentralisation both because these were important issues in themselves, but also because they influenced considerably the ability of the system to provide education of high quality. Many of the questions posed must be understood on this background:

- Due to the wealth from the petroleum industry, the authorities might have initiated ambitious reforms. The wealth could have pushed sensible planning and conscious development into the background. The panel asked if the authorities thought that it was possible to reach their goals in a situation where demographic and economic conditions were changing or if the practical policy had to be modified in such a situation.

- The panel asked for a closer consideration of the ambitious policy to decentralise power. On the one hand, they were uncertain if the central authorities had kept sufficient influence on the policy-making and if they had enough analytic background information. On the other, they asked if the small local units were able to handle their extended responsibility. An administrative structure with many small municipalities might fail to reach the objectives of the national educational policy, be unable to give the schools sufficient support, and stimulate self-evaluation and development within the teaching profession.

- The panel thought that a more thorough analysis of the use of resources could have positive effects. The question was if resources could be used more effectively without reducing local influence and geographical distribution of schools.

- Norway lacked a strong database as a platform for calculations of the costs and the efficiency of the educational system. The authorities did not have figures making it possible to analyse expenditure and to relate those estimates to an analysis of educational results and quality. Norway should make a forceful effort to stimulate systematic and professional research within the comprehensive field of educational policy.
- To a large degree the educational system was without control and evaluation functions after the reforms in the 1980s. Having these functions was even more important when power was devolved from the Ministry to local authorities. The panel therefore challenged the authorities on this point and asked how such functions could be distributed between the Ministry, the Superintendents of School, central expert commissions and the local authorities in order to provide evaluation, control and self-development in the whole system.
- In higher education the OECD report suggested a consideration of amalgamation of the many small institutions and for closer ties between universities and other institutions. Further, the report invited a debate on whether the universities should be given more long-term economic security and more autonomy related to staffing. As part of a bargain the universities should make their objectives explicit in a consultation with the authorities.
- There seemed to be an imbalance between the needs of working life and the educational system. Schools did not have adequate equipment and the teachers' qualifications were lagging behind the development in the industry. General education was given higher priority than vocational training. Closer connections between companies and educational institutions could contribute to reducing the cleft. Norway should further reconsider the number of lines and courses the pupils could choose.
- Adult education could contribute to realising the policy of equality, regional distribution of educational provisions and vocational training. These facts should secure that adult education became an integrated part of the educational policy.
- Teacher training seemed to be fragmented since the students had to study ten subjects. Neither was the relationship between practical work in placement periods and theoretical studies satisfactory.

In their conclusion the OECD panel recommended that Norway shift focus from changes in structure to the quality the system provided in the next reform phase. In a situation where the Ministry had devolved parts of its traditional power, it would be necessary to establish new forms of influence through knowledge, information about good practice and critical evaluations of the whole system. The universities should provide parts of their budgets through contract research and teaching, but retain a certain freedom through state funding. They should carry out basic research and critical surveys, and simultaneously have an open eye for the needs of society and working life.

The recommendations of the panel have had great impact on the development of the Norwegian education system in the 1990s. The emphasis on relevance to working life and the reduction in lines and courses in upper secondary education are in accordance with the panel's recommendations. The amalgamation process in higher education has, together with greater institutional autonomy, its roots in the panel's suggestions. The evaluation of educational reforms has been strengthened, information system and better statistics have been introduced and reporting of results has been underscored. The establishment of the National Education Offices is part of the answer to the question of how to provide evaluation, control and self-development in a decentralised system.

Statistics

Statistical information is of vital importance for the functioning of society in general. Statistics describe numerically the status and changes of society; its objective is to give useful information for a wide range of purposes. Statistics Norway is responsible for producing official statistics in Norway. They prepare statistics on almost all principal sectors in society. For most of the topics, statistics contain information related both to national and regional level (county and municipality).

There is a running collection of information about the conditions in the educational system. Information about compulsory education is collected in GSI (*Grunnskolens informasjonssystem*) and about upper secondary education and training in VSI (*Videregående skoles informasjonssystem*). Statistics Norway has, in general, quality data concerning the whole "public" education system, but they lack data for analysing student progression.

The statistics cover almost all public educational activity at different education levels, from primary school to higher education. At present, educational statistics focus most upon the number of pupils, apprentices and students attending different educational levels and courses. These statistics include distribution by gender, age, mother language and type of educational line/stream. Further statistics give information about the number of schools, size of schools and classes, number of staff, staff per pupil, and class and financial resources used per pupil and class and in special education. There is also information about the number of applicants, the system's performance measured by the pupils' marks and number of diplomas, the time spent in different educational activities, classes and schools/colleges/universities and the personnel in different categories. Some of this quantitative information is used as indicators of quality and goal achievement. The statistics will be extended to include information on teachers' formal qualifications and economic conditions.

The official statistics are based on different databases. Concerning upper secondary education, the counties are responsible for giving comprehensive and systematic reports on the educational activities in the field. To this purpose a database called Linda has been established. Information about higher education and continuing education is collected in a database called DBH (Database for higher education) administered by Norwegian Social Science Data Services in Bergen. The Norwegian Institute for Studies in Research and Higher Education (NIFU) is responsible for the Norwegian doctoral degree register and also the database for R&D activities in higher education. The Directorate of Labour maintains its own register on the unemployed taking part in labour market training and disabled persons receiving rehabilitation benefits or taking part in a programme.

As shown in Chapter 5, there are some statistics related to the "adult education area". This covers information about adults attending primary, secondary and tertiary education and training, the number obtaining their diplomas, attending labour market courses and courses run by study associations and distance study institutions. The authorities also collect statistics about public resources allocated to adult education.

The overall picture, however, is that the statistics are rather incomplete and fragmentary. At present, no statistics give the full picture of the total investments in competence development. Neither does the Ministry have sufficient information about how municipalities and counties use the block grants to provide learning opportunities for adults.

There are many reasons for this. The public statistics on adult education that contained adult education in different voluntary associations, in compulsory education and in upper secondary education, ceased from the school year 1984-85 (Engesbak, 1995, p. 12). Furthermore, there are few public education institutions targeted especially at adults. As mentioned, the responsibility for adult education is shared between public authorities, study associations and other actors as distance education institutions, folk high schools, etc. In addition, actors like specific trades, business and enterprises also play important roles in adult education through internal educational programmes or in-service training. The voluntary and private organisations do not always deliver statistics over their course participants and investments in competence development. The authorities are aware of the weaknesses concerning statistical information, and, according to several public documents, development of relevant and reliable statistics within adult education is given high priority.

Research and evaluation on the reforms of the 1990s[1]

The educational sector manages a large part of society's resources, and it is necessary to be able to document the relationship between the input of resources and the capacity to meet the national objectives for the sector. An OECD report from 1988 focusing on the Norwegian educational system concluded that there was very little documentation and control data that could indicate to what extent educational policy goals were achieved. The Ministry of Education, Research and Church Affairs has followed up many of the proposals made by the OECD experts.

As mentioned earlier in this report, there have been reforms on all levels of the Norwegian educational system recently. In order to acquire knowledge of high quality and to enlighten more qualitative aspects of the educational system, the Ministry has initiated several research-based evaluations as supplements to the running reports. These have examined the extent to which the changes introduced have contributed to realising the stated goals. Since the lifelong learning perspective is a concern of all levels in the educational system, almost all of these evaluations have touched upon the field. The evaluations have also been necessary because the phenomena are complicated and the result shall be used in political processes. The evaluations give legitimacy and can contribute to a more qualified debate.

But the evaluations also have additional functions. They are organised in such a way that those involved in the reforms shall learn from the reform process. The evaluations therefore take into consideration the planning, the implementation and the carrying out of steps and projects. In other words, the evaluations follow the process from planning an educational reform through the point at which the user has passed through the system. Further, evaluations are an instrument to govern the educational system towards a higher degree of goal achievement and to disclose if the effects benefit the user of the educational system.

Evaluation of Reform 94 (upper secondary education): The most relevant evaluations and research studies in the field of lifelong learning were done in connection with the reform of upper secondary education (Reform 94). The Ministry of Education commissioned seven different research institutes[2] to monitor and evaluate various aspects related to the reform. The reform was subject to research-based analysis and the evaluation finished in 1998/99. The evaluation was designed to document to what extent the superior aims of the reform have been realised. In addition, it was important through the evaluation to provide the authorities with information in a form that made it possible to effectuate rapid adjustments and corrections in order to achieve more fully the aims of the reform.

Topics covered by the studies were: 1) the initial cohort's flow through the various levels of courses and the qualifications they obtain; 2) the division of responsibility among education authorities at different levels and the way they interact with each other; 3) the organisation and content of the vocational educational programmes; 4) the impact of the reform on young people with special needs and on adult applicants; and 5) the effectiveness of the follow-up service for early school leavers. Important aspects are the reform's consequences for marginal groups, such as adult pupils, ethnic minorities and apprentices with special needs, and the functioning of the statutory follow-up service.

More than 40 research reports have been published, and the main results are published in a common anthology (Kvalsund, Deichman-Sørensen and Aamodt, 1999). A complete literature reference list from the evaluation can be found in the anthology. All research institutes that were involved in Reform 94 are also today more or less active in the research field of lifelong learning.

Evaluation of the State University College reform: The reorganisation of the regional college system in 1994 is the most comprehensive reform ever in higher education. Over a period from 1994 to 1999 three research institutes evaluated the reform.[3] This resulted in one final report, 10 reports and 18 working papers. The final report gives a summarised analysis of the development in the college system related to the objective of the reform and other guidelines for the activity at the colleges. The report publishes results concerning the academic activity – teaching and research – at the college as a whole and academic activity related to individual programmes. This comprises data about co-operation, cross-disciplinary activity and time used on teaching and research. It contains information about governing and managing the colleges including division of responsibility between the different organisational levels and academic and administrative leaders and users' satisfaction with different administrative services. Data about the effect of the reform on recruitment, the adults' situation and on the institutions' connection and collaboration with industry and public services in the region are absent from the report.

Evaluation of Reform 97 (compulsory education): There are four main elements in Reform 97: 1) the school entrance age is lowered from seven to six and the compulsory education is extended from nine to ten years; 2) the school shall contribute to give children rich impulses through play and learning and company with adults having different roles; 3) according to the intentions small children shall be taken care of before and after ordinary school-hours when needed; and 4) the culture of the neighbourhood and region shall be an integrated part of school's everyday life.

The reform will now be evaluated over a period of five years dated from 1999 in a research-based programme directed by the Norwegian Council of Research. The objectives of the programme are to map changes and development that can give basis for further planning, adjustment and implementation of the reform. It shall evaluate if the chosen solutions are suited to reach the targets of the reform, disclose strong and weak aspect of the reform and point at unintended positive and negative consequences. Finally, it is expected that the projects shall bring forth proposals to improve the results of Reform 97.

In order to involve the best qualified researchers six research groups were invited to co-ordinate the projects, and some are already given financial support. The programme is organised around three topics: 1) the curriculum, subjects and educational practice; 2) co-operation, leadership, learning environment and learning results; and 3) comprehensive school, equality and cultural diversity. According to conditions stated by the Parliament, the evaluation of the new subject "Christianity, Religion and Life-stance" was given priority.

Research and evaluations concerning adult education: There was also a certain research activity in connection with the Buer Commissions' work in 1997. The main contributors were the Foundation for Research in Economics and Business Administration (SNF) and the Centre for Economic Analysis (ECON).

In the 1970s, researchers as well as politicians focused on adults with little formal education and their participation in the educational system. Much research was carried out by the Norwegian Institute of Adult Education Research, established in Trondheim by the Ministry of Education.

From the 1980s, politicians and researchers focused more on competence development in working life, particularly employee education paid by employers. Researchers from the Norwegian School of Economics and Business Administration published studies on employee education with data covering both firms and individuals. Studies in the 1990s were occupied with collaboration between firms and local higher education institutions (Nordhaug, 1991), and also with some municipal services (Larsen *et al.*, 1997) in realising employee education.

Researchers from the Norwegian Institute for Studies in Research and Higher Education studied employee education in firms (Brandt, 1989). Furthermore, they have studied different providers of continuing professional education for managers and engineers (Brandt, 1991, 1995) – the later as part of the OECD project "Recent Developments in Continuing Professional Education" (OECD, 1995). They found that more courses in management, sales and service were "tailor made" for firms. Commercial course agencies, often also consultants in these fields, made up a majority of the providers. However, higher education institutions in business administration and technology were also active providers of customised commissioned management courses through their centres of continuing education.

Distance education has become a more and more popular field of research in the 1990s. The typical distance education student in Norway has been described as between 35 and 45 years-old, he/she is working full-time, is married, has children and has some higher education. The spouse has completed higher education. In a study of distance students in Northern Norway, most had taken work-related courses for years, and their employers in public sector have paid for their studies (Støkken, 1993).

Notes

1. This section is partly based on an article from Brandt (2001).

2. The following research institutions participated in the evaluation of Reform 94: Work Research Institute (Arbeidsforskningsinstituttet – AFI), Group for Work Research at University in Bergen (Gruppe for flerfaglig arbeidslivsforskning ved Universitetet i Bergen), Institute for Applied Social Science (Forskningsstiftelsen FAFA), Volda College/Møre Research (Høgskolen i Volda/Møreforskning), Lillehammer College (Høgskolen i Lillehammer), Norwegian Institute for Adult Education (Norsk voksenpedagogisk forskningsinstitutt – NVI), and Norwegian Institute for Studies in Research and Higher Education (Norsk institutt for studier av forskning og utdanning – NIFU).

3. The participating institutes are: Norsk institutt for studier av forskning og utdanning (NIFU), Møreforsking Molde and Institutt for administrasjon og organisasjonsvitenskap at the University of Bergen.

Bibliography

ÅRANG, M. (2000),
Education in Norway, Ministry of Education, Research and Church Affairs, Oslo, May.

BORGE, A.I.H. (1998),
Barnets verd og barnehagens verdier, Oslo.

BRANDT, E. (1989),
"Vi satser på kompetanse: opplæringspolitikk i tolv høyteknologi- og servicebedrifter",
No. 7, NAVFs utredningsinstitutt, Oslo.

BRANDT, E. (1991),
Continuing Education for Managers and Engineers: From a study of Norwegian firms and course providers, No. 91, NAVFs utredningsinstitutt, Oslo.

BRANDT, E. (1995),
"Norwegian contribution" to Continuing Professional Education of Highly-Qualified Personnel,
OECD, Paris.

BRANDT, E. (1999),
"Higher Education Institutions and the Market for Lifelong Learning in Norway", in
OECD, Higher Education Management, Vol. 11, No. 2, Paris.

BRANDT, E. (2001),
"Lifelong Learning in Norwegian Universities", European Journal of Education, Blackwell
Publishers Ltd, Oxford, UK and Boston, USA, September, Vol. 36, No. 3, pp. 265-276.

BRISEID, O. (1995),
"Comprehensive Reform in Upper Secondary Education in Norway", European Journal of
Education, Vol. 30, No. 3.

ENGESBAK, H. (1995),
"Voksne i videregående. Reform 94 og konsekvenser for voksne", Evalueringsrapport 1/
95, Norsk voksenpedagogisk forskningsinstitutt.

GRØGAARD, J.B. and MIDTSUNDSTAD, T. (1999),
"Oppfølgingstjenesten – Quo Vadis?", in R. Kvalsund, T. Deichman-Sørensen and P.O.
Aamodt (eds.), Videregående opplæring – ved en skilleveg? Forskning fra den nasjonale evalueringen
av Reform 94, Tano Aschehoug, Oslo.

KVALSUND, R., DEICHMAN-SøRENSEN, T. and AAMODT, P.O. (1999),
Videregående opplæring – ved en skilleveg? Forskning fra den nasjonale evalueringen av Reform 94,
Tano Aschehoug, Oslo.

KYVIK, S. (1999),
Evaluering av høgskolereformen, Sluttrapport, Norges forskningsråd, Oslo.

117

LARSEN, K.A. (1996),
Rekrutteringsundersøkelsen 1995. Søkning og rekruttering til ledige stillinger, Arbeidsdirektoratet, Oslo.

LARSEN, K.A., NYSETH, T. and VRALSTAD, K. (1997),
Kompetanseheving i kommunesektoren, No. 10/97, Nordlandsforskning, Bodø.

LYSKLÆTT, F.T. (1999),
"Background Paper from the Ministry of Education, Research and Church Affairs to Nordic Transition Conference 1st-2nd November 1999", Oslo.

MICHELSEN, S., HØST, H. and GITLESEN, J.P. (1999),
"Mot en ny fagopplæringsordning", in R. Kvalsund, T. Deichman-Sørensen and P.O. Aamodt (eds.), Videregående opplæring – Ved en skilleveg?, Tano Aschehoug, Oslo.

MINISTRY OF EDUCATION, RESEARCH AND CHURCH AFFAIRS (KUF) (1999),
"Følge opp – eller forfølge", Evaluering av Reform 94, Oslo.

NORDHAUG, O. (1991),
The shadow educational system, Norwegian University Press, Oslo.

NORWEGIAN INSTITUTE FOR STUDIES IN RESEARCH AND HIGHER EDUCATION (NIFU) (1998),
Gjennom videregående opplæring, Sammendrag av i Evaluering av reform 94, Report No. 19.

NORWEGIAN INSTITUTE FOR STUDIES IN RESEARCH AND HIGHER EDUCATION (NIFU) (2000),
Veksten i høyere utdanning: Et vellykket arbeidsmarkedspolitisk tiltak, Report No. 2.

NORGES FORSKNINGSRÅD (1999),
Det norske forsknings- og innovasjonssystemet – statistikk og indikatorer 1999, Oslo.

NOU (1986),
Livslang Læring. Kirke- og undervisingsdepartmentet, Norwegian Royal Commission Report No. 23, Oslo.

NOU (1997),
New Competence – The Basis for a Comprehensive Policy for Continuing Education, Norwegian Royal Commission Report No. 25, Oslo.

NOU (1999),
Forberedelse av inntektsoppgjøret, Norwegian Royal Commission Report No. 14, Oslo.

NOU (2000a),
Frihet med ansvar: Om høgre utdanning og forskning i Norge, Norwegian Royal Commision Report No. 14, Oslo.

NOU (2000b),
Mellom barken og veden – Om fagskoleutdanninger, Norwegian Royal Commision Report No. 5, Oslo.

NORWEGIAN INSTITUTE OF ADULT EDUCATION RESEARCH (NVI) (1998),
På rett vei, uten rett, Reform 94.

OECD (1995),
Continuing Professional Education of Highly-Qualified Personnel, Paris.

OECD (1996),
Lifelong Learning for All, Paris.

OECD (1998),
"Thematic Review of the Transition from Initial Education to Working Life – Norway, Country Note", Paris.

OECD (2000),
"Thematic Review on Adult Learning, Norway – Background Report", Paris.

OECD (2001),
Education at a Glance – OECD Indicators, Paris.

PAPE, A. (2000),
Fagbrev gjennom dokumentasjon av realkompetanse i Norge, FAFO-notat, pp. 12-13.

SALVANES, K.G. (1996),
Job Creation and Job Destruction in Norwegian Manufacturing and Service Sectors 1976-92, SNF.

SKAALVIK, E. and ENGESBAK, H. (1996),
"Selvrealisering og kompetanseutvikling: Rekruttering til vokseopplæring i et tjueårsperspektiv", in Fra lov til reform, NVI, Trondheim.

SKULE, S. and REICHBORN, A.N. (2000),
Lærende arbeid – En kartlegging av lærevilkår i norsk arbeidsliv, FAFO-Report 333, Oslo.

SØBSTAD, F. (2000),
"Barnehagen inn i et nytt årtusen" (unpublished article).

STATISTICS NORWAY (1999),
Befolkningsstatistikk. Innvandrerbefolkningen; Folkemengde, etter landbakgrunn 1970-1999.

STOKKEN, A.M. (1993),
Fjernstudenten, No. 9, Arbeidsforskningsinstituttet, Oslo.

TELHAUG, A.O. (1997),
Utdanningsreformene – Oversikt og analyse, Oslo.

TØSSE, S. (1996),
Det statlege engasjementet i vaksenopplæring. I Fra lov – til reform, Trondheim.

Part II
THE EXAMINERS' REPORT

Executive Summary

The review was undertaken to assess Norwegian progress towards implementing "lifelong learning". The concept of lifelong learning that has guided the Norwegian authorities and the Review Team includes several key aspects:

- a truly "cradle to grave" view – recognising that motivation to learn needs to be instilled early on, and learning needs to continue beyond initial education and training;

- coverage of all forms of learning – be they formal or informal – irrespective of the setting in which they occur;

- paying attention to multiple transitions between learning, working and living throughout life;

- placing the learner at the very centre – a shift of focus from teaching to learning, and an emphasis on addressing the learning needs of *all* individuals; generating a capacity for self-directed learning; recognising that the sources, types, and the settings of learning are becoming diversified, especially due to ICT;

- a shift of policy focus from supply orientation to the demand side, which implies that learning is well integrated with the needs of the economy and society; and

- a wide and deep involvement of all actors in the process of teaching and learning.

With this conception of lifelong learning in mind, the Review Team set out to investigate a number of five broad questions that were agreed to in advance by the Norwegian authorities and the OECD Secretariat:

- How is lifelong learning defined, and whose views does it represent?

- What difference does the concept and practice of lifelong learning make to the individual learner?

- Is public policy-making coherent with the aims and implementation of strategies for lifelong learning?

123|

- What roles do the social partners play in implementing strategies for life-long learning?

- What is being done to ensure that lifelong learning is affordable?

The Norwegian decision to forge ahead with articulating and implementing a bold vision of lifelong learning was not taken in a vacuum. It represents a next logical step for a highly-developed country with a highly-educated population, confronted with challenges ranging from economic re-structuring, to an increasingly diverse society and an ageing workforce. The context is a "knowledge society" – a world in which information, knowledge and information and communication technology (ICT) play a large and growing role in work, leisure, and home life.

Unlike many OECD member countries, Norway approaches the challenges of the "knowledge society", and of implementing a system of lifelong learning from a position of exceptional strength:

- It has one of the highest standards of living of any country in the OECD; from an economic perspective, its past performance appears to rest on strong foundations and to be durable and sustainable in the future. The windfall from the North Sea petroleum reserves is being husbanded, and there is awareness of the need to ensure that economic growth can continue in the long-term without petroleum.

- Norway aims to achieve lifelong learning for one of the most highly-qualified populations in the world. Young and old alike have high levels of educational attainment. Judging from the results of the International Adult Literacy Survey, the output of the formal education system is good.

- On a political level there is strong support for education, judging from the share of GDP and the share of public expenditure devoted to education, and judging from the ongoing initiatives to reform and improve education. The view that it is important to strengthen learning opportunities seems widely shared, within Government and by social partners.

Nonetheless, existing institutional arrangements and policies fall short of a systemic approach to lifelong learning. The most obvious shortcomings concern adults. Though the Competence Reform aims to redress them, there are formidable challenges to its implementation. Ministerial responsibilities, institutional roles and individual behaviour need to change, and daunting issues regarding the finance of adult learning need to be addressed. There also is need to further understand the interaction between different stages of lifelong learning and what that implies for policy and practice. For example, it would appear that reforms in secondary education have not resolved the difficulties faced by a non-negligible number of young persons who leave education before acquiring any qualification. It remains to be seen whether these problems can or will be addressed through preventive interventions at an earlier age, and/or remedial interventions for poorly-qualified adults.

Perhaps the most unsettled issue is leadership. As with past education reforms that have been led by the Ministry of Education, Research and Church Affairs, the Ministry is leading the Competence Reform. But in contrast to past education reforms, the Competence Reform agenda requires concerted action by multiple ministries *as well as* the social partners. A critical question is whether the available instruments for leadership will be sufficient.

Choice, equity and quality are in many cases conflicting, and decisions about priorities often must be made. The equity criterion is the most important in the first phase of educational participation. For the young, and especially for minority groups, it is the prime focus of the responsibility of the Government. Further on in the educational system the importance of the other criteria increases. There is no exact line to draw; it is a matter of further discussion and deliberation to find out what is the most appropriate in the Norwegian context. Norway is advanced, relative to other countries, in the development of new politics regarding the knowledge society. Indeed, the Review Team believes that if lifelong learning is to succeed anywhere, Norway is one of the most likely places in view of its history of reforms, co-operation among bodies, high educational standards and outcomes. While the Norwegian approach is not a model to copy, lessons from the experience with this approach can be usefully applied in other settings.

The Review Team is most impressed by the ambitions of Norway to become a society where lifelong learning is a reality to the benefit of its citizens and society at large, and by the systematic way it has created the pre-conditions.

Chapter 1

Introduction

1.1. Why a review of lifelong learning?

When Ministers met in January 1996, they argued that "lifelong learning will be essential for everyone as we move into the 21st century…". In so arguing, they neither under-estimated the challenge they laid down, nor over-stated the importance of the role of international co-operation in sharing understanding and strategies for meeting that challenge:

Strategies for lifelong learning need a wholehearted commitment to new system-wide goals, standards and approaches, adapted to the culture and circumstances of each country. OECD Education Ministers agreed to:

- *strengthen the foundations for learning throughout life* (…);
- *promote coherent links between learning and work* (…);
- *rethink the roles and responsibilities of all partners* (…);
- *create incentives…to invest more in lifelong learning* (…).

In *developing these strategies, Ministers affirm the importance of international co-operation and the value of the exchange of views and information that take place in the* OECD… (OECD, 1996, p. 21).

In the spirit of "international co-operation and… the exchange of views", the Norwegian Ministry of Education, Research and Church Affairs (KUF) invited the OECD Secretariat to undertake an examination of lifelong learning in Norway that would permit sharing their experience and learning from others. The review was organised within the framework of the OECD's education policy reviews.

After agreeing to terms of reference, in 2000 the Secretariat assembled a Review Team,[1] in consultation with the Norwegian authorities, to assess the efforts of the Norwegian society to make lifelong learning for all a reality. The Norwegian authorities supervised preparation of a background report that provided the Review Team with information on the historical, cultural, social, economic and policy context within which lifelong learning was being implemented. The Review Team also benefited from other background material provided by the Secretariat;

127

this included the most recent economic survey of Norway (OECD, 2000d), the most recent review of educational policy, carried out in 1988 (OECD, 1990); a report on financing lifelong learning in Norway, and material from a number of "thematic reviews" of early childhood education and care policy, transition from initial education to working life, tertiary education, and adult learning. The team visited Norway[2] to carry out a number of interviews to gather further facts and solicit views on a range of issues related to lifelong learning in Norway.

1.2. Terms of reference

The review was undertaken to assess Norwegian progress towards implementing "lifelong learning". The concept of lifelong learning that has guided the Norwegian authorities and the Review Team includes several key aspects:

- a truly "cradle to grave" view – recognising that motivation to learn needs to be instilled early on, and learning needs to continue beyond initial education and training;

- coverage of all forms of learning – be they formal or informal – irrespective of the setting in which they occur;

- paying attention to multiple transitions between learning, working and living throughout life;

- placing the learner at the very centre – a shift of focus from teaching to learning, and an emphasis on addressing the learning needs of *all* individuals; generating a capacity for self-directed learning; recognising that the sources, types, and the settings of learning are becoming diversified, especially due to ICT;

- a shift of policy focus from supply orientation to the demand side, which implies that learning is well integrated with the needs of the economy and society; and

- a wide and deep involvement of all actors in the process of teaching and learning.

With this conception of lifelong learning in mind, the Review Team set out to investigate five broad questions that were agreed to in advance by the Norwegian authorities and the OECD Secretariat:

- How is lifelong learning defined, and whose views does it represent?

- What difference does the concept and practice of lifelong learning make to the individual learner?

- Is public policy-making coherent with the aims and implementation of strategies for lifelong learning?

- What roles do the social partners play in implementing strategies for life-long learning?
- What is being done to ensure that lifelong learning is affordable?

1.3. Structure of the report

Chapter 2 reviews the social, economic, political and institutional context in which Norway has articulated its vision of lifelong learning. Chapter 3 examines the goals and objectives of lifelong learning in Norway, who it is for, and who it involves. Chapter 4 examines unfinished aspects of the lifelong learning agenda in Norway, with a focus on integration of learning and working life. Chapter 5 addresses the issue of implementation of lifelong learning across multiple public policy areas and in co-operation with the social partners. Chapter 6 discusses overriding principles to guide formulation and implementation of further policies for lifelong learning. Annex II.A lists recommendations by chapter and section.

1.4. A word of thanks and warning

The Review Team and the OECD Secretariat would like to express its appreciation to the Norwegian authorities, representatives of the social partners and non-governmental organisations, academics, and citizens who shared their knowledge, experience, and views during meetings in Oslo, Trondheim and Tromsø. Their co-operation and input was invaluable. We also would like to thank Minister Trond Giske for welcoming this review, to Trond Fevolden, Hanna Marit Jahr, and Jan S. Levy for putting at our disposal the resources of the Ministry of Education, Research and Church Affairs, and to Per Kjøl for preparing the background report. We are particularly grateful for the efforts of Kari Østvedt of the Ministry of Education, Research and Church Affairs who supervised the preparation of the Background Report, and organised the Review Team's visit, and accompanied the team. This visit took place in October 2000. Since then much policy development and implementation has taken place, decisions have been made in Parliament and action has followed. Therefore some of our observations have been taken over by developments.

Notes

1. The team was chaired by Ingrid Moses, Vice-Chancellor, University of New England, Armidale, New South Wales, Australia. Other members were Ferdinand Mertens, Inspector General for Education, the Netherlands; Åsa Sohlman, Director, Ministry of Industry, Employment and Communications, Sweden; and Mark van Buren, Director of Research, American Society for Training and Development, Alexandria, Virginia, United States. During its visit to Norway, the team was accompanied by Abrar Hasan, Head, Education and Training Division, and Gregory Wurzburg, Principal Administrator, Education and Training Division of the OECD.

2. Preparations for the review and scheduling of the team's visit were co-ordinated by Kari Østvedt of the Ministry of Education, Research and Church Affairs. The review team visited Norway from 1-10 October 2000. The team met with government officials, service providers, academics, and representatives of the social partners, learners and non-governmental organisations; these meetings took place in Oslo, Trondheim and Tromsø.

Chapter 2

Lifelong Learning in Norway: The National and International Context

The Norwegian decision to forge ahead with articulating and implementing a bold vision of lifelong learning was not taken in a vacuum. It represents a logical next step for a highly-developed country with a highly-educated population, confronted with challenges ranging from economic re-structuring, to an increasingly diverse society and an ageing workforce. The context is a "knowledge society" – a world in which information, knowledge and information and communication technology (ICT) play a large and growing role in work, leisure and home life.

This chapter examines the broader context within which Norwegian society is attempting to realise its vision of lifelong learning. After providing an overview of the country, it examines first the social and demographic factors that provide much of the impetus for the initiatives for lifelong learning. Then it considers the economic factors at work that intensify the demand for lifelong learning, as well as providing the financial means for making it happen. Throughout this discussion, the Norwegian situation is compared to that in other OECD member countries. The chapter then considers the institutional and policy context out of which the present initiative is growing, and in which lifelong learning is being implemented. Concluding comments summarise the main challenges, and introduce the chapters that examine them.

2.1. Overview

Norway is a geographically rugged Nordic country that straddles the Arctic Circle; it shares borders with Finland, Russia and Sweden on the east, and faces the North Sea on the west. It has a population of 4 445 million, of which a fifth lives in the 3 largest cities, Oslo (503 000), Bergen (227 000) and Trondheim (147 000). Compared with other OECD countries (see Table 2.1), Norway is wealthier, better educated, and healthier. It also does extremely well, in comparison to other OECD member countries, in providing opportunities for lifelong learning (OECD, 2001, Chapter 2 "Lifelong Learning for All: Taking Stock", pp. 65-66). Norwegians are

Table 2.1. **Main features of Norway compared to other countries**

(data for 1998 unless otherwise indicated)

	Norway	OECD
Land area (1 000 km^2)	324	
% in agriculture	2.7	
% in productive forests	19.2	
Population density (inhab./km^2)	14	32
Population total (x 1 000)	4 418	1 100 546
% under 15	19.8	20.9
% 15-64	64.6	66.4
% 65 and over	15.7	12.7
Foreign population in %[1]	3.7	7.0
Life expectancy at birth (1997)		
women	81.0	
men	79.6	
Labour force (x 1 000)	2 317	521 104
Female participation rate in %	76.3	
Foreign labour force in % (1997)	2.8	
Unemployment rate in %	3.2	6.7
GDP growth in %		
(1998-99)	0.6	2.8
(1995-99)	3.0	2.7
GDP per capita in $ US (adjusted for PPP)	27 600	22 300
Total tax receipts as % of GDP	42.6	37.2
After tax income of average production worker (spouse + 2 children), % of gross pay	74.8	79.6
Gross domestic expenditure on R&D as % of GDP	1.68	2.21
Public education expenditure on institutions as % of GDP (1997)	6.6	5.1
Adults 25-64 with upper secondary education or more in %	83.0	61.2

1. % of total population that is foreign or foreign born (OECD, 2000, *Economic Outlook*, Paris).
Source: Unless indicated, OECD (2000), OECD *in Figures*, Paris.

taxed relatively heavily to help pay for this good life; but citizens in many other countries get considerably less for the same or even greater tax burdens.

One can imagine a near-limitless number of explanations of Norway's good fortunes, that range from snowy mountains, to stormy seas, to trolls, to abundant sun in the summer, to long nights in the winter, to the beauty of the *aurora borealis*. But, of course they do not really explain what one sees in Norwegian society, and they are not of much help in addressing the problems that even society in Norway encounters.

Indeed, the interest of Norway and Norwegians in lifelong learning seems driven in substantial part by recent developments and concern about an uncertain future and the problems it may hold, and the conviction that lifelong learning offers a strategy to better equip Norwegian society to deal with those uncertainties. If external and internal circumstances and developments risk posing problems, lifelong learning is seen as part of the solution.

The sources of concern stem from social and demographic factors that are changing the fabric, values, and expectations of Norwegian society. Norway is considered to be an ageing society. It has fewer young and more older citizens than most OECD countries. Although it has been relatively homogeneous in its cultural and ethnic composition, Norway does have some ethnic minorities who have not had equitable access to opportunity. Additionally, Norway, like many other OECD member countries, has experienced large influxes of foreigners recently, many of them refugees. Concerns also stem from factors in the Norwegian economy, and developments and trends in the larger global economy within which Norway competes. North Sea oil reserves, a unique source of wealth for Norway, are finite. The anticipated exhaustion of those reserves combined with intense international competition in other markets promises substantial economic restructuring. The following sections examine these and related factors in some detail, and relate them to the view that lifelong learning needs to be strengthened. Except where indicated otherwise, references to the Background Report refer to a report (KUF, 2000c) prepared under supervision of the Ministry of Education, Research and Church Affairs (KUF), and intended to inform the deliberations of the Review Team.

2.2. The changing face of Norway

Lifelong learning is seen as something that can enhance society's capacity to stimulate and accommodate transitions. Aside from the interactions with some of the obvious economic developments that are discussed in the next section, there are important changes in Norwegians themselves, in *who* they are.

2.2.1. Educational attainment and literacy

The emphasis on lifelong learning is justified not simply as a strategy to update qualifications of adults, for example, but to respond to the demand of a highly-qualified population for still more learning. In the case of Norway, it is "the learning-rich wanting to get richer". Moreover, given the strong commitment in Norway to overcoming sources of social division, lifelong learning strategies have a crucial role to play. Figures 2.1a and 2.1b present data on educational attainment levels by age group and gender for Norway and the average for all OECD countries. It shows not only high overall levels of educational attainment compared to the OECD, but a longstanding pattern of relatively high attainment rates. Thus, while young Norwegians are better educated than older Norwegians, the differences between the younger (25-34-year-olds) and older (55-64-year-olds) in Norway tends to be much smaller than those found in most other countries. The gaps in educational attainment between men and women are much smaller for

133

Figure 2.1*a.* **Percentage of the population that has attained at least upper secondary education, by age and gender, 1998**

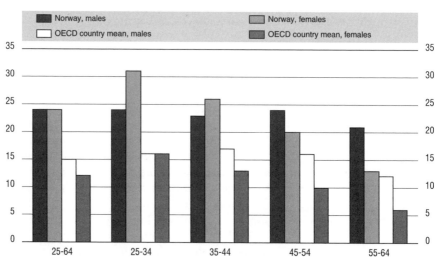

Source: OECD (2000), *Education at a Glance – OECD Indicators*, Paris.

Figure 2.1*b.* **Percentage of the population that has attained at least upper tertiary education type A,[1] by age and gender, 1998**

1. Theorical studies leading to first and advanced university degrees.
Source: OECD (2000), *Education at a Glance – OECD Indicators*, Paris.

older persons in Norway than in other countries; among persons under the age of 45 differences by gender are virtually non-existent or favour women.

Data on formal educational attainment suggest that Norway has a population that is well qualified by international standards. However, since educational attainment data do not always capture equivalent achievement levels, it is useful to compare measures of actual outcomes to interpret the educational attainment data. Data gathered through the International Adult Literacy Survey permit comparing outcomes by providing estimates of *literacy levels* of the adult population. Figure 2.2 presents data on actual educational achievement (proxied by literacy level) of younger persons who have exited the formal education system. It also provides data on literacy levels for older adults who have only a secondary education; this serves as a proxy for learning by adults after leaving the formal education system. The data from Figure 2.2 show that, on average, Norwegians who have completed upper secondary education score slightly above the OECD average for upper secondary completers. Another way of evaluating learning is to assess literacy levels of older persons who left formal education years ago. The last group of

Figure 2.2. **Literacy levels[1] in Norway and the OECD[2]**

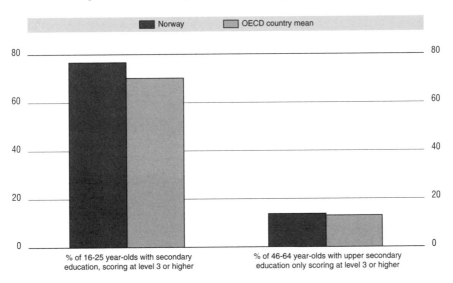

1. Mean score on document scale, IALS.
2. Australia, Belgium (Fl.), Canada, Czech Rep., Denmark, Finland, Germany, Hungary, Ireland, Netherlands, New Zealand, Norway, Poland, Portugal, Sweden, Switzerland, United Kingdom, United States.
Source: OECD (2001), *Education Policy Analysis*, Paris.

135|

columns of the figure shows the proportion of 46-65-year-olds who have an upper secondary and no more, and yet score relatively high on the IALS. Again Norway shows up slightly above the OECD average. But here, as in the first case, there are several countries in which adults score higher on average. This would suggest that the success of the Norwegian approach derives more from its *inclusiveness* (capacity to provide high levels of educational attainment to a larger proportion of the population), than in its *quality* (capacity to achieve high level outcomes for a given level of educational attainment).

High levels of educational attainment of the Norwegian population do not appear to be translating fully into high rates of participation in lifelong learning. Figure 2.3 shows that highly-qualified adults comprise a relatively large share of tertiary level enrolments, substantially above the OECD average. But those levels are not particularly high compared to other countries with a large proportion of persons holding tertiary qualifications. In other words, Norway's performance with respect to providing further learning opportunities for highly-qualified persons is *not* exceptional by international standards. What is more worrisome is that the forces that have led to high levels of initial qualifications have not had much effect on pushing up participation by adults with lower levels of initial qualifications. In

Figure 2.3. **Adult share of total enrolments in education institutions, 1998**

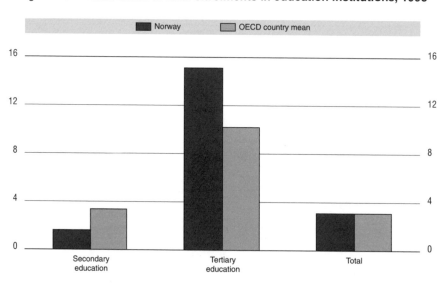

Source: OECD education database.

Norway their share of enrolments in secondary level institutions is, in fact, slightly below the OECD average. The picture is brighter at the other end of the age spectrum, where Norway's commitment to learning translates into relatively high levels of participation of young children in structured early childhood education and care activities. 67% of 3-year-olds participate compared to an OECD average of 50% (OECD, 2001, p. 46). This is all the more impressive in view of the facts that, until recently, children in Norway did not begin formal education until age 7, and that there are substantial payments for families choosing to keep young children at home.

2.2.2. An ageing population?

One can expect there to be considerable demand for lifelong learning opportunities solely on the basis of the fact that the population is so highly and equitably educated. But it is argued that it is essential to strengthen lifelong learning also *because* the Norwegian population is ageing. As older workers take up a larger share of employment in a world in which qualifications requirements change rapidly, lifelong learning provides a means for ensuring a source of renewal of the labour force. To what extent is this true, and how does Norway compare with other countries?

The population in Norway is ageing, as in nearly all other developed countries. In the case of Norway it is due to a combination of rising life expectancy (particularly among men), and declining birth rates. As data from Table 2.1 show, 15.7% of Norway's population is 65 or older, a figure that is higher than all the other Nordic countries except Sweden, and more than 3 percentage points above the average for the OECD total. 19.8% of the population is under 15, slightly below the OECD total.

But the trends in Norway are not as straightforward as they appear at first glance. First, fluctuations in the composition of the population in Norway have been more gradual than in most other countries. The increase since 1960 in the proportion of persons 65 or over has been more gradual than about half of OECD member countries. The decrease in the population under age 15 was far slower in Norway than in five out of six other OECD countries. Moreover, over the longer term it would seem that Norway, with the sixth highest fertility rate of OECD countries, will age comparatively slowly. For these reasons, it could be unhelpful if preoccupations with the ageing population are given excessive weight as drivers of policy, including policy for lifelong learning.

2.2.3. Ethnic diversity and immigration

Until recently Norway was seen as relatively homogenous with respect to the ethnic composition of its population. The Saami, the indigenous people in

Norway, have always lived in Norway; there have also been different national minorities in Norway for several hundred years. Accurate statistics on the population size of the Saami and the national minorities of Norway are not available. However, it has been estimated that there are between 50 000 and 100 000 of Saami descent in Norway. In 1970 only 1.5% of the population had parents born outside Norway. Of those, more than 5 in 6 had their roots in other Nordic countries, Western Europe, North America, and Oceania.

By 1999, the foreign population had risen to 5.9% of the total population. The proportion from countries sending most immigrants in the past dropped to a bit more than 2 in 6. In the meantime, persons from Eastern Europe and Turkey, Asia, and Latin America increased their share of the foreign population from 1 in 6 to nearly 4 in 6. In 1997, net migration constituted more than two-fifths of the population growth in Norway (OECD, 2000d, p.7). These developments are part of a more general trend in the OECD towards increasing immigration. Table 2.2 presents data on changes in the share of foreign or foreign-born persons in the total population between 1988 and 1998. During that period, Norway was below the average for the OECD countries for which data are available, with respect to the foreign share of the population, and the proportional change between 1988 and 1998. However, the trend may be accelerating. In 1998, annual arrivals of foreigners in Norway stood at 6 per thousand inhabitants, the third highest level in selected OECD countries, behind only Switzerland and Germany (OECD, 2000c, p. 187).

These changes are being felt already in the formal education system. In 1998, foreign children (first language not Norwegian) comprised 4.7% of the early childhood enrolments, about 6% of enrolments in compulsory education, and 4% of enrolments in upper secondary education. It seems inevitable that they will have quantitative and qualitative impacts on the demand for learning opportunities for adults as well.

Table 2.2. **Trends in foreign or foreign-born share of the population in Norway and OECD,[1] 1998**

	Thousands		Percentage	
	1988	1998	1988	1998
Norway	136	165	3.2	3.7
OECD	43 677	56 872	5.7	7.0

1. Selected countries; dates vary for some countries.
Source: OECD (2000), "Trends in Migration and Economic Consequences", in OECD *Economic Outlook*, No. 68, Paris, pp. 185-203.

2.3. The economy and labour market

The enthusiasm in Norway for lifelong learning rides not just on cultural and social arguments, but on economic arguments as well. There is a belief – widely shared by the Government as well as by the social partners – that the high level of educational attainment of the Norwegian population is not enough to satisfy the shifts in the demand for labour in the coming years. It is argued that lifelong learning is a crucial strategy for upgrading the skills and qualifications requirements of poorly-qualified adults and updating those of more highly-qualified individuals to both accommodate and minimise the adverse social consequences of structural economic change. The discussion below overviews the more salient economic and labour market developments.

2.3.1. *Strong long-term macro-economic performance of a diversified economy*

Norway has a strong, balanced, technologically advanced and productive economy. In 1999, gross domestic product (GDP) reached NOK 1 189 348 million. GDP growth in Norway accelerated in the early 1990s and, during the period from 1993-97, averaged 4.2%, compared to an average for other OECD countries of 2.9%. In the late 1990s, annual GDP growth dropped from 6.4% in 1997 to –0.9% in 1999 (OECD, 2000c, p. 218) (also see Table 2.1). The sharp slowdown is attributable to a number of inter-related factors including a sharp drop in investment, a rise in interest rates and rising labour costs. Norway's comparatively low levels of investment in research and development may have been a contributing factor. The economy recovered in 2000, with GDP growth rising to 2.2% thanks in large part to rises in oil prices and stronger growth in oil activities. In the future growth is expected to decline slightly, though there are two areas of uncertainty. One is the worry that wage increases, after a period of restraint through the late 1990s, will outpace productivity growth, thus hindering Norwegian competitiveness in international markets. The other concerns the price of oil and the volume of output. The implications of these issues for lifelong learning are discussed further below.

Thanks to the long-term overall performance of the Norwegian economy, helping and helped by the relatively high levels of qualifications of Norwegian workers, Norway enjoys one of the highest standards of living of any country in the OECD area. In 1999, per capita GDP in Norway was US$ 27 600 (using current purchasing power parities). This was well above the average per capita income for all OECD countries of US$ 22 300, and was exceeded by only Luxembourg and the United States.

But the long-term sustainability of such performance is open to question for reasons that are directly relevant to lifelong learning, namely declines in productivity. In the 1960s and 1970s, annual productivity growth in Norway ranged between 3.5 and 4.7%. The average over the two decades since then has been closer to 2% – on a par with productivity growth in the United States but lagging behind the rates in many European countries. It dropped from 3.5% in 1990 to 1.3% in 1998 (Background Report, Chapter 2). Furthermore, against this backdrop of declining productivity, labour costs in Norway have been rising at more than double the rate of the OECD as a whole (OECD, 2000c, p. 223). Indeed concern about this lacklustre productivity growth has been one of the motivating factors behind the concerted efforts of the social partners to address questions of human capital investment, and behind the support for the government's effort to strengthen strategies for lifelong learning.

2.3.2. Particular structural features of the Norwegian economy

The overall structure of the Norwegian economy is similar in many respects to the other advanced economies. The share of total employment in agriculture and fishing is under 5%, under 25% in industry, and more than 70% in services. The components of services that have grown most are business services, education, health and social services. During the period 1993-99, employment grew by 240 000, with 90% of this growth occurring in the private sector. Nonetheless, industry, including fish products, paper and wood products, and machinery, is a key element of the Norwegian economy. Norway's sectoral contributions to gross value-added from agricultural/fishing and services are slightly below the average for other OECD countries, while that from industry is slightly above. Although it is generally accepted that the labour market currently is more volatile in terms of skills and qualifications requirements, there has been considerable reallocation of labour in the past. A study of employment in Norwegian manufacturing and service sectors found that during the period from 1976-1992, annual job creation and job loss was equivalent to 7-9% of total employment.

Norway is different from other countries in ways that have material consequences for the goals and objectives that are attached to lifelong learning and the strategies for financing and implementing it. The first and most particular can be summed up in a word: petroleum. The second, shared with certain other countries, is the important place occupied by small- and medium-sized enterprises.

Norway first discovered oil and gas reserves on the continental shelf below the North Sea in the late 1960s. Though Norway possesses only 1.1% of total gas and oil reserves in the world, they are seventh largest producer in the world, and the second largest net exporter, behind Saudi Arabia. At current extraction rates, and with current technology, it is estimated (in 1999) that oil reserves would last for 18 years, and gas reserves for 85 years. The discovery and subsequent exploitation of the North Sea oil and gas resources has had a profound impact on the Norwegian economy and society (OECD, 1999, pp. 132-136). Although a number of other countries have substantial oil and gas reserves (Canada, Denmark, the Netherlands, the United Kingdom, the United States), Norway is unique among OECD countries with respect to the size of petroleum sales as a share of GDP, and the fact that nearly all the extracted petroleum is exported. In 1999 crude oil and natural gas accounted for 35% (and in 2000 46%) of Norway's exports. The North Sea oil industry also provided a basis for the development of related industrial and service exports related to oil platforms and ships, exploration and drilling equipment and know-how and related technical services. It has had important positive effects by further ensuring energy self-sufficiency (Norway already enjoyed considerable independence thanks to abundant hydro-electric capacity; in 1998 fully 45% of Norway's energy supply was hydro). The downside has been that, with a large share of its exports exposed to the vagaries of the world petroleum market, Norway's economy is vulnerable to an extra source of turbulence. The slide down in oil prices in the late 1990s led to a reversal in the annual growth of petroleum-related investment from 23.5% in 1998, to –8.8% in 1999, to –22.0% in 2000. In 2000, declines in such offshore investment are estimated to have reduced mainland GDP by 1½ percentage points (OECD, 2000c; and updated figures provided by the Norwegian authorities).

Another consequence of North Sea oil, one that is more pertinent to the implementation of lifelong learning in Norway, is revenues it has generated for the State. Such revenues are raised through a tax and surtax on profits of oil producing companies, royalties, leases and licenses. The stream of revenues has varied over time between 3 and 15% of GDP, because of variations in price, the relative value of the US dollar (international oil sales are priced in US dollars) and output levels fluctuations. In view of the fluctuating nature of petroleum revenues, and the fact that when reserves are exhausted future generations will be deprived of a source of revenue, the State established a Petroleum Fund in 1991. It is a trust fund financed out of oil revenues, and intended to benefit future generations by serving as a source of revenue to be transferred to central Government budget at the discretion of the Parliament (see *www.norges-bank.no/english/*). The petroleum reserves and the Petroleum Fund provide the basis for a longer-term view of the role of the State in undertaking investments that can generate net positive returns only over the long run.

Another structural factor that seems likely to influence the strategic and tactical dimensions of lifelong learning is the relatively large role that small- and medium-sized enterprises play in the Norwegian economy. It is perhaps not too surprising that Norway is dominated by small- and medium-sized enterprises. Because of the small overall population and its relatively wide dispersion (thanks in part to regional development policies, less than 20% of the population is found in the three largest cities), economies of scale are hard to achieve. Although some large companies have multiple small sites, most enterprises are small. Table 2.3 presents data

Table 2.3. **The place of small- and medium-sized enterprises in Norway and selected OECD countries**

Manufacturing sector

	Norway	Austria	Belgium[2]	Finland	Sweden[2]
	1995	1995	1997	1996	1996
Distribution of enterprises by size					
1-9 employees	80.8	67.4	67.7	84.5	71.3
10-99 employees	16.5	28.1	28.3	13.1	24.8
100 employees and over	2.7	4.5	4.0	2.4	3.9
Distribution of employment by enterprise size[1]					
1-9 employees	12.2	9.7	8.1	8.8	8.5
10-99 employees	30.1	28.8	29.8	22.4	24.5
100 employees and over	57.7	61.5	62.1	68.8	67.0
Distribution of economic turnover (production) by enterprise size					
1-9 employees	6.7	4.9	5.3	4.3	5.2
10-99 employees	25.4	21.0	23.3	15.2	19.2
100 employees and over	67.7	74.0	71.4	80.4	75.7

1. Excluding sole proprietors in Sweden.
2. Excluding size class "0 salaried employees" for enterprises and production.
Source: OECD database on statistics relating to small- and medium-sized enterprises.

for the mid-1990s on the distribution of enterprises, employment and turnover by size of firms; data are presented for Norway and, for comparison, two other Nordic countries and two other relatively small countries. In 1995, more than four out of five firms in Norway employed fewer than 10 employees. These small-sized firms employed 12.2% of all workers in Norway, and generated 6.7% of the economic turnover. Comparatively speaking, Norway does not have the largest share of enterprises taken by small- and medium-sized firms; Finland has that honour. But in the mid-1990s large firms in Norway employed a smaller share of all workers than similar-sized firms in the comparison countries, and generated a relatively smaller share of total output than in other countries. Norwegian authorities believe that SMEs "have a greater problem in maintaining the level of competence among leaders and staff members" (Background Report, Chapter 2). This is because SMEs in Norway, as in other countries(Eurostat, 1997), train far less than other employers. Lifelong learning is conceived as a strategy to overcome the unequal opportunities for work-related training that are found in firms of different sizes.

2.3.3. *Labour market conditions and developments*

Actual and anticipated labour market developments have had enormous influence in shaping current thinking in Norway about lifelong learning. With unemployment in Norway averaging 3.3% in 2000 (half the average for the OECD, and ⅓ the average for the European Union), social partners and public authorities have been preoccupied for a number of years with the risk of labour and skills shortages and mismatches. Lifelong learning is championed as a remedy for enhancing the capacity of the current labour force to adapt to change, and for expanding labour supply. What is the evidence of the nature and severity of such shortages and mismatches? Aggregate labour supply is the easiest to evaluate.

In comparison to other countries, Norway's labour supply is running at close to full utilisation. Figure 2.4 shows that in 1999 the labour force participation rate of persons 16-64 years old was 80.6%, third highest of any OECD country. By 2000 overall participation rose to 81.5%, the highest level ever attained in Norway and second highest in the OECD. It is expected to rise slightly in 2001 (OECD, 2000c). High rates of participation extend to older workers as well. With an official retirement age of 67 years, Norway shares with three other countries the highest retirement age in the OECD area (OECD, 1997). Partly because of the later retirement

Figure 2.4. **Labour force participation rates, OECD countries, 1999**

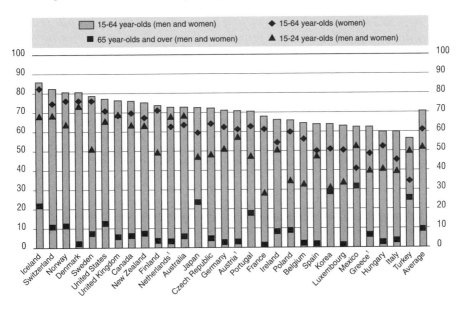

1. Data for 1998.
Source: OECD labour force statistics database 2000.

age, participation rates of workers 65 years of age and older also are relatively high. However, overall activity rates for older persons are expected to decline. Since the early 1990s, the social partners have been entering into early retirement agreements that allow persons to retire as early as 62 years of age. These agreements, which now cover 60% of all employees, have reduced activity rates among older workers. Among Norway's younger population, labour force participation rates are high relative to past patterns, and relative to participation rates in other countries.

The squeeze on labour supply in Norway might be relieved through two general strategies:

- One strategy, alluded to in the preceding sub-section, is to raise productivity growth from its present levels that are low relative to past experience, and low relative to other countries. This would enable output to grow faster than labour input (or to grow even while labour supply is declining).

- The other strategy is to increase labour supply.

In the 12 years from 1989 through 2000, annual labour force growth in Norway has averaged a bit more than 0.6%. Raising this to 1% through delayed retirements and increased participation of older workers would be hopelessly difficult, requiring an increase in participation of persons 65 and older, of more than 17 percentage points. But such an increase could be achieved through only a 2% rise in labour force participation among 15-24-year-olds , or a 1% rise in their labour force participation and a doubling of net immigration (OECD, 2000b and OECD, 2000c; Secretariat calculations).

Another source of increased labour supply is among women. Although Norway has the fourth highest labour force participation rate in the OECD area among women aged 25-64 years, they are relatively more likely to work part-time (see Figure 2.5). In 1999, 35% of Norwegian women worked part-time, compared to 30.3% in the European Union, and 26.4% in the OECD at large. This is changing, though; since 1990, the incidence of part-time employment among Norwegian women has declined by nearly 4 percentage points (while their labour force participation rates were rising). It remains to be seen whether increasing labour force participation through more full-time employment reduces the comparatively high birth rates in Norway. However, it is conceivable that participation rates of women might be raised if work were less polarised by gender. It is estimated that in Norway 80% of women work in the 10 occupations that are most heavily female dominated, compared to an OECD average of 60% (Background Report, Chapter 2).

Finally, in theory, the labour supply squeeze might be eased through increased annual hours worked. Data on average annual hours of work need to be interpreted with care because definitions vary from country to country. With that caveat in mind, published figures suggest that average annual hours worked in

Figure 2.5. **Employment rates in Norway and the OECD, 1999**
Percentage

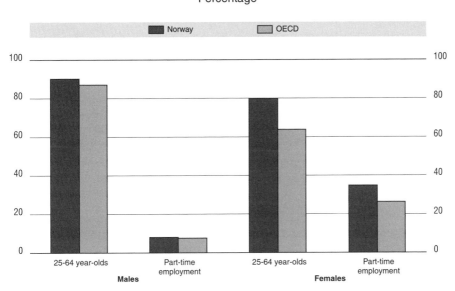

Source: For 25-64 year-olds, OECD (2000), *Education at a Glance – OECD Indicators*, Paris. For part-time employment, OECD (2000), *Employment Outlook*, Table E, p. 218, Paris.

Norway are very low when compared to other countries (OECD, 2000*e*, p. 219).
However, it is questionable whether average hours of work are susceptible to
being prolonged. It can be argued that shorter hours are part of the dividend,
agreed to by social partners and supported by high qualifications levels, high levels of investment and the management of petroleum and other natural resources.
In any case, it would be easy to imagine that short average annual hours are part of
the appeal of employment, and that the negotiated increases would be accompanied by off-setting drops in labour force participation.

Thus, overall, it would appear that remedies to possible labour shortages
depend on: *i*) higher participation rates on the part of younger persons, prime-age
persons and older persons; *ii*) more full-time employment by women, preferably
helped by less occupational segregation by gender; and *iii*) higher levels of output
per worker. Lifelong learning potentially could play a role in all these areas.

Before considering evidence on skills and qualifications mismatches, it is useful first to consider overall qualifications levels of the Norwegian population.
Figure 2.6 shows that the qualifications levels of the Norwegian population are

145|

Figure 2.6. **Educational attainment of the 25-64 year-olds in Norway[1] and the OECD, 1998**

Percentage

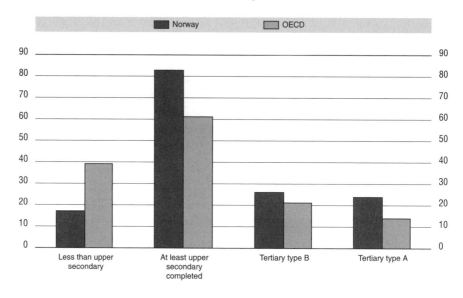

1. Data for 1997.
Source: OECD (2000*), Education at a Glance – OECD Indicators*, Paris.

substantially higher than the average for all OECD countries. The proportion of adults in Norway with less than an upper secondary education is less than half the average for all OECD countries. The proportion with tertiary qualifications is nearly one-and-one-half times higher in Norway. More detailed data show Norway to have some of the highest levels, based on the (low) proportion of persons with less than an upper secondary education, and the (large) proportion with some form of tertiary qualification (OECD, 2001). Moreover, Table 2.4 suggests that relatively high levels of educational achievement have been a longstanding feature in Norway; younger persons are only slightly more likely than older persons to have completed at least upper secondary education or some form of tertiary education.

How well does this highly-qualified population and labour force correspond to what employers look for in workers, and to what the economy needs to expand? Two ways of judging are to examine evidence on unemployment rates and earnings by level of educational attainment. Insofar as employers seek more qualified individuals, one would expect to see persons with higher levels of qualifications to have lower unemployment rates and higher earnings, relative to less qualified

Table 2.4. **Progress towards achieving a minimum educational attainment level and tertiary qualifications, 1998**

| | A. At least upper secondary education | | | |
	25-64 year-olds	25-29 year-olds	50-54 year-olds	Ratio 25-29/50-54
Norway[1]	83	92	76	1.21
OECD average	61	72	52	1.56
	B. At least tertiary education			
	25-64 year-olds	30-34 year-olds	50-54 year-olds	Ratio 30-34/50-54
Norway[1]	26	29	23	1.23
OECD average	21	24	18	1.44

1. Data for 1997.
Source: OECD (2001), *Education Policy Analysis*, Paris.

individuals. In fact, one finds from data in Table 2.5 that in Norway, as in most other OECD countries, the higher the educational attainment level is, the lower the unemployment rate, and the higher the relative earnings.

Table 2.5. **Labour market outcomes by level of educational attainment in Norway and the OECD**

		Norway[1]	OECD average[2]
Unemployment (%)			
Less than upper secondary	*males*	4.2	8.9
	females	3.8	10.0
Upper secondary	*males*	2.9	5.3
	females	3.4	7.6
Tertiary type B	*males*	1.7	4.3
	females	1.6	5.2
Tertiary type A	*males*	1.8	3.3
	females	1.6	4.6
Relative earnings of 25-64 year-olds (ISCED 3/4=100)			
Less than upper secondary	*males*	85	
	females	84	
TOTAL		85	78[3]
Tertiary type A	*males*	138	
	females	140	
TOTAL		138	161[3]

1. Data for 1997.
2. Data for 1998.
3. Mean value for 18 countries; data for late 1990s.
Source: OECD (2000), *Education at a Glance – OECD Indicators*, Paris.

147|

But the picture emerging from Norway is not as straightforward as that emerging from other countries. First, the reduced risk of unemployment associated with higher levels of educational attainment are not as great, proportionately, in Norway as in OECD countries on average. Moreover, unlike the case in other OECD countries, there is evidence that there is little difference between unemployment rates of persons with ISCED $^5/_6$ A and B (between more academically oriented and more technically oriented studies); in other countries persons with ISCED $^5/_6$ type A qualifications have slightly lower unemployment rates than those with more technically oriented type B qualifications. As unemployment rates in Norway are so low, it is important not to read too much into small differences. However, the apparent pattern is not at odds with other evidence. In Norway, the earnings of persons with upper secondary education completed relative to those without upper secondary education, are slightly less than the average for OECD countries. The gains for persons with tertiary qualifications are substantially below the average. These smaller differentials are due in part to the wage and salary structure that is more compressed in Norway than in many other countries. However, in comparing the relative wages in Norway to those found in other Nordic countries with similarly compressed wage and salary structures, one finds that the relative earnings of tertiary graduates are well below the average of even those countries.

This international statistical evidence is not inconsistent with country-specific evidence, such as the study of Norwegian manufacturing and services referred to earlier. That survey found that between 1993 and 1995 the proportion of jobs in which secondary education was regarded as most productive increased from 35 to 44%. That same survey found that the proportion of jobs best adapted to tertiary qualifications declined from 59 to 50% (Background Report, Chapter 2).

Another way to evaluate evidence of skills mismatches is to consider the "returns" to participating in continuing education and training, by seeing whether participants who upgraded and updated their qualifications enjoy a premium in the labour market. Table 2.6 compares the likelihood of individuals participating in continuing education and training to the likelihood of them having above average earnings (proxied here by having earnings in the top two earning quintiles), controlling for level of educational attainment. The data show that the relationship in Norway is similar to that found in most other countries, with the least qualified enjoying the greatest earnings premia. But the magnitudes of such premia are modest compared to what is seen in other countries, except Denmark. Although compressed wage and salary structures might dampen the differentials, the fact that one observes larger differentials in two other Nordic countries with similar structures would suggest that the returns to further education and training that are observed in Norway do *not* support the assertion that there are important skills mismatches in Norway.

Table 2.6. **Earnings and participation in continuing education and training, Norway and other countries**

	Highest level of educational attainment achieved	Participants in continuing education and training (CET)		
		Likelihood of participating (%) = A	Likelihood of having high earnings[1] (%) = B	Earning "premium" for CET participants = B/A
Norway	**Less than upper secondary**	**33**	**40**	**1.21**
	Upper secondary	**47**	**53**	**1.13**
	Tertiary	**68**	**71**	**1.04**
Denmark	Less than upper secondary	52	43	0.83
	Upper secondary	59	58	0.98
	Tertiary	74	76	1.03
Finland	Less than upper secondary	48	60	1.25
	Upper secondary	67	76	1.13
	Tertiary	79	89	1.13
Sweden	Less than upper secondary	28	43	1.54
	Upper secondary	50	61	1.22
	Tertiary	66	74	1.12
All[2]	Less than upper secondary	24	39	1.63
	Upper secondary	43	53	1.23
	Tertiary	62	68	1.10

1. Likelihood of participants being in top two earning quintiles.
2. Belgium (Flanders), Canada, Czech Republic, Denmark, Finland, Germany, Hungary, Ireland, Italy, Netherlands, New Zealand, Poland, Sweden, Switzerland, United Kingdom, United States.
Source: International Adult Literacy Survey.

This would suggest that the questions in Norway about the extent and nature of skills mismatches, trends in qualifications requirements and the appropriate economic role of lifelong learning all merit further investigation. At a minimum, it would appear that the eventual economic goals of lifelong learning in Norway do not need to be confined to continuous *upgrading* of qualifications, but should be extended to *updating* of existing qualifications. The fact that the social partners have invested so much in competence development (discussed in the following section) would indicate that they attach importance to broader objectives.

2.4. The changing institutional and policy landscape

The current concerns in Norway with lifelong learning are not new. Rather they are an extension of inquiries and reforms that are a familiar feature in a near-permanent process of continuous improvement, and were intensified during the 1990s. Nor are the concerns isolated. They are closely related to developments that cut across ministries within the Government and to initiatives launched by the social partners. More fundamentally, the concerns with lifelong learning should be viewed as further application of the "Nordic [or Scandinavian] Model".

That "model", though hardly identical across the Nordic region (Denmark, Finland, Iceland, Norway, and Sweden) has a few recurrent features (Background Report, Chapter 2):

- at the national level, the Nordic countries have long democratic conditions, rather centrally regulated economic regimes, and strong systems for social protection with an egalitarian redistributive bias;

- politically there is a strong social-democratic tradition, a strong and cohesive union movement, centralised tripartite co-operation between public authorities and the social partners;

- at the enterprise level, there is a strong tradition for negotiation and problem solving, high levels of unionisation, high degree of membership by employers in confederations, low levels of labour disputes;

- in education policy the Nordic model is progressive and pupil-centred, emphasising pupil activity in the tradition of John Dewey and the German concept of *Arbeitsschule*.

The discussion below considers recent and ongoing reviews and reforms, and relates them to the main themes of the lifelong learning debate in Norway. The discussion first considers developments on the Government side, and then examines what the social partners have been doing.

2.4.1. Education reforms related to lifelong learning

Since the 1950s, there have been a number of reforms in the formal education system that have aimed to better co-ordinate educational pathways, to increase participation in formal education, and to reinforce the comprehensive school system (*enhetsskolen*). Taken together, the various measures have helped create over time an education system that embodies four features (Background Report, Chapter 3):

- equitable access to education resources in all regions;

- pupils exposed to a common Core Curriculum and taking part in a common culture;

- children in schools in their neighbourhood (limits on school choice, private or public); and

- schooling experience individualised according to the needs of children.

Those early reforms could be characterised as improving the performance of the education system and its capacity to achieve long and widely accepted policy goals. Reforms since the late 1980s and through the 1990s, discussed in more detail below, appear to be fundamentally different in character, aiming to re-define the very goals of education policy. They explicitly situate initial education as a first stage in a continuous process of *lifelong learning* in which subsequent learning may not necessarily take place within the formal education system. They explicitly recognise distinct economic, social, cultural and personal purposes that such learning needs to serve. Though important elements of various reforms occurred at different times over the last decade or so, they are discussed below in their order in the life-cycle, *i.e.*, starting with pre-school and finishing with adults.

- **Early childhood education and care.** Until the 1990s, compulsory education did not begin until age 7, and prior early childhood education and care was viewed as a family concern. In 1994 a national programme was enacted to help parents develop and strengthen parenting skills and to otherwise ensure a healthy and stimulating home environment for young children. This was based on establishing a dialogue between parents and relevant social service agencies. The Day Care Institution Act of May 1995 established the *barnehage* to provide pre-school age children with an institutional setting for development and activity. In 1999, 62% of all children aged 1-5 years were enrolled in *barnehage*; more than three-quarters were aged 3 or older, probably because of the extensive provisions for parental leave during the first year or so after birth of a child. With evaluations showing a strong positive relationship between participation in early childhood education and subsequent school performance, the Government is now committed to ensuring that there is sufficient capacity by 2005 to accommodate all children whose parents want them enrolled. The *barnehager* are the responsibility of the Ministry of Children and Family Affairs. Administration and supervision of institutions has been largely transferred to municipalities; *barnehager* are operated by the municipalities themselves or private non-profit associations. The institutions are financed with contributions from the national ministry and parents, and, sometimes, the municipalities; private *barnehager* often are subsidised by the municipalities. The introduction in the late 1990s of a cash benefit scheme (*kontantstøtten*) was another reform aimed at providing families with a cash benefit of NOK 3 000 per month when children are 1 to 3 years old, to make it easier for working parents to stay at home with their children or to make alternative arrangements for care (other than *barnehager*). Evidence so far suggests that most families take advantage of the benefit. Its availability has reduced work or study activity for some mothers, but for very few fathers (Background Report, Chapter 3). A research programme conducted by the Research Council of Norway was implemented in order to reveal effects of the cash benefit on gender equality, day care centres, labour force and deprived children. Evidence so far suggests that the cash benefit seems to have had little impact on these issues. While the majority of parents report that they would prefer arrangements that provide more time with their children, and three out of four children in the eligible age receive the cash bene-

151|

fit, the reform has not to a great extent effected parental behaviour when it comes to organising child care and participation in the labour force. Care by parents has increased to some degree, and availability of the benefit has reduced work activity for mothers by an average of 1.5 hours per week. Fathers' working hours have not been affected, and in this respect the cash benefit has not proven to have had a positive effect on gender equality. However, the cash benefit seems to have achieved more economic equality among families with small children.

- **Primary and lower secondary education.** Schools in Norway have been undergoing a steady transformation in governance, with more authority shifted to the municipal authorities. But centralised curricula and syllabuses, and limits on local discretion are still the rule. Reforms targeted at this level have been limited. The Norwegian Parliament lowered the starting age for compulsory education from age 7 to 6, effective 1 July 1997. There were a number of reasons for the change. One was economic. The emergence of the knowledge society required higher level competence and skills; an earlier starting age was seen as one way of better equipping young persons. Other reasons included the wish to more fully utilise excess capacity in primary schools, while freeing up space in *barnehager* to meet the growing demand for pre-school education; to overcome the inequities in opportunities that some 6-year-olds were experiencing because of the uneven availability of pre-school programmes for them; and to bring Norway in line with international experience. From July 1998 all municipalities were required to offer voluntary programmes in music and the arts for children and adolescents (Background Report, Chapter 3).

- **Upper secondary education.** Reform 94 brought important changes in the objectives, content and delivery of upper secondary education in Norway. Its overall objectives were economic, heavily influenced by perceived changes in skills and qualifications requirements. The reform aimed to raise the general competence level of the population, increase labour force flexibility, and increase participation in upper secondary education. The strategies for achieving these objectives include strengthening and simplifying vocational programmes and apprenticeship training, achieving better balance between practical and theoretical training, and involving enterprises in the last 1 or 2 years of study through a combination of training and work in the enterprise.[1] (Background Report, Chapter 3).

- **Intermediate education.** This sector consists of institutions that provide education or training of more than 2 months duration, but are not regulated by the legislation concerning public schools, universities and colleges. Though it is small, with enrolments equalling only about 5% of the college and university enrolments, the sector is growing. The Berg Commission, appointed by the Government in 1999, acknowledged the value of such institutions and recommended that they be recognised and organised as an autonomous sector (Background Report, Chapter 3). A subsequent white paper did not follow up on this proposal, however, leaving it to colleges to meet these educational needs.

- **Tertiary education.** There have been far-reaching reforms in the tertiary sector. In 1994 a total of 98 colleges, many of them small and specialised, were amalgamated into 26 larger, multipurpose *state university colleges* for the purpose of raising academic standards in the non-university sector, to reduce barriers between programmes of study and to make better use of resources in different regions. In addition a network among the various institutions (*Network Norway*) was established to rationalise divisions of responsibility among institutions and to facilitate students choosing different courses in different institutions.[2] The 1994 reform left the university sector largely untouched, though it allowed, in principle, mobility of students from the State university colleges into universities which had occurred at a small scale from the 1980s. From 1996, too, there was a new common act for both universities and colleges. In 1998, in anticipation of broader reform in the whole higher education sector, a royal commission was established to undertake a broad study of the adequacy of universities and colleges as institutions of education and research. The Commission, chaired by Professor Ole Mjøs, has adopted recommendations that address issues ranging from the responsiveness of the system to workplace and economic change, to the structure of degrees, to the efficiency of education and research (NOU, 1999) (Background Report, Chapter 3). The Government has prepared a white paper that indicates how it proposes to implement ideas recommended in the Mjøs report (KUF, 2001).

- **The Competence Reform.** Other reforms have dealt with issues that impact, for the most part, on fairly traditional education ground. Although such reforms move in the direction of aligning education policy with the goals of lifelong learning, *The Competence Reform* is the first initiative that can be characterised as a head-on attempt to redefine institutional arrangements for lifelong learning. In response to a 1996 Parliamentary mandate for the Government to prepare a white paper on competence development, the Government appointed a commission, chaired by Lars Buer, on adult education and the development of competence in working life and society. The Buer Commission delivered its report in October 1997. After public debate, the Government presented its Report to the *Storting*, "The Competence Reform", in May 1998. That paper committed the Government to pursuing lifelong learning policies. The goals were to encourage acceptance that further learning serves individual development for varied purposes; guarantee

153

a right to primary, lower and upper secondary education; document and recognise non formal learning by adults; give employees rights to learning leave; remove tax disincentives to learning; and, restructure public education to meet workplace learning needs. The Competence Reform also engages the labour market authorities, the *Aetat* (public employment service) in particular, in providing better information to individuals on occupations and learning opportunities. Within the Competence Reform there is an on-going project to develop a system for assessing qualifications related to the demands of the enterprises. *Aetat* will be able to contribute to assessment of informal qualifications when the results of this project are implemented. It also is intended that the Competence Reform take account of relevant initiatives by the social partners in the workplace (discussed below). The Government established an inter-ministerial forum, with input from the social partners and providers of education, for the purpose of guiding implementation of its mandate.[3] Although the Competence Reform established new objectives for government in the area of lifelong learning, it leaves certain issues un-addressed, particularly those related to resources and financing of subsistence during leave of absence to participate in education and training. A commission was established in late 2000 to address such issues (Background Report, Chapter 3).

- **Competence development in the workplace.** The Government's Competence Reform initiative was stimulated in some part by an earlier initiative by the social partners. In the mid-1990s, employers and trade unions agreed to accept, as part of the central 5-year industrial relations agreement, a strategy to identify long-term trends in competence requirements in the workplace and to develop and implement competence development strategies to address the trends. In 1997, the employers federation and the trade unions agreed to set aside an initial NOK 191 million to finance a job-oriented further education system; different trades allocate additional resources. This amounts to less than 2% of the amount it is estimated to be spent each year on in-service training. No additional funds were allocated in 1998 and 1999, though it was agreed in principle that in the future employees would have a right to paid training leave. There are still unresolved issues of who will pay for training leave for competence development in the workplace. This is the subject of continuing negotiation between the social partners themselves, and between them and the Government; it depends as well on the outcome of deliberations by the newly appointed commission on financing of subsistence during education and training leave (Background Report, Chapter 3).

- **A *word on adult education*.** Many of the reforms outlined above work around a prized feature of the Norwegian education landscape, namely the arrangements for adult learning outside the labour market. These include adult enrolments in primary and secondary education at the municipal and county level; education resource centres, often linked with upper secondary schools; study associations, distance education and folk high schools. These institutions provide a broad range of opportunities for individual development, not just for vocational purposes. "Schools for life", the term used to describe the Folk High Schools, can be applied to all these institutions. Implementation of the current reforms implicates these institutions in a number of ways. First, the new initiatives are intended to support lifelong learning for multiple purposes, not just vocational. Second, insofar as they favour recognition of learning outcomes *regardless of whether they are in formal education programmes*, they favour learning settings that are closer to the home, and perhaps less structured than a traditional school setting. Third, in that they endorse learning for multiple purposes, they further affirm the rationale for the establishment of these institutions and the reason for their success.

Recent reforms in Norway are re-orienting existing institutions in a way that is intended to strengthen the foundation that initial education provides for further learning, and to facilitate mutually supportive action by such institutions and the social partners in order to make more accessible further learning opportunities. The following chapters review evidence on how well these initiatives are achieving their aims.

2.5. Concluding remarks

Unlike many OECD member countries, Norway approaches the challenges of the "knowledge society" and of implementing a system of lifelong learning from a position of exceptional strength:

- It has one of the highest standards of living of any country in the OECD; from an economic perspective, its past performance appears to rest on strong foundations and to be durable and sustainable in the future. The windfall from the North Sea petroleum reserves is being husbanded, and there is awareness of the need to ensure that economic growth can continue in the long-term without petroleum.

- Norway aims to achieve lifelong learning for one of the most highly-qualified populations in the world. Young and old alike have high levels of educational attainment. Judging from the results of the International Adult Literacy Survey, the output of the formal education system is good.

- On a political level there is strong support for education, judging from the share of GDP and the share of public expenditure devoted to education, and judging from the ongoing initiatives to reform and improve education. The view that it is important to strengthen learning opportunities seems widely shared, within Government and by social partners.

155|

Nonetheless, existing institutional arrangements and policies fall short of a systemic approach to lifelong learning. The most obvious shortcomings concern adults. Though the Competence Reform aims to redress them, there are formidable challenges to its implementation. Ministerial responsibilities, institutional roles and individual behaviour need to change, and daunting issues regarding the finance of adult learning need to be addressed. There also is need to further understand the interaction between different stages of lifelong learning and what that implies for policy and practice. For example, it would appear that reforms in secondary education have not resolved the difficulties faced by a non-negligible number of young persons who leave education before acquiring any qualification. It remains to be seen whether these problems can or will be addressed through preventive interventions at an earlier age, and/or remedial interventions for poorly-qualified adults.

Perhaps the most unsettled issue is leadership. As with past education reforms that have been led by the Ministry of Education, Research and Church Affairs, the Ministry is leading the Competence Reform. But in contrast to past education reforms, the Competence Reform agenda requires concerted action by multiple ministries *as well as* the social partners. A critical question is whether the available instruments for leadership will be sufficient.

The following chapters address the questions. Chapter 3 examines the overall policy vision for lifelong learning and how current institutional arrangements fit in with that vision. Chapters 4 and 5 consider the initiatives that have been put in place for better realising that vision. Chapter 6 suggests broad themes to guide future actions to make lifelong learning a reality for all Norwegians.

Notes

1. For further information on this reform and related reforms in other OECD member countries see OECD (2000), *From Initial Education to Working Life: Making Transitions Work*, Paris.

2. The OECD review of tertiary education was carried out shortly after this reform was implemented; the experts' report noted the need for special attention being given to *i*) ensuring that autonomous institutions could rationalise national with local and regional objectives; and *ii*) improving teaching and curriculum. See OECD (1998), *Redefining Tertiary Education*, Paris.

3. For further details on Competence Reform, see Kirke, utdannings og Forskningsdepartementet (2000), *The Competence Reform in Norway: Plan of Action 2000-2003*, May, and earlier status reports.

Chapter 3

Norway's LifeLong Learning Vision: Learning from Cradle to Grave

The concept of *lifelong learning* in Norway is all-embracing and totally inclusive – learning is ubiquitous, life-important and occurs from the cradle to the grave. It covers formal and informal learning in the home, in society, in educational institutions and at work. The boundaries between the different venues for learning and modes of learning are fluid. The learner's capacities, needs, motivation, active involvement and potential contribution to society are at the centre of policies. As such learning is well integrated with the needs of the economy and society.

The Ministry of Education, Research and Church Affairs has the overall responsibility for administering and implementing the national educational policy. Certain portions of the lifelong learning agenda are under the auspices of other Ministries. Pre-school education is organised and funded by the Ministry of Children and Family Affairs, and education for displaced workers seeking new employment falls under the care of the Ministry of Labour and Government Administration.

In this chapter we describe the comprehensive network of learning opportunities in Norway. It is clear from our conversations that much of Norway's lifelong learning agenda is already well in place. This chapter is focused primarily on the provision of learning through to early adulthood. In comparison to the workplace as an arena for learning where the lifelong learning agenda remains unfinished, these provisions are well established. Therefore, while we comment on most types of providers, we have made recommendations only where we observed clear gaps in provisions or in the realisation of the learning opportunities.

3.1. Youth education

With Norway's strong emphasis on education for all, the reforms of the past decade in particular have provided a legal framework for the current youths of the country – their learning opportunities are guaranteed by law, are provided for through the school system and lead in later years to a variety of pathways of institution-based and other learning, including in the workplace. During these critical early years the foundations for lifelong learning are established.

3.1.1. Early childhood education

Background: *In Norway, pre-school children have the opportunity to be looked after by their parent(s) or other care-giver at home or in one of the municipal or private barnehage. A cash benefit option introduced in 1998 allows parents who choose home-care to receive a cash benefit for children at the age of 1 and 2 years equivalent to the amount of the State subsidy for sending each child to a barnehage. Parents who use part-time care are entitled to a reduced amount. By 1999, according to the Background Report (Chapter 3), 62% of all pre-school children aged 1 to 5 years attended barnehage, with 82% of the 5-year-olds. By 2000 11% of all 1- and 2-year-olds attended barnehage part-time and were thus entitled to reduced cash benefit; 23% of all 1- and 2-year-olds attended full-time barnehage and were not entitled to any cash benefit.*

Clearly, the State wishes to balance parents' and children's rights with the strong belief backed by research, that children reap long-term intellectual, social and personal benefits through attendance at barnehage. The goal of the Government is to offer barnehage to any child whose parents ask for a place by the end of the year 2000.

Norway has grappled with the question of who should provide early childhood care and education within the context of its national goals and national values. At present early childhood education falls under the care of the Ministry of Children and Family Affairs.

The curriculum reforms have led to a healthy holistic perspective in early childhood education. However, we heard legitimate concern that those who need access to early childhood education may not make use of it or be able to make use of it.

We note that recent immigrants are a group which provides particular challenges. Immigrants in Oslo represented in 1999 18% of the city's population, concentrated mostly in the inner East of Oslo. In primary and lower secondary school, 29% of pupils in 1999 had a non-Nordic language as their native language. We were impressed by the efforts of the Toyen Primary School to address the educational needs of immigrant children. We were told that around Toyen Primary School there are free kindergarten places for five- and six-year-olds to enable the children to acquire Norwegian more easily.

Helping immigrant children take advantage of learning opportunities requires more than simply sending them to school or providing them with the necessary language skills. In the inner city of Oslo-East, for example, there are family programmes centred around schools. Schools receive NOK 10 million per annum to achieve a better life for the immigrant children and families. Breakfast, homework assistance, courses for the family are provided (*e.g.*, swimming for Muslim girls, aerobics, cooking, courses in Norwegian for the parents). Another example is earmarked grants given by the State to support the wages of bilingual assistants in ECEC institutions with immigrant children. In close co-operation with the Municipality of Oslo, the Ministry of Children and Family Affairs finances a programme for all 4- and 5-year-olds living in a district that is heavily populated by ethnic minorities, to increase integration and improve language skills before starting school. Nearly 100% of children in the target area participate.

Recommendation:

The state should work closely with each municipality to ensure that all children have access to appropriate early childhood care and education and to use a bundle of assistance programmes to achieve equitable educational and social outcomes simultaneously.

3.1.2. Primary and secondary education

Background: *Compulsory school education stretches from six to sixteen years through primary and lower secondary school. The State has delegated this responsibility to the 435 municipalities. This formal education is guided by a national framework which provides detailed curricula and syllabuses to help develop a set of skills and attributes in all school children. As illustrated in Chapter 2, Norway's academic success rate is high as measured on literacy rates.*

While compulsory schooling finishes at 16, all young people between the ages of 16 and 19 have a statutory right to three years of upper secondary education which would lead to eligibility for higher education or a journeyman's certificate. Upper secondary schooling, reorganised in Reform 94, has been delegated to the 19 counties.

According to the Background Report (Chapter 2), in 1998 as many as 223 800 pupils attended upper secondary education. In 1996 approximately 94% of the 16-year-olds were enrolled in grade one in upper secondary education. Similarly, 94% of the 17-year-olds and about 88% of the 18-year-olds were pupils in secondary education.

In upper secondary education we find a strong cross-link with enterprises and institutions for training of apprentices. Apprentices learn both at school and at work, with the last two years completely through on-the-job training. In 1999, 16% of the cohort were apprentices. In addition, some schools organise visits for students to local municipalities and enterprises to acquaint them with the world of work.

While nearly all primary and lower secondary pupils attend public schools, 4% of upper secondary students are enrolled in a private school. In 2000, there were 83 private primary schools with 9 435 pupils and 56 upper secondary schools with 7 325 pupils. Approved private institutions can award diplomas and receive grants from the State. They receive a public subsidy equal to 85% of the per student expenditure in public schools; some of them charge fees and also get support from organisations, church societies, etc.

159|

We received very few comments on primary and lower secondary education. However, in discussion it emerged that not all students experience the transition to upper secondary smoothly. Some students in upper secondary education seem to have made choices which suit neither their abilities nor interests. Career counsellors were seen as playing a very important role in both assessing and assisting students in their course choice prior to entering upper secondary schooling.

Recommendation:

Career guidance in lower secondary schools particularly for those pupils choosing the vocational stream is seen as needing some improvement.

Upper secondary schools have multiple roles, notably educating young people for higher education, vocations and apprenticeships, as wells as providing adult education. There were few comments on the general course leading to university entrance. But there were many on the vocational streams.

Since 1976, vocational training has occurred in upper secondary education. Those entering the vocational track are provided mainly with apprenticeship training leading to a journeyman's certificate or, for a small number, school-based vocational training.

One of the criticisms we heard was that the curriculum of vocational training has become too academic. Apprentices who struggled academically in the past, struggle more in the new system. Among school principals from one of the counties, with whom we met, there was disagreement on whether there was an academic drift following the 94 Reform. While some thought that a lot of training had moved from "hand to head" because the latter was less expensive, others thought that the academic drift had more to do with the move towards a knowledge society and economy where very high skills levels such as critical thinking were needed. Indeed, the social partners for this reason had supported the principle of more theory in the training. Regardless of the reasons, students are dropping out because of the increase in academic content in upper secondary school.

Although employers use apprenticeships as a means of recruitment, they are seeking differently qualified apprentices than those being produced by the current system and want more influence on vocational upper secondary education. Indeed, they questioned why vocational education is largely located in schools with their bureaucratic structure. According to employers, schools seem unwilling or unable to accommodate the flexibility they desire in the apprenticeship system, despite the trades having heavy influence on structure and content of training in their particular field through a central body (RFA) and twenty national boards. The difficulties with vocational education and the apprenticeship system are no doubt part of the reason that there are 6 000 dropouts from upper secondary schools per annum. Even though students have different options to dropping out, *e.g.* choosing a new track, individual arrangements between school and work, and indeed the option of training in industry from the beginning, the dropout phenomenon was seen as a serious issue.

Even though we are aware of alternative options and small numbers in some of the "dead ends", we agree with the observations made in the Norway Country Note of the Thematic Review of the Transition from Initial Education to Working Life (OECD, 1998c, p. 23):

"There are three groups for whom present pathways run the risk of leading to side tracks or dead ends. These are:

- those who fail to obtain an apprenticeship and are offered an alternative school-based vocational course;

- those who fail to obtain an apprenticeship and take, as an alternative, a general education course; and

- those who appear to have exhausted their statutory right before either obtaining a vocational qualification or, having obtained one, before having qualified for higher education entry."

Part of the 94 Reform was a commitment and funding for systematic follow-up of dropout students from upper secondary school with the aim of re-integrating them while they still have a statutory right to education. Regional institutions have the responsibility for follow up. While this can work, and the OECD provides a good overview (OECD, 2000, p. 22), we were told that the communication and co-ordination between the services within municipalities and regions (counties) is not optimal.

The experiences after the upper secondary school reform which produced the current general and vocational streams raise several questions: Is there an assumption underlying the reform that everyone learns in the same way (*e.g.* abstractly)? Is the dropout due to the increase in academic content within vocational training? Is institutional learning appropriate for everyone? The focus of the reforms was on the individual learners. Not all are equally motivated, and hence those who choose not to continue learning in a formal setting can get documentation of partial competence, *i.e.* a description of skills obtained.

As adult uptake of lower and upper secondary education shows that people will return to study, it might be advisable to allow non-motivated, non-performing upper secondary students to exit early and return later. In a lifelong learning system earlier exit should be possible with encouragement for those exiting to return when they are ready. Unlike other countries, Norway has a relatively highly-developed infrastructure for reaching adults. Thus, allowing an early exit is not tantamount to policy makers turning their backs on those who leave early, but would accentuate the importance of ensuring that lifelong learning arrangements do meet the needs of early leavers. In fact those arrangements could be evaluated on the basis of whether they succeed in keeping early leavers "in the loop".

There are obvious risks in accommodating early exits from the school system at a time when virtually all OECD countries are aiming for universal completion of upper secondary education. However, a number of facts persuade us that such a strategy merits serious consideration. First, universal completion remains in Norway, as everywhere else, an unachievable ideal, given the constraints on financial resources, pedagogical know-how, and flexibility of schools, and the preferences of some young persons. Second, for now, labour shortages in Norway strengthen incentives for even unqualified youths to leave school. Third, Norway has well developed institutional arrangements for adult learning, as well as a strong tradition of popular adult education and solid commitment of the social partners to continued learning. Thus, we find in Norway a rare opportunity to transform the choice that traditionally has faced young people between learning and working. Instead, they should be given the choice of *when* to learn and *when* to work.

We are aware that there is concern in Norway about the length of time students take to get into the workforce. But we believe that a preoccupation with getting 100% of a cohort through upper secondary education ignores differences in individual motivation, aspiration and capabilities, and stigmatises those who do not reach the goal.

Indeed, the paper *The Competence Reform in Norway: Plan of Action* 2000-2003 (KUF, 2000a) acknowledges that groups may be marginalised, in particular those unemployed. "In the transition to a knowledge society, there is a clear tendency that large or small groups can be marginalised, and that serious knowledge and competence gaps can develop if no inclusive education policy is formulated and implemented" (p. 13).

Recommendations:

The Review Team suggests that those upper secondary students who leave the education system before they have used up their statutory allowance be credited for the equivalent costs of the remainder years on a learning account in order to achieve the relevant learning outcomes.

Furthermore, we suggest that these students be given an exit certificate which details their achievements, explicitly describes their entitlement to: a) obtain future upper secondary education; b) have experience outside the school system (work, volunteer activity, etc.) assessed and accredited for the purpose of subsequent entry into education or the workplace (leaving open the possibility of never returning to secondary education); and c) receive whatever financial support might be made available once the financing strategy is in place.

3.1.3. Educational institutions on an intermediate level

Background: *There are a number of educational institutions on an intermediate level which do not fall under the regulations of the Education Act, the University and College Act or the Act of Private Education. In 1999 there were about 250 providers, many of these technical schools offering vocational education within different trades and occupations. Included are also about 52 bible schools. A total of 13 000 students were enrolled in 1999. About 75% of these students are enrolled in the private sector.*

Educational institutions at an intermediate level were the subject of the Berg Commission. The Commission recommended a recognised and regulated level of educational institutions between school and higher education. Courses should be developed as modular units so that people can study and work sequentially. The duration of these courses should be between one and two years equivalent. Presently technical schools of one to two years do not provide credits towards colleges, though the path from technical school to certification for engineering is one year shorter.

The Berg Commission believes that the system needs to be flexible but contained. But, in the present political climate, we were told, there was not unanimous support for a level between secondary and higher education. The Commission also recommended that the public authorities take financial responsibility for this intermediate level. Already, many of the foundations or non-for-profit institutions receive state funding.

We had few comments on the intermediate sector. Employers valued the flexibility which private providers demonstrated. Particularly in the IT area, the flexibility of intermediate institutions has been helpful. Their training was seen as "just in time," not "just in case" as higher education institutions do with their degree programmes. The perceptions of flexibility and responsiveness no doubt come from several aspects of intermediate education. One is the short length of their programmes. We met with the Norwegian Correspondence School (NKS) and learned how students at the school prefer their programmes of 1-4 semesters over spending up to 5-7 years in higher education.* Flexibility also comes from the availability of distance education as an option. The Norwegian Knowledge Institute (NKI), for instance, provides 50 different programmes through the Internet.

Despite the growth of this sector of education during the 1980s and 1990s (Background Report, Chapter 3), we found very few available statistics on the sector. The lack of information likely reflects the fact that private institutions and organisations dominate this sector, and information on the private sector in general is notably absent. We found that information on both the extent and the quality of intermediate institutions could be greatly enhanced. The issue of

---

* State colleges also offer 2-3 year programmes of study.

163|

information on quality is especially important as employers increasingly turn to these institutions to meet their labour needs.

Recommendation:

With the increase in importance of the intermediate sector and its many private players, a national agency needs to collect data on intermediate institutions and disseminate the data more broadly.

3.1.4. School management

The responsibility for primary and secondary education has been delegated to municipalities and counties. We accept that in a country as geographically vast as Norway decentralised education provisions together with national curricula provide an equitable and common foundation for the road to lifelong learning for all its citizens.

While decentralisation does provide greater autonomy to the municipalities and counties, the Review Team was concerned that, at this level of education, school management and leadership seemed to be unevenly encouraged and developed. We observed great variations between counties. For instance, we heard that headmasters in Oslo have on-line budgets and the authority and means to affect change whereas those in other counties did not.

In trying to understand the concerns around school management, our focus turned to the role of the National Education Offices. The National Education Office in each county represents the State. Their mandate is to provide information and guidance to the municipalities, many of which are very small indeed. They are involved in quality assurance and co-ordination (particularly of adult education), leadership training for headmasters, and in seeing the Government's regional and national agendas implemented.

We found concerns about whether and how the National Education Offices support school management, both principals and headmasters. We sensed that the offices may dis-empower the school management in its attempts to provide leadership *vis-à-vis* teachers within the broader external community, even though the Offices have had important co-ordinating roles in the arrangement of leadership training for headmasters in all counties. The National Education Offices do not appear to provide school managers with sufficient voice in the national discourse around the lifelong learning agenda, and in particular, how it is achieved at primary and secondary level.

Recommendation:

We recommend that school principals be included in the national dialogues on policy development and implementation.

We wonder whether state offices add value in a system where the State delegates autonomy to the municipalities and counties.

Recommendation:

We recommend that the relationships between state, county and municipalities be re-examined to ensure that bureaucratic structures are aligned to current and future practice in management and, particularly, in quality assurance.

3.1.5. Teachers

Teachers comprise one of the main stakeholders in public education. At the time of the review, they were represented by two unions: Teachers' Union Norway and the Norwegian Union of Teachers. Teachers are employed by the municipalities or counties, but their salaries and conditions are fixed centrally.

The teachers unions support lifelong learning and indeed the Competence Reform. Until now, the teachers unions have played an important though informal part in the development of the lifelong learning agenda. The teachers unions feel they should be partners in the Competence Reform along with the social partners, but that the current tripartite co-operation has not always included them. They are, however, represented in the Forum for Competence Building and in the Reference Group for the Competence Reform.

Their members have a number of concerns. They are concerned that in the Competence Reform, for example, the Government-owned system (*i.e.*, the public education system) might be marginalised in favour of more commercial aims and institutions. They believe that the market will or might decide on courses to be offered and the content of those courses, shifting the balance of education to work-related lifelong learning to the detriment of other areas of learning (*e.g.*, civic responsibility, life skills, etc.)

They also fear that private providers will want to place an excessive emphasis on the working world in education. This, of course, is officially on the agenda, and while one might reject the union's concerns as outdated, they do reflect the tension between education as personal, social and intellectual development towards being an effective citizen and education for employment.

There was some fear expressed that the move towards greater diversity in education and training provision and the concomitant increase in choice for the individual learner could have undesirable consequences, such as:

- public schools may decline if more affluent parents send their children to private schools, impoverishing the public schools;
- the decline in public schools may lead to a decline in nationally held values which are normally transmitted via the public school system, and thus will

lead to less social cohesion and a fragmentation of the population in terms of values;

- teachers may put even more of their energy into teaching through resource centres or private providers – withdrawing their energies, commitment and creativity from their fulltime, publicly funded work;

- universities and colleges, unless they are given additional funding, may divert their energies to development of programmes for adults – this might lower the standards and education for the age cohort; and

- diversification in delivery (*i.e.*, through ICT or more distance education) may disadvantage the regions if more people choose higher status providers (*i.e.* courses from the University of Oslo).

These are legitimate concerns which should be addressed.

Recommendation:

We recommend that the concerns of teachers unions be fully considered in the discussions concerning the future of the education system, its composition, funding and goals, and in the implementation of the Competence Reform.

There were many comments on the inflexibility of schools and teaching arrangements. The collective agreements for teachers are inflexible and highly egalitarian. One consequence is that it is very hard to get after-hours delivery of courses. We heard that the teachers unions are negotiating with the State for pilot programmes of agreements at local levels, and, indeed, that in Oslo and other areas this is already possible.

We found it disturbing that teachers were "moonlighting", were prepared to be flexible in their working arrangements when working for private providers or resource centres but through the union agreements stuck to fairly inflexible conditions. We understand that the new agreements will provide for much needed flexibility in exchange for higher salaries.

Indeed, the Teachers' Union reported that they are entering a three-year period in which they are trying to develop quality in school, including flexibility. Therefore working hours are on the agenda. This is particularly important in view of the role of schools and of teachers in the provision of adult education.

The Teachers' Union has submitted a paper to the Government arguing for national quality standards. They believe that standards should not be left to counties. The National Education Offices in each county assure quality and review schools, though are not inspecting schools. The Ministry of Education, Research and Church Affairs looks upon the aims defined in the curricula as guarantee for national standards. Examinations are partly common national exams, partly common for schools in the county. There are national guidelines for both.

Furthermore, there are recruitment difficulties for the teaching profession. We heard of past innovative schemes in Troms county where there had been a teacher shortage. We heard that primary and lower secondary schools with large numbers of immigrant children do not get many qualified teachers. Rosenhof Upper Secondary School, in contrast, which teaches adults has no problems in attracting qualified teachers.

Part of the challenge in obtaining qualified teachers concerns teacher education. The State Education Office in Tromsø reported that teacher training was seen as too theoretical, and that teachers suffered reality shocks when they came to schools. Colleges seem to isolate themselves from schools. Tromsø has decentralised training since the 1980s using flexible teaching approaches, including ICT.

Though many school teachers have been teaching adults in continuing education context, it is important that as a standard part of their teacher training they become familiar with theories of adult learning. We understand that the new curricula included adult education theories as a regular part both of primary and secondary education. At the same time, we see positive signs concerning other aspects of teacher education. We understood that the level of in-service training was increasing, more funds had been allocated to ICT-delivered teacher training, and the training was helping teachers become more learner-centred.

Recommendations:

We recommend that teacher education be reviewed to ensure an adequate supply of appropriately qualified teachers for all schools.

We recommend that the role of teachers be redefined to include, where possible, responsibilities for the education of adults through the school system. At the same time, teacher training, especially for teachers of upper secondary schools, needs an increased emphasis on adult learning.

We further recommend that teachers' bilingual capacity in schools with immigrants be counted as a qualification for salary purposes.

We also recommend that the emphasis on ICT in teacher training be expanded to ensure that all teachers and administrators understand ICT, its appropriate uses, its potential benefits and drawbacks.

3.2. Adult education providers

The field of adult education as a source of lifelong learning opportunities and implementation of the Competence Reform is diverse and complex. Official responsibility for public adult education within the education sector is shared between the counties, the municipalities and higher education institutions. Adult education makes use of public sector educational institutions, a host of for profit and not-for profit organisations, employers and Aetat. It is here more than any-

167

where else that various educational reforms with their laudable intentions have met key challenges in their implementation.

Adult education is especially important as Norway seeks to expand lifelong learning opportunities beyond the formal educational sector. Indeed, the country has already been successful in increasing the level of adult education over the last 4-5 years. Since most of this education is taken for work-related reasons, it is not surprising that work-related courses dominate adult education. Such education tends to differ from traditional education in a number of important ways. Courses taken for work tend to be shorter, the students display greater levels of motivation, and the studies tend to be paid for by the employer.

3.2.1. Higher education

Background: *Those who enter higher education have a choice of 4 universities (75 000 students), 6 specialised university colleges (7 000 students), 26 state university colleges (75 000 students) and 2 colleges of arts and crafts. These public institutions are funded by Parliament in the form of a block grant through the Ministry of Education, Research and Church Affairs.*

In addition to the public higher education institutions, 30 private colleges provide education mainly in ICT and business administration, as well as theology, for about 16 000 fee-paying students.

For adults who have been denied opportunities in the past or were unable to make use of existing ones, a legal framework provides access to elementary and lower secondary education, to upper secondary education with both an academic or vocational paths, leading either to tertiary entrance or to a skilled trades certificate, and to a comprehensive assessment of non-formal learning in relation to attainment levels at school.

Higher education institutions continue to be seen by many stakeholders as ivory towers. Yet those institutions of which we met representatives were very much attuned to the necessity for lifelong learning and acknowledged the role higher education institutions could play in it. Indeed, we were impressed by the relationships the University of Tromsø and Tromsø College had with the region and its public and private employers. We also sensed that the regional colleges are seen as important actors in innovation and in regional development. Small- and medium-sized enterprises have a very high rate of employee turnover, and regional colleges were seen to provide knowledge relevant to the needs of these enterprises.

The shift from detailed prescriptions by the Ministry to a broad framework as advocated in the Mjøs Commission and by the Network Norway Council (an advisory committee to the Minister on building up competence on evaluation and accreditation) was generally welcomed by the University of Tromsø (and we assume the university sector) as providing higher education institutions with more autonomy. There is an expectation that greater autonomy will lead to greater flexibility and opportunities for experimentation with the organisation of learning.

The Mjøs Commission also advocated schemes for admission to higher education on the basis of non-formal learning. The University of Tromsø already received special dispensation to accept any adult of a given age (30) regardless of qualifications and has preliminary results that such students perform no differently than ordinary students. Not surprisingly, the Rector expressed some reservations about being required to use non-formal learning assessments to decide which adults to accept. She believed that adults should make their own assessment of their qualifications and whether they were ready for university study on the basis of information given to them. Indeed, new constraints would diminish the empowerment which lifelong learning can and should provide to individual citizens.

Recognition of prior learning and assessment of non-formal learning, of course, are also means of reducing the length of study. The Government is concerned about the long duration of tertiary studies as well as the late entry of graduates into the labour market. Norway has signed the Bologna Declaration and we urge a commitment to its implementation. The Bologna Declaration, *inter alia*, recommends Bachelor length courses followed by Master courses where appropriate. Within the lifelong learning agenda shorter study courses followed by periods of work and study make sense.

In Chapter 2 we referred to increasing globalisation and international co-operation. We heard from the College Students' Association that they were promoting student mobility within Norway and abroad to help students learn about other cultures. However, there were pressures to keep students in their home regions, and there were more students going abroad than foreign students studying in Norway. They also commented that movement from college to university can be difficult – universities do not recognise all subjects. Officially, the transfer system is very good but as universities have different programmes, getting advanced standing for all subjects done can be difficult.

We note that the Mjøs Commission promotes the international orientation of institutions and individuals and recommends a variety of strategies to open Norwegian education to international perspectives, co-operation and students.

Recommendations:

We suggest that the higher education system be encouraged to implement the Bologna Declaration by introducing Bachelor and Master courses, where appropriate, and to align the degree structure to that of many other OECD countries.

We further suggest that the recommendations of the Mjøs Commission promoting the international orientation of institutions and individuals be adopted.

169

For any institution to be responsive to its clients (*i.e.*, to students in the case of higher education institutions and external stakeholders), its needs to have management structures which encourage timely responsiveness, responsible decision-making, and accountability. For any institution to be innovative (*i.e.*, in teaching, research and service in the case of higher education institutions), it needs to have management structures which encourage ideas, responsible risk-taking and leadership.

Norway's university management structures still follow the traditional collegial model, a model which has served the university system well world-wide. But in many countries it has been realised that in a mass higher education system which needs to be internationally attractive and competitive, management structures have to change. For instance, it has become the practice in most countries to strengthen the position of the rector/president/vice-chancellor.

Higher education institutions are responsible to many communities, including the international disciplinary bodies. But as publicly funded institutions they also need to be relevant to the needs of the knowledge society. They need to be in touch with society to ensure that societal demands are met. External input can be systematically sought via course advisory committees and other committees. At the management level it has become common in many countries to establish a governing board with a limited membership, the majority of the members being external appointments.

Recommendation:

We recommend that universities and colleges establish governing boards with a majority of members from outside the institution; the exact composition and terms of reference to be negotiated between the Ministry, the Norwegian Council of Universities and Colleges and other organisations, if appropriate.

3.2.2. Other adult education providers

Various adult education providers, some with long traditions, others new, complement the provisions by the formal education providers.

Education resource centres

In addition to one state-run centre catering for more than 1 800 students, counties have established about 250 resource centres in connection with upper secondary schools. They provide competence development for both private and public clients (Background Report, Chapter 5).

Study associations

Between 680 000-800 000 people study each year a variety of subjects through study associations. The largest group of students engage in art and craft studies, followed by organisational and management studies, with humanities and religious studies, economics and computer based studies, and use of nature, ecology and environmental studies all drawing significant numbers of students.

Twenty-two study associations receive public subsidies, among them the Folk University and the Workers' Educational Association (AOF). In addition to general education courses, study associations also aim their courses at the labour market and indeed at students who prefer to learn through them rather than through the formal education system. There has been an increase from 1995-98 of 461 to 734 courses which form part of compulsory education; an increase from 13 658 to 18 099 in courses at upper secondary level, and an increase from 33 229 to 47 829 at higher education level. There is also an increase in the courses preparing private candidates for examinations in the formal education system (Background Report, Chapter 5).

Folk high schools

The 82 folk high schools in Norway provide residential annual courses mainly geared at young people and a variety of short courses for adults spanning social, creative and communication subjects.

Employers

Employers provide a variety of learning opportunities. In addition to paid study leave, employers provide various forms of staff development and training via in-house capacities, external consultants, or public and private education providers. Employer-provided learning relies to a large degree on private suppliers which are prepared to develop tailor-made courses.

In both the public and private sector, collective wage agreements require that employers document the need for continuing training and to develop training plans. Several of the organisations in working life offer alone or together with their counterpart job-oriented education at different levels (Background Report, Chapter 3).

Private providers

About 1 000 companies with 10 000 employees offer their training and consultancy services to companies and trades.

Labour market authorities

Of course, lifelong learning also has to extend to those adults who are unemployed or marginalised in relation to the labour market. The Ministry of Labour and Government Administration aims, in 2001, to mobilise unemployed individuals to fill vacant positions, to counter increased unemployment due to industrial and geographic imbalances, and to raise the qualifications in groups of unemployed and vocationally disabled who have problems entering and getting a foothold in the labour market.

The *Aetat*, formerly Public Employment Services (PES), offers for this purpose job-oriented training to the unemployed. These labour market courses are free and run about 15 weeks on average. Due to a buoyant labour market, there has been a decline in participants and courses since 1989, with 30 261 participants in 2000.

In 2000 there were on average 57 400 people registered as "vocationally disabled"; on average 45 200 took part in vocational rehabilitation measures. Just over half of those who completed vocational rehabilitation started work, education or became job seekers like other job seekers. In 2000 20 000 disabled jobseekers took part in ordinary education mostly at upper secondary level and were funded by the Social Security Scheme. We comment further on *Aetat* in Chapter 4.

3.2.3. Distance education

Background: *Distance education has a long tradition in Norway. In 2000, 14 institutions received financial support from the public authorities to provide flexible learning opportunities for those who could not easily participate in institution-based learning. While some courses are available at upper secondary level, many lead to work-related qualifications. More than half of the courses cover subjects related to social and health care, management and economics and technical subjects. In 1998, 45 000 students completed a course via distance education* (Background Report, Chapter 5).

Distance education is one medium of instruction which can be used to reach adults. The Government has high hopes for ICT and distance education in general. Distance education can work at upper secondary level for motivated adults if complemented by face-to-face interaction. However, there remain some important obstacles to making distance education a viable option for adult education

First there is the issue of geography and regional development. Norway is a country where educational institutions are dispersed as part of the country's regional development policy. Learning in people's mind is associated with physically going to courses, which is geographically feasible. Hence distance education is not the preferred option for many students. Furthermore, there is the concern that ICT and more distance education might lead to inter-regional competition between universities and colleges as they seek to attract students from a dwindling pool.

Even though SOFF (the Norwegian Agency for Flexible Learning in Higher Education) has given grants for pilot projects over a ten-year period, universities and colleges have been slower to offer distance education in the past for several reasons. Universities and colleges are willing to offer existing courses via ICT but not to develop tailor-made ones. There appears to be few incentives for universities to develop such courses and the field is already occupied by private providers.

On the whole, with some exceptions, universities and colleges cannot afford to invest in distance education courses or other adult education courses which are not cost-effective. From what we have heard, many are not cost-effective even now, and those which are not developed with project funding from the Government must be subsidised by the regular students. Indeed, smaller and remote colleges are especially disadvantaged, as they are funded on the same basis as other institutions but have higher per unit costs. Nevertheless, a few are making serious efforts to develop new courses, both extramural and taylor-made.

We comment further on ICT and distance education in Chapter 5.

3.2.4. *Secondary education for adults*

Since 2000, adults have had the right to complete their upper secondary education (their statutory right to complete primary and lower secondary education will become effective in August 2002). Adults constituted between 25 to 35% of students in upper secondary education before the 1994 reform, now they are one-eighth. Counties report fewer adult applicants but also say they give preference to those potential students with a statutory right, *i.e.* the 16- to 19-year-olds. The schools of the municipalities and counties seem ill-prepared to meet the needs of adults. Adults, of course, do not have to go to schools – the municipalities and counties are obliged to provide for flexible education and they can use other providers like study associations or distance learning institutions.

For example, we were presented with a project report in Tromsø, a part of the larger funded project on assessment of scope and testing of models that meet adult learning needs at primary and lower secondary level. In the area, 74 people registered interest in a range of subjects. They were geographically dispersed and wanted to learn at different times and in different ways.

However, at the time no funds had yet been set aside to address the diverse needs of adults such as these 74 people. Funding the educational needs of adults is a considerable challenge for municipalities and counties. Each municipality has to offer elementary education to adults and, we were told, is responsible for finding funds to address the Competency Reform within its block grant. We have since been informed that Parliament has decided that the State shall cover the extra costs related to adults' right to primary and lower secondary education.

To meet the needs of adults who are looking for upper secondary education, counties must reconcile individual needs and societal needs for competence, and indeed set their priorities between education and health and other social concerns. The economic situation in counties is such that education fights for its share of the budget. Moreover, in the 1980s, part-time study for adults after working hours became too expensive for counties and decreased. While counties can and do contract with private providers to supply education for adults, this is not a preferred option for the teachers unions.

3.2.5. Seniors

We received relatively few comments about seniors and those in post-retirement groups and their position *vis-à-vis* lifelong learning and the Competence Reform. The official retirement age is 67. But many people take the option to retire at age 62 or transfer into part-time work. There is a change in pensioner expectation and the behaviour expected. From a labour market perspective, there are obvious mismatches in the labour market. There are regional differences in getting work. But people prefer to get pensions where they live rather than move to where work is available. There also seems to be a considerable number of people on disability pensions.

The Graduate Association is developing a senior policy (for people 60 plus). They are looking at the last years of employment, aiming to provide incentives for individuals to stay longer in their jobs while giving them more flexible working time. In the State sector, where the focus has been strongest on people engaged in the labour market, too, the policy is to try to keep people in the system.

For the post-retirement age groups the question arises to what extent they wish to be involved in employment, be self-employed or be open to new activities. It is not known whether people retire early because of lack of competence or ability to re-skill. However, seniors' skills could be utilised in informal roles as mentors or advisers to younger employees.

While the labour market might increasingly seek their skills, other opportunities or reasons for learning should also be available. Avenues for learning open to them, apart from the workplace, include travel, courses at university, library services, senior internet cafes, senior centres, activity centres for small jobs and senior clubs for retired people.

Recommendation:

With the increase in average life expectancy it is important that the State address how to engage seniors in life and work and how to provide them with learning opportunities to make the last years of life meaningful, fulfilling, and productive.

Chapter 4

The Unfinished Agenda:
Integrating Learning and Working Life

An important, if not *the* most important, principle underlying the notion of life-long learning is that individuals should continually acquire and learn new skills, knowledge and competencies. Initial education's ability to equip people once and for all with the skills they require through the rest of their lives is diminishing. To enable continual learning, as described in the Background Report (Chapter 1), "Lifelong learning for all requires a connection between [the] formal educational system, experience and learning in working and in every day life".

Given the importance of learning throughout one's adult years, the growing recognition of the workplace as an arena of learning, and the centuries-old perspective of viewing education and work as separate spheres of life, it is critical that Norway address what appears to be the portions of the lifelong learning agenda which remain relatively unfinished. This chapter pays special attention to the efforts in Norway to integrate the spheres of learning and work.

4.1. The Competence Reform

Much of the unfinished business in the lifelong learning agenda falls in the province of Norway's Competence Reform. Work on the Competence Reform began in 1996 as a response to the rapid pace of change in society, technology, internationalisation and the economy.* Among the areas of focus are:

- flexible learning;
- framework conditions for individuals;
- a competence-building programme;
- documenting and evaluating non-formal learning;
- "popular enlightenment" and democratic participation;
- a new chance – primary and secondary education;

---

* A full elaboration of the Competence Reform was provided in KUF (1998a). Its principal objective is "to help meet the need for competence in society, in the workplace and by the individual" (KUF, 2000, p. 6).

- structural changes to the public education; and
- motivation and information.

Efforts in each of these areas are at varying levels of advancement. Elsewhere in this review, we comment on each area to some extent.

As we noted in earlier chapters, Norway's formal educational system is highly-developed and, indeed, well-regarded. Norway is among the leading nations in the provision of primary, secondary and tertiary education to its citizens. Although we have made recommendations concerning the formal educational system in Chapter 3, none of them require revolutionary changes in the system.

By contrast, work-related learning and its provision, as in most countries, has received comparatively less attention until recent years. There is growing recognition that a competent workforce, whether such competence is received through an employer or through other educational providers, is critical to creating a knowledge society and ensuring competitiveness in a global economy.

Indeed, the Ministry of Trade and Industry, while it does not focus so much on the learning of individuals but on the learning enterprise, recognises the importance of a competitive workforce. Continuous upgrading of knowledge and skills is seen as necessary for industry to adapt to changes in technologies and markets. The basis for the Competence Reform therefore should be the need of the labour market as well as of the society and the individual.

4.2. Learning in working life

Working life is increasingly seen as a key arena for learning. Employers acknowledge the value of training their employees and stimulating them to enhance their competence. Employees and organisations that represent them acknowledge the importance of learning for advancement, career mobility, and achieving a fulfilling life in and out of the workplace. The social partners see responsibility for learning in the workplace as a joint partnership between employers, employees and their organisations.

The Background Report (Chapter 3) admits that workplace learning, or in-service training, has received comparatively less attention from researchers. Thus, reliable and precise statistics on the extent of such learning are difficult to find. Nonetheless, there are several measures of workplace learning including:

- Conservatively, about half of all adult education in terms of participants takes place in working life.
- Participation in work-related adult education grew from 11 to 30% between 1978 and 1996.
- About ⅓ of workers attend courses organised by their employers each year. In a five-year period, 75% of workers report that they participated in one or more courses.

- An estimated 11.5 – 18 billion NOK was set aside by working life for competence development in 1996.
- Approximately 3-4% of employers' wage budgets go to employer-provided training each year.

75% of employees in the State sector have participated in courses. The investment in workplace training is higher in the public sector than the private sector. Generally, also, younger people are more likely to participate and graduate.

The amount and type of competence development varies widely by type of company and the types of workers they employ. About half (49%) of the courses are given by external providers, with the figure being higher in smaller enterprises. The types of providers include:

- professional course providers and consultants (used by 53%);
- public and private educational institutions (used by 41%); and
- customers/providers (used by 36%).

It is also estimated that the trade associations within the employers' federation presently offer another 1 000 courses.

4.3. Current bridges between work and learning

The issues of competence in a framework of lifelong learning cannot be addressed by treating the formal educational system and other means of learning, including the workplace, as separate spheres of activity. To its credit, Norway has recognised the importance of integrating these spheres and has begun to make progress on certain points. While the Government views the Competence Reform as a gradual process, in recent years a number of mechanisms for linking learning (*i.e.*, education institutions) and work (*i.e.*, the labour market) have been formed which provide a foundation for moving forward. Here we briefly review some of these mechanisms.

4.3.1. Resource centres

Resource centres are one link between education and working life. The intention of the Ministry of Education, Research and Church Affairs and the Ministry of Local Government and Regional Development had been that centres contribute to developing forms of co-operation between upper secondary schools and local industry and working life to enhance competence and thereby encourage regional development.

Although there is no standard form, resources centres are normally associated with one or more upper secondary schools or other autonomous institutions. Most upper secondary schools tend to have a resource centre, sometimes administratively as part of the school, sometimes as a separate business unit. In some counties independent resource centres have been established.

The resource centres are commercial business enterprises providing, for a fee, training and consultancy services to private and public organisations, including PES. They provide courses primarily to those in working life. The centres often use teachers from their upper secondary schools for these additional activities with the profits being expended on staff development or equipment.

While in cities like Trondheim school-industry links do not depend on resource centres, in the country, sometimes strong links are established. While there might be a general mistrust of schools by industry organisations, there have been highly successful examples of co-operation through resource centres. Indeed the resource centres can be more pro-active and responsive than schools. Their arrangements are flexible in contrast to the school system which employers generally regard as inflexible in school year, timetable, and course content.

4.3.2. Business-at-school programmes

The NHO (the Norwegian Confederation of Industry and Business) offers another mechanism for linking work and learning through a national project of "business-at-school" projects. These projects are long-term (3-4 years) formal agreements between schools and employers to guide students' schooling and career choices. The programmes are intended to:

- give the pupils and students better knowledge of the role played by business and industry as generator of wealth;
- improve young people's rationale for choosing education and career;
- assist employers in recruitment; and
- exploit the knowledge of schools and working life to improve the quality in developing schools and companies.

These agreements vary and may include:

- company representatives as resource persons;
- structured company visits;
- case and project work;
- work experience for pupils;
- teachers' placement in business and industry;
- teachers' participation in internal company courses; and
- company representatives as permanent consultants for pupil enterprises at school.

Launched in the 1996-97 school year, there were already over 3 000 such agreements in Norway. In Tromsø alone, we were told of 120 agreements. The potential benefits for employers and schools are relatively clear. Schools may be able to achieve greater alignment between general and vocational education, improve the knowledge and skills of teachers, and become more involved in their local communities. Employers may obtain a more qualified workforce, improve their public image and help shape school curriculum to better meet the needs of working life.

Unfortunately, not all projects are successful. In Tromsø, a large employer tried to initiate an agreement with two schools but eventually gave up when it met what it saw as a lack of interest in schools. In this employer's enterprise, 25% of the employees were unskilled and were barely coping with job requirements. The employer has arranged for unskilled employees to get a certificate following training, half of which occurred during work time and half in leisure time. This training was not provided by an educational institution. Due in part to the difficulties experienced in providing these employees with the necessary skills, in the future it intends to recruit only skilled workers; unskilled work will be automated.

While we heard from schools and businesses of good will and intentions on each side, it was clear that much planning was needed to ensure that these co-operative agreements are worthwhile for the students and teachers and for the business partners. Above all, clear objectives for each component of a partnership need to be established and integrated in school or business plans.

4.3.3. Young Enterprise Norway

Young Enterprise Norway is another attempt to link schools and workplaces. It relies on building networks and anchoring agreements in official plans of schools, municipal plans for development of schools and business and industry, strategic plans for counties, national curriculum and pedagogic instructions, and national plans for development of business and industry – a huge co-ordination task.

4.3.4. The Aetat

Discussed briefly in Chapter 3, the Aetat is another key provider of training and education for competence in working life. The Norwegian Public Employment Service changed its name to Aetat in February 2000. The traditional role of the Aetat has been to implement the Norwegian labour market policy. It includes vocational guidance and advice, job placement, regular labour market measures, vocational rehabilitation (including benefits), and unemployment benefits. Table 4.1 describes the labour market measures and the number of persons participating in 1999.

Table 4.1. **People in regular labour market measures,
by type of programme, 1999**

Public service employment	37
Wage subsidies to employers	1 577
Skill training measures	6 651
Of which: Labour market courses	4 529
Practice positions	2 122
Temporary posts	119
Total	8 384

Source: Aetat – The Directorate of Labour.

In 1999 the situation on the labour market was characterised by low unemployment so the volume of labour market measures was rather low. During the 1990s labour market courses reached a peak in 1994 and thereafter the number of participants has been reduced. Due to the increasing lack of personnel in certain sectors, particularly the health sector, the Aetat has recently been involved in recruiting personnel from abroad.

The purpose of the labour market courses is to qualify job seekers for ordinary work and reduce the imbalance between the needs of the labour market and the skills of the job seekers and to motivate the unemployed to undertake further education or training. Target groups are unemployed and vocationally disabled people and also people in insecure employment situations. Prioritised groups are the long-term unemployed with low educational attainment. The minimum age is 19 years.

For the vocationally disabled, training could also include upper secondary education and higher education in the ordinary education system. This is not the case for other unemployed persons. Short courses and vocational training are emphasised but the courses can also cover general subjects and lead to, or build up to, a final apprentice exam. The upper limit to labour market training courses is 10 months. Average length in 2000 was 15 weeks. During training the individuals should be available for job placement. This does not apply to the vocationally disabled. There are, however, few examples where course-participants have had to quit a course due to a job offer.

The labour market training is publicly funded. The unemployment benefit/Social Security Scheme is used to finance the subsistence of participants, vocationally disabled or otherwise. The right to the benefits is earned by taking part in paid work. The recipient is reimbursed 60-70% of the former wages. The individual benefit therefore depends on the size of the former earnings. For this reason the economic conditions for prime age or older workers when taking part in labour market training will often be better than for students in ordinary studies, when the benefit payments are higher than the total amount of grants and loans from the State Education Loan Fund. Participants in labour market training who have small or no benefit rights may receive a daily cash benefit which is more or less equivalent to the smallest total amount of grants and loans from the State Education Loan Fund. Books and travel costs related to participating in labour market training are also covered by the Aetat. However, the unemployment benefit dependent has to adhere by rules and regulations for job seeker activities, otherwise benefit payments may be cut off.

The labour market training courses take place in separate resource centres associated with upper secondary schools (mentioned above) or with private suppliers/organisations. They are, for instance, run by school authorities, study associations or private providers. The provider is selected after a tender.

According to the reform that was introduced on July 1st 2000 the Aetat's monopoly on job placement was abolished and the general ban on the hiring out of labour was lifted. The Aetat was allowed to receive payment for specific services that it provides for employers that go beyond straightforward job placements. Temporary employment service within the Aetat was established to administer the hiring out of temporary workers. The payment based services would supplement Aetat's free services and administrative functions. All services for job-seekers will remain free of charge.

The Review Team discussed the Aetat and its involvement in the implementation of the Competence Reform at ministerial level, national level and county level. It was evident that so far its role and the future extent of its involvement were unclear to the actors concerned and that the preparations for its participation had not really started yet.

Counselling and assessment of the participants' qualifications are also part of the different programmes conducted by the Aetat. Some actors, however, expressed certain doubts about the assessment capacity of the Aetat. In some cases apparently the Aetat bought such services, e.g. from resource centres associated with upper secondary schools. How far the development of assessment programmes within the Aetat had progressed was unclear to the Review Team. In Tromsø, the municipality wanted to include the employment services in its reference group for its project on assessment of informal qualifications in relation to secondary training.

Recommendation:

To the Review Team the most evident task for the Aetat in the Competence Reform would seem to be to provide:

- *information to the unemployed and job-seekers about the opportunities offered by the Competence Reform. As the target group for the Aetat are individuals with a weak position on the labour market it would appear very natural and valuable for the Competence Reform to use the contacts and networks of the Aetat.*

- *the education and training unemployed individuals will need to get a job, and to get a foothold in working life.*

- *assessments of the qualifications of individuals. Useful experience in this field must have been acquired by the Aetat that could be used in the Competence Reform. Especially its knowledge about assessment of informal qualifications may be helpful.*

Related to the information, communication, and career guidance responsibilities of the Aetat in the Competence Reform is the question of wider co-ordination of such activities between the Aetat, the schools, employers and welfare services (*e.g.*, the social security and social insurance offices). Adult education involves many actors, with much responsibility in the counties. At county level, we were told, closer co-operation is needed by the different actors. We were told that both Labour and Education Departments sometimes are handling the same adults seeking secondary education. Adults now have to initiate the contact with the Education Department if they want access to a particular course. However, the expectation locally is that many will not do so and will fail to obtain the necessary skills to re-enter the workforce.

Individuals need to cut across three systems – social welfare, labour and education. More co-operation and facilitation are needed on behalf of individuals by departments. A one-stop shop for groups risking marginalisation in society would assist individuals as they attempt to understand and navigate the provisions of these organisations and to keep them from "falling between the cracks". A pilot project in this area (in Röros) was mentioned to the Review Team. The findings of such projects should be disseminated and applied as soon and as far as possible.

Recommendation:

We suggest that one-stop shops be established which include in their services information and advice on education and training options for groups outside the public education and labour market system.

4.4. Perspectives on bridging work and learning

While it is clear that there are noteworthy efforts to more closely align the spheres of work and learning, interstices between the domains remain troublesome for employers, employees, and educational institutions alike.

4.4.1. The employers' perspective

Although the Competence Reform has focused much attention on workplace learning and learning throughout working life, concerns from the employers' point of view are embodied in the perspectives of the social partners. Employers, for one, believe that the present educational system does not yet provide appropriately qualified workers in a timely, flexible and efficient manner. Adult education in the upper secondary school system is perceived as conservative and school centred. Part of the challenge is building more effective bridges between the labour system and the formal educational system.

In looking at the labour market, employers are also worried that much needed employees will withdraw from the labour market to engage in training. Ideally, they would like to see work and study combined. With ICT and other distance education teaching and learning methods, this possibility is certainly becoming more realistic. Employers are actively addressing these concerns through activities like the NHO-sponsored programme described above and by developing e-learning courses and promoting e-learning with universities and firms as partners.

4.4.2. The employees' perspective

The Review Team did not meet with individual employees, but received some insights about what employee organisations provide in lifelong learning opportunities. We heard from one vocational organisation for white-collar workers with 250 000 members which was concerned with how to motivate members to upgrade their skills. Its ultimate concern was that the gap between the highly-skilled and less skilled could widen. The organisation itself is providing study opportunities for its members to address this concern.

By contrast, we met with an organisation for professional graduates. It was clear that this organisation's more highly-educated members will make greater use of the upgrading opportunities it provides through its own further and continuing education.

Employee organisations had concerns that mirrored those of employers. For instance, they were frustrated by a lack of flexibility on the part of schools created by centrally established standards and centrally negotiated contracts between the Teachers' Union and the State. They also expressed interest in creating closer ties between schools and their local communities and enhancing the flexibility of the educational system through ICT-based learning. Since many vocational employees do not have access to computers at work, it was suggested that municipalities should be able to provide facilities for all types of workers (e.g., ICT-based courses could be delivered through schools).

4.4.3. The educational system's perspective

We discussed many views and concerns of the formal educational system in Chapter 3. It is evident that the Competence Reform has presented challenges for

183

schools and other educational institutions that will result in changes on their part. However, from the perspective of the educational institutions, particularly those of the teachers' union, the social partners and the State must accept the need for changes on their behalf as well.

4.5. Challenges in bridging work and learning

To create smooth and effective transitions between the systems of education and working life that address the concerns of the actors involved means overcoming certain challenges. While the broader challenges with implementing the lifelong learning agenda are covered in Chapter 5, here we discuss several challenges specific to connecting education and working life in the context of lifelong learning. They include a system or framework of qualifications, a means of documenting competence gained outside formal education and a focus on the outcomes of learning.

4.5.1. Competence or qualifications framework

The Competence Reform faces as one of its critical challenges the development of standards for recognising competencies acquired through either education and working life. Without such standards, actors in the two sectors will continue to speak in their distinct languages. Currently, the educational system describes competencies primarily in terms of years of schooling, courses completed and credentials, whereas employers and employees describe competencies in terms of skills, knowledge, experience and expertise. The net effect is to hinder the optimal transfer of individuals between the two sectors, as one sector does not understand what competencies an individual brings from another sector.

Standards for recognising competencies require the development of several tools. The first is a standard framework in which to situate and categorise competencies or qualifications. A competence or qualifications framework would greatly facilitate the integration of competencies acquired both through formal education and through formal and informal learning at the workplace and in civic life.

This is crucial from two perspectives. From an equity perspective, similarly skilled individuals should have their competencies equally recognised, regarded and rewarded, no matter how those skills were obtained. From a national labour market perspective, both employers and other institutions which provide adult education courses (except those at a primary education level) need to ensure that a recognised level of competency has been reached and certification is awarded at a consistent standard.

International experiences with developing national competence or qualification frameworks, however, illustrate that the task is fraught with complexities and difficult issues. Therefore, such a framework is best worked out in consultation with other nations and the OECD. By working cross-nationally, Norway will ensure its compatibility with emerging frameworks elsewhere. Compatibility may aid considerably in the ability of individuals from outside to transfer into Norway's educational system and labour market. Working with other nations will also enable Norway to avoid some of the pitfalls that others have encountered and perhaps even shorten the period of time it takes to complete such a framework.

Recommendation:

We recommend that a national framework be developed to ensure transparent national standards of competencies.

4.5.2. Documentation of non-formal learning

The second set of tools required to standardise competencies across education and working life is a common process for measuring and documenting competencies. The means and occasions for documenting competencies have long existed in the educational system, typically in the form of tests and grades upon completion of courses. However, documenting competencies acquired in other arenas such as working life and through non-formal learning (*e.g.*, experiences outside of the workplace) presents a substantially greater challenge.

The challenge, therefore, is two-fold: first, to develop means for formally documenting competencies obtained outside of formal education, and second, to ensure that the resulting documentation has legitimacy both in the workplace and in the educational system. Such documentation ideally would be portable across both sectors. Hence the need is for documentation processes which rely on transparent and consistent assessment criteria.

According to the Plan of Action for the Competence Reform, one of its principal objectives is "to establish a national system for documenting and evaluating the non-formal learning of adults, with legitimacy both in the workplace and in the education system" (KUF, 2000a, p. 12). This includes learning attained through paid and unpaid employment, organisational involvement, and organised training.

As another important objective, the Competence Reform intends to recognise non-formal learning in a manner that allows individuals to obtain credit toward educational requirements in upper secondary and higher education. The Ministry of Education, Research and Church Affairs has initiated a number of pilot projects to assess and recognise non-formal learning with respect to the requirements of upper secondary education. Employee and employer organisations, the public education system and the various providers of education are collaborating on this task. In higher education several institutions have on their own initiative been allowed to admit applicants on the basis of documentation of non-formal qualifications (see Box 4.1).

Box 4.1. Documentation of non-formal learning

We were presented with one effort in the County of Trøms to document non-formal learning gained through non-school activities and experiences. Non-formal learning was defined as the competence a person has built up through paid or unpaid work, continuing education or leisure activities.

A reference group was appointed, consisting of principals, teachers' organisations, the employment service, the social partners, local education centres and the county authorities. The project leader, from the Department of Education, was responsible for achieving the project's objectives and ensuring quality. The project consisted of working with local education centres (OPUS) that registered adults who wanted their non-formal learning recognised as stepping stones for further formal upper secondary education.

The project had the following objectives:

- develop a total system for recognition of non-formal learning using both interview and software technology as tools in the process of documentation;
- start with subjects within health and social science, expand towards other subjects during the project;
- reach the target group through efficient information;
- provide adult education on the basis of the recognition of non-formal learning and the needs of the target group; and
- develop flexible education models to meet the needs of the target group.

At the time of our meeting, October 2000, documentation consultants had been appointed and a system of documentation of non-formal learning was close to having been established. Two upper secondary schools offered adult education courses in the area of health education. Exam preparation courses were being developed for employed or unemployed individuals with non-formal learning relevant to health work and were administered using software technology and the Internet. Financing of the adult education was done in co-operation with the employment service.

We were informed that numerous other similar, yet separate, projects were being conducted around the country at the county level between 1999 and 2002. Despite the progress these projects have made to date, the Review Team was concerned about several aspects of the overall approach in Norway to documenting non-formal learning. We were concerned with the apparent piecemeal approach to the documentation and evaluation of informal learning, although we have been assured that eventually there will be an evaluation of the projects and formation of national standards. National standards are the prerequisite for transferability of documented non-formal learning, and its acceptability in the workplace and education system.

While this effort is being co-ordinated on a national level in conjunction with the Social Partners and the counties, our concerns essentially re-iterate some of those raised in the recently completed "Thematic Review of Adult Learning" in Norway by the OECD (2000f). Namely:

- there appeared to be no overarching framework for co-ordinating the various projects;

- few, if any, common definitions and terms were used across projects; and

- it was unclear how the projects would result in common, nation-wide processes for documenting non-formal learning.

As with the competence framework, the efforts to establish this system of documentation will benefit greatly from similar efforts outside Norway. We were pleased to learn that Norway had already arranged an international conference in May 2000 on the documentation of non-formal learning.

Recommendations:

We support the recommendation of the Competence Reform that a system for documenting and evaluating non-formal learning be established and disseminated.

We recommend a review of the current process for developing national consistency in the documentation and evaluation of non-formal learning.

4.5.3. Shifting the focus from inputs to outcomes

A third, critical component to the development of national standards for competencies recognised by both education and the workplace involves the object of measurement. The question is what exactly should be documented and evaluated. The notion of "competence", although currently interpreted differently from one setting to another, must be the same concept in both education and working life to facilitate the movement of individuals between both systems.

Heretofore, the educational system has relied on accreditation of formal institutions to provide a measure of an individual's qualifications. While accreditation can in many cases serve as a measure of quality, and therefore an individual's competence, it suffers from focusing the attention on inputs into the learning process instead of the outcomes. While employers have used the credentials of the institutions attended by job applicants as a measure of competence, in the end, what they need to know most is what applicants know and are able to do.

187|

The Review Team was especially concerned that, in the initial efforts to document and evaluate non-formal learning which it reviewed, the terms of reference for the measurement are those of the educational system (namely, the national curriculum). Indeed the Plan of Action for the Competence Reform's objectives surrounding this documentation are only aimed at translating competencies gained outside of formal education into units of measurement recognised only by the educational system. For such a system to succeed, the units of measurement (*i.e.*, the competencies) must be recognised by educational institutions and employers alike. The bridge between education and working life goes both ways, not simply from working life back into education.

As above, our concerns mirror many of those of the "Thematic Review of Adult Learning," including:

- a lack of evidence that the signalling of competencies will be transparent across all institutions;

- an exclusive reliance, thus far, on the school curriculum to measure competence;

- placing *lead* responsibility in the hands of educators while sharing leadership with representatives from working life; and

- a lack of means of external assessment to validate not only the initial assumptions behind the efforts, but also the effectiveness of the resulting processes and measures.

Recommendations:

We recommend that the documentation of competencies focus on assessing the outcomes of learning in a manner that translates both into job qualifications as well as school credits, and that it be capable of recognising these competencies wherever or however they have been acquired.

The learning outcomes should not be expressed in terms of grades, course content, or performance ratings, but rather as descriptions of what an individual knows and is able to do. Taken together this is no simple task; it will certainly require creativity and hard work on the part of willing and committed representatives from both sectors. Again, we suggest that Norway look to international experience in assessing the outcomes of learning to aid its own efforts.

Chapter 5

Bringing About the Lifelong Learning Agenda

In this chapter we will concentrate on the implementation of the lifelong learning agenda. First we discuss in general terms the role of the State, the social partners and other actors, the "enablers" of the process. Then we go on commenting on our observations as to actual implementation practices in Norway – the many projects started to promote lifelong learning, the innovation and research systems, the evaluation and dissemination activities and distance education and ICT. The funding problems encountered in financing the lifelong learning agenda are also discussed. Finally some information needs are highlighted.

The sum of practices and provisions described and commented upon in Chapters 3 and 4 do not necessarily add up to a coherent lifelong learning agenda. First of all leadership is needed (Section 5.1). A central control mechanism is required to keep the different parts and experiments together and linked to an overall implementation strategy. Moreover, an interdependent, collaborative approach is needed in both policy-making and execution. The State has an essential role to play, but partnership with other actors is necessary to advance the lifelong learning agenda. The social partners can help bridge the gap between education and working life.

Educational providers, teachers and students have to be involved in developing the learning and teaching arenas. Other preconditions are also explored – development incentives (Section 5.2), well functioning research and innovation (Section 5.4) and evaluation systems (Section 5.5); a shift from teacher-centred to student-centred learning (Section 5.3) as well as a shift from central steering to market mechanisms (Section 5.6), funding (Section 5.7), and information systems (Section 5.8).

5.1. Roles

5.1.1. *The role of the State*

Leadership

Major reforms which cut across a number of ministerial portfolios need leadership which has been explicitly delegated and communicated. This review of lifelong learning policies was initiated by the Minister for Education, Research and Church Affairs who has the main carriage for the implementation of the lifelong learning agenda. However, the actual operational responsibility for progressing the agenda is distributed over several ministries.

In Chapter 6 we make a case for a strong role by the State and for the State through the Prime Minister to delegate leadership explicitly.

We became aware of a great need for this leadership to bring to fruition through the difficult process of implementing a vision that will benefit all of society.

There are several pressure or critical points where the credibility of the Government's commitment to lifelong learning is at stake. The Government approach has to be communicated, properly organised and funded.

Creating arenas for dialogue and inquiry

Norway with its strong and old democratic traditions has involved relevant stakeholders whenever social or educational reforms were mooted. The past decade has seen a number of Royal Commissions, OECD reviews and white papers.

The Review Team had access to a number of summaries, translations and full reports from different recent commissions:

- the Buer Commission, Norwegian Royal Commission Report (1997);
- the Mjøs Commission, Norwegian Royal Commission Report (1999);
- the Aamodt Commission, Norwegian Royal Commission Report (1999);
- the Berg-Commission, Norwegian Royal Commission Report (2000).

The Review Team found them most relevant.

It had also access to the Summary of parts of the Report to the *Storting* No. 42 (KUF, 1998b) concerning the Competence Reform and to the various OECD reports on Norwegian educational policies:

- Reviews of National Policies for Education (1988);
- Thematic Review of the First Years of Tertiary Education (1997);
- Thematic Review of Early Childhood Education and Care Policy (1998);
- Thematic Review of the Transition from Initial Education to Working Life (1998);
- Thematic Review on Adult Education (preliminary version, 2000).

All of these are relevant to the lifelong learning agenda. The reports have all contributed to making lifelong learning the overall policy framework. They have contributed to policy formation and debate and eventually form a mosaic of measures and reforms, which, as noted above, only need a framework to hold them in shape.

The use of Commissions and Reviews is an excellent way of involving stakeholders, as they are normally sent out for comments by large numbers of stakeholders. However, this does not always seem to be enough to engage the general public, even if the policies under consideration concern them. The Review Team was told that there has been little discussion in Norway on lifelong learning and adult education and the associated challenging issues of globalisation and the impact on society of the greater influence of markets, commercialisation and privatisation. A more instrumentalist view of education may be a threat to democratic values and quality. However, intellectuals and politicians have shunned the debate and people outside the labour market do not make themselves heard. In contrast to adult education and lifelong learning, the Mjøs report on higher education is widely debated.

Despite the Government's commitment to the lifelong learning agenda as demonstrated in the present OECD review of Norwegian lifelong learning policies, the Review Team gained the impression that this was not appreciated everywhere. Instead it was pointed out to the Review Team that the pace of change had slowed somewhat with the implementation of lifelong learning policies, notably the Competence Reform, as the hard questions are finally rising to the surface asking to be addressed. The Buer-Commission presented its report in October 1997. In Spring 1999 the Prime Minister wrote a letter to the employer and employee organisations announcing the Government's willingness to partly finance a competence-building programme but so far the Competence Reform has not really reached the awareness of the general public.

Communication with the different stakeholders and potential clients is crucial. We note that at the time of the Review Team's visit in October 2000 the Forum for Competence Building had not met since the new Government took office earlier that year. The group is made up of representatives from 10 ministries, the social partners and providers of education. It was established in May 1999 as an arena for discussing professional and political issues relating to competence building. The Minister of Education is the chairman of the Forum and the nine other ministries are also represented at a political level. However, the Reference Group, consisting of representatives from the same institutions, has kept on meeting once a month since the two groups were established.

Still, various stakeholders in the reform – ranging from other ministries to the social partners – expressed in many interviews the demand for more and clearer communication between the different actors, and indeed the demand for more appropriate arenas for discussion, dialogues and implementing the reforms.

Information and communication at the system-wide level are important to keep up the momentum of the reform, to demonstrate commitment to the reform, and to ensure that the reforms progress inclusively and are owned by all the stakeholders.

Recommendation:

We recommend that high-level communication channels be established or re-established between the different stakeholders in the lifelong learning and Competence Reform agenda.

5.1.2. The role of the social partners

The social partners, especially NHO (the Norwegian Confederation of Industry and Business) and LO (the Norwegian Confederation of Trade Unions), have recently been very active in the field of education and training. They have pushed for introducing vocational education at upper secondary level and a modern apprenticeship system, which became a reality with Reform 94. They were also very active in the Buer-Commission. In the collective wage agreement in 1998 the partners accepted the right of individual employees to leave for educational purposes. The partners also required that persons without upper secondary education should be given a statutory right to such education and public support to cover living costs.

In 1999 leave for educational purposes became part of the Norwegian legislation and effective as of 2001. A statutory right to upper secondary education became effective in 2000 and a statutory right to primary and lower secondary education was to become effective as of 2002. A Commission was set up by the Government to study the unresolved issue of financing subsistence during leave for study.*

The social partners – LO, Akademikerne (Trade Union for University Graduates), YS (Confederation of Trade Unions for employees at middle level), NHO, HSH (Confederation of employers in trade and services) and KS (Confederation of Local Governments) – are represented in the commission. Represented are also the Ministry of Education, Research and Church Affairs, the Ministry of Finance, the Ministry of Local Government and Regional Development and the Ministry of Labour and Government Administration. The latter provides a Secretariat.

---

* In the meeting with the OECD Education Committee to discuss the review, the Norwegian authorities reported that the Commission was unable to resolve the issue of how to cover the cost of living during training or who should pay; it was suggested that the problem might not be serious for persons employed by large companies; and that the problem might be side-stepped in the case of individuals employed by small- and medium-sized enterprises, through greater use of short studies and modular education programmes once individuals have acquired a bachelor's level degree.

In the 1997 wage negotiations the social partners set aside 191 million NOK to finance a job-oriented further education system. However, this was not repeated either in 1998, 1999 or in 2000. The Government agreed to co-finance the Competence Building Programme with a total of 400 million NOK over two to three years.

The controversial issue in this area is where to draw the dividing line between what should be financed by the social partners and the State respectively. On the one hand basic education is seen to belong to the public domain while employers should finance firm-specific vocational training. On the other hand, the difference between these two types of training has become blurred, especially in cases when adults return for vocational upper secondary schooling, and SMEs find it difficult to finance any type of learning.

Examples of other areas where the social partners to varying degrees have shown interest in having a dialogue are:

- The supply of public education and training.
- The flexibility of public providers.
- The steering mechanism for the lifelong learning agenda.
- How to bridge the gap between the formal education system and informal learning in working life.
- Competence documentation.
- Open universities and e-learning. (The social partners have set up the Competence Net. It provides e-learning services to its members. The social partners also participate in financing the Norwegian University Network for Lifelong Learning.)
- Academic drift in upper secondary and higher education.
- Employees' access to the Internet.
- The actual combination of decentralised and centralised standards.
- The recruitment of teachers.

Recommendation:

We recommend that the interest of the social partners in lifelong learning be utilised and the demarcation lines between the responsibilities of different actors be clarified.

5.2. Progressing through funded projects of distance and ICT-based education

Funding policies for the achievement of lifelong learning and the Competence Reform emerged as a major concern of all stakeholders. Achievement of the Competence Reform is for the time being funded to a large extent through a variety of projects with funding made available through the Ministry of Education,

193|

Research and Church Affairs. This type of more or less *ad hoc* Government funding is a proven way of rapidly providing incentives for change.

There are also initiatives funded by independent (though publicly funded) bodies such as the Research Council of Norway, SND (the Norwegian Industrial and Regional Development Fund) and SOFF (the Norwegian Agency for Flexible Learning in Higher Education). Indeed, distance education and e-learning provide good examples of the interaction of different funding mechanisms.

Research and innovation also feed into change and progress but are normally slower processes. The experiences in these fields gained by the Ministry of Trade and Industry and the Ministry of Education, Research and Church Affairs are discussed in Section 5.4.

We also devote a special Section 5.5 to evaluation and dissemination of project results. These aspects are critical factors when it comes to assuring optimal effects of projects, research and innovation.

Examples of projects directly financed by the Ministry of Education, Research and Church Affairs are described below. We devote some space to projects in the area of "Flexible and Distance Education Learning – A New Chance" and the "Competence Building Programme". But there are some other funded *ad hoc* projects concerned with documenting and evaluating non-formal learning.

Initially the Ministry of Education, Research and Church Affairs had organised a project involving documentation and evaluation of non-formal learning directed at education at the upper secondary level. A project group with representatives from the ministries, employer/employee organisations and the education system has been set up. NOK 20 million was allocated for 2000.

Pilot projects were funded where the requirement of upper secondary education for admission to higher education may be replaced by documented non-formal competence. When the Review Team visited the University of Tromsø, some 100 students were already studying there without formal qualifications.

Many projects revolve around ICT and distance education in general. Norway has had a long tradition of distance education and there are many examples of experimentation in this area with the application of ICTs.

In 1990 a co-ordinating body SOFF (the Norwegian Agency for Flexible Learning in Higher Education) was set up under the Norwegian Ministry of Education, Research and Church Affairs. In 2000 NOK 12 million was allocated to SOFF for the development of new distance learning programmes within higher education. In 2001 the corresponding sum was NOK 18 million.

The Ministry of Education, Research and Church Affairs is also implementing a Plan for ICT in education 2000-2003 with regard to the development of net-based educational programmes for adults with ICT as a subject and ICT as part of other subjects. Moreover, NOK 30 million will be allocated to ICT and the building of competence among teachers.

The Ministry of Education, Research and Church Affairs also disposes of an Innovation Fund of NOK 130 million, which has also been used for the promotion of ICT.

SOFF's main task is to promote the development of flexible learning and distance education based on pedagogical use of information and communication technologies. But SOFF is also looking to promote an overall strategy for change within the higher education institutions. It is supposed to stimulate – in collaboration with the Norwegian Research Council, research institutions and other relevant parties – research and development within flexible learning and distance education and contribute to the dissemination of the results from this research.

For adult learners needing to "catch up", the following flexible learning provisions were funded (KUF, 2000a, pp. 8-9):

- Assessment of scope and testing of models that meet adult learning needs at primary and lower secondary level – NOK 10 million in 2000.

- Development of educational models within upper secondary education that are adapted to the needs of adults – NOK 10 million to county municipalities for the development of flexible models with regard to time, location, duration and progression, within upper secondary education.

- Reduction in charges made to people who pursue a secondary education or take a craft certificate under the auspices of study associations and distance learning institutions – NOK 10 million in 2000.

- Development of decentralised educational programmes at colleges – NOK 30 million for colleges (for example programmes adapted to individuals in the offshore industry who have been given notice or laid off); plus NOK 5 million for decentralised nursing training.

The Competence Building Programme focuses on the labour market and the development of education and training to help produce innovation. It was funded with NOK 50 million in 2000 and NOK 100 million in 2001. The Norwegian State Institution for Distance Education (NFU) administers the funds. The Ministry of Education, Research and Church Affairs appointed the governing board in February 2000 at the suggestion of employer and employee organisations and the implicated ministries. NFU has since then been integrated into VOX as further described in Sub-section 5.4.2.

The programme gives priority to projects that contribute to (KUF, 2000a, p. 11):

- The development of new forms of training and teaching methods for continuing education courses.

195

- Continuing education and training being held more often in the workplace.

- The development of cost-efficient and educationally effective competence-building methods, through, among other things, the increased integration of ICT and multimedia.

- Making primary and secondary education more accessible for adults.

In addition, projects will be supported that have an impact on the system, *i.e.* that produce innovation and "have a learning and transfer value that reaches beyond the individual competence-building project".

Of the 67 projects approved in the Competence Building Programme at the time of the Review Team's visit to Norway, 18 belonged to the public sector and 19 to the private sector, while educational providers were responsible for 30 projects.

Of the public sector ones, seven were in health care. The projects by educational providers were distributed about equally between private and public providers on the one hand, and for vocational and general courses on the other.

Fourteen projects aimed at introducing ICT in existing courses. While, on the whole, projects did not seem to be a breakthrough for the workplace as a learning arena, some of the projects were directed towards quality development and teamwork and based on practical work.

It was noted in the State budget 1999 that SOFF also should contribute to the implementation of the Competence Reform, in particular by funding projects that meet the following criteria:

- Courses should be adapted to the needs of adult learning.

- The learners' workplace should be used as an arena for learning.

- Competence building relevant to employment has priority.

- Educational institutions should collaborate with enterprises, organisations or other actors within working life.

However, distance education and ICT are not a panacea for all problems in learning or in access. There is a body of knowledge about when ICTs are best used for learning and how they can complement and enhance other forms of learning. We know, for example, that distance education is unlikely to be the optimal learning medium for school dropouts. In the follow up to the 94 Reform researchers found that school dropouts have less self-direction. Distance education typically relies to a greater extent on self-directed learning.

A study conducted by the NKI (and funded by the Ministry of Education, Research and Church Affairs), "Recruitment Barriers to Learning on the Internet" (Rekkedal and Møystad, 1999) examined attitudes to technologies necessary for Internet-based distance learning, experiences in using this technology and access to a PC and the Internet among active distance education students and prospective ones. Its results are instructive (pp. 57-58):

"Nearly 60% of the distance students say that they certainly or probably would enrol in Internet-based studies if that were their only choice. More than 50% of the prospective students say that Internet studies are suited to their needs.

These answers do not, however, mean that Internet studies are preferred before more traditional "low technology' distance study. It is clear that both groups favour aspects of distance study concerned with individual freedom, non-pacing and flexibility, which can be implemented in both Internet-based and "correspondence' based distance studies.

It seems clear that access to the Internet from home is seen as a necessary condition for enrolling in Internet-based distance study programmes.

There are large differences in experience of using technology, access to technology and interest for studying on the Internet between men and women, between different age groups, between persons with different educational backgrounds and between persons studying different types of courses."

Recommendation:

The Review Team recommends that funds continue to be allocated to study and evaluate how ICTs might facilitate learning for different groups and in what instances it should be utilised.

While with face-to-face teaching the Government opted for a standard Core Curriculum but geographically dispersed providers, distance education is meant to overcome the barriers of geography. Instruction could be delivered centrally with regional support in study centres and with linkages to industry. We are aware of the Government's reluctance to establish an Open University in view of its policy of decentralised regional education on which it has expanded billions of dollars. The Norwegian University Network for Lifelong Learning is the response for the request for an Open University. It was established by the Norwegian Council of Universities and Colleges, itself a recent merger of two separate councils, one for Universities and one for Colleges and the social partners.

We are also aware that counties fear that students might take distance courses from Oslo in preference to courses offered by regional colleges. Clearly educational efficiency conflicts with the policy imperative of regional education. This is a political decision. Nevertheless the Review Team believes that some rationalisation is possible.

Recommendation:

The Review Team recommends that learning institutions and enterprises work toward standards for the development and delivery of ICT facilitated learning that ensure it is of the highest

197

quality possible instead of letting all organisations develop their own manner of ICT-*delivered learning.*

In view of the globalisation of education and since the Internet knows no geographic boundaries, institutions and organisations should co-operate with each other in their involvement to develop international standards for distance education using ICTs.

SOFF could serve as the overall co-ordinating body due to its already wide involvement in distance education.

Recommendation:

The Review Team recommends that the Government review the adequacy of the institutional arrangement concerning funding, research, evaluation and dissemination of results of distance education and ICT-based methods.

Many vocational employees do not have access to a PC at their workplace. While access at work and in the home is improving, everyone in the knowledge society should have a PC or access to one and know how to use it. In order to deliver educational programmes, widespread broadband access is needed. It seems clear that access to the Internet from home is seen as a necessary condition for enrolling in Internet-based distance study programmes.

Recommendation:

The Review Team recommends that the Government review access to PCs and broadband.

5.3. Shifting from teacher-centred to learner-centred learning

Another national ambition, and in accordance with international trends, is a shift from teaching to learning. While the Scandinavian model may have as one of its tenets "pupil-centredness", the new emphasis on learning rather than teaching is a relatively new emphasis at all levels of the education system and beyond. For the child it does not mean that the child decides what he or she wants to learn, but that the child has an opportunity to create meaning, to learn in ways that stimulate creativity, curiosity and involve him or her actively.

For the adolescent it means increasingly more choice, building on the common foundation all children have built, expanding interests, knowledge, learning repertoires and active engagement.

For the adult the emphasis on learning means that they have a say in what they learn, how they learn, when they learn and where they learn, after they themselves have decided why they want to or need to learn.

The Competence Reform, of course, puts these individual ambitions into a societal context and therefore also addresses the need for incentives.

We found enthusiastic support for the concept and the emergent practice of learner-centred education. Teachers noted the benefits of problem-based learning and project work in their attempt to motivate students, provide opportunities for integrative and holistic learning. Industry was making use of action learning programmes developed for and with them for their employees by university educators. Active learning in all arenas was supported.

The Review Team noted the enthusiasm but also supports use of a wide variety of teaching strategies enabling the development of an appropriate repertoire of learning strategies for all learners.

Members of the College Students' Association told the Review Team that the shift of focus from teaching to learning was much needed. Many still have knowledge transmitted to them when they want to seek it. They would prefer to work in small groups on problem solving tasks with easy access to staff and to information. Students coming into higher education are now used to student-centred learning, but the higher education sector is slow to change its practices in spite of official exhortations to improve quality.

In addition to that we would like to make another remark: the way providers organise their education is more than ever up to them. Therefore we have to accept that there is not one right way for the suitable educational provision for the different learners' needs. Variety is essential and the professionals have to decide what will be the most appropriate way that is suitable for the different learning needs.

Recommendation:

Previous OECD *reports have commented on the state of teaching in tertiary education institutions (see "The design and delivery of the curriculum: teaching and learning" in* OECD, *1998a, pp. 55-68). We recommend implementation of their recommendations.*

5.4. Innovation and research

Despite its concerns about the future of a number of industries, Norway sees its future as a society very much as a knowledge society.

Lifelong learning is a prerequisite in a knowledge society. Indeed, the knowledge society must be a learning society, where the system, organisations and individuals learn from own experience, from each other and indeed from experiences and developments abroad.

This means that the State, organisations and individuals must have access to knowledge which is meaningful in their quest for innovative ways of organising society, Government, work, education, life and of anticipating and tackling issues facing them.

Moving towards a knowledge society presents challenges. We have already noted some of the tensions which Norway experiences between traditional ways of organising society and the demands of a modern society, between traditional ways and values and the necessity to connect to the world and external experiences.

The Mjøs Commission in its report, *Freedom with Responsibility* (NOU, 1999) notes, "In combination with the democratic social development, knowledge has created new options that were previously restricted by customs, traditions or nature. This challenges our value system. Knowledge development does not only have political consequences; it creates new political, cultural and moral dynamics, and is in itself an arena for decision-making that transforms our lives." (Chapter 2, English translation).

The Ministry of Education, Research and Church Affairs and the Ministry of Trade and Industry both sponsor innovation and research relevant to the lifelong learning agenda. In the first case the Research Council of Norway is the most important player. In the second case important intermediate actors are the Research Council of Norway and SND (the Norwegian Industrial and Regional Development Fund) with its many local branches.

In research policy the approach has often been top-down while innovation policy has had more of a bottom-up approach. Research used to be seen as preceding innovation while nowadays a more common attitude is to see them as parallel processes. It is easier to transfer research results if the users have been alerted to participate in innovation projects.

5.4.1. *Innovation*

Innovation is one of the key concepts in a knowledge economy, a subset of the knowledge society. Innovative projects both at schools and in industry, innovative teaching delivery and innovation within the lifelong learning system are promoted within the Competence Reform. Not only learning individuals are needed but also learning enterprises and learning schools.

Since approximately 97% of all Norwegian businesses are small (less than 20 employees) – less than 1% of the businesses have more than 100 employees – Government innovation support is mainly directed towards SMEs. The Research Council and SND are both involved in the implementation of the Government's Action Plan for Small- and Medium-sized Enterprises (1999-2002) (see Box 5.1).

In the document, "The Programme for Bridging the Gap Between Industry and Research: Strategic Platform" (Research Council of Norway, 1998, p. 4), innovation

Box 5.1. **Action Plan for Small- and Medium-sized Enterprises**

The Government's Action Plan for Small- and Medium-sized Enterprises (1999-2002) aims to stimulate an entrepreneurial culture and improve the business environment for smaller enterprises, making it easier to set up and run a business in Norway.

The main policies and priorities in the plan are:

1. Less red tape

2. Innovation, technology and research

3. Better terms and conditions for recruiting and employing staff

4. Better public information

5. Access to venture capital for start-ups and innovation

6. Tax regulations better suited to small business

7. Internationalisation

8. Changing attitudes to small business.

Individual measures under these headings complement provisions in the Competence Reform, *e.g.* The Government will work to simplify the various sets of regulations while maintaining a register which contains all the businesses' formal official reporting obligations. One of the aims of the register is to encourage various authorities to collaborate in the field of information gathering and help them to develop forms which request only essential information in a straightforward manner.

The Government will also provide an effective scheme for post-qualification and further education, based on distance learning and other flexible types of training adapted to the needs of small businesses. And it will prioritise the assistance for technology transfer, innovation and skills development given to small businesses by the Norwegian Research Council and the Norwegian Industrial and Regional Development Fund.

Indeed, the partners in this initiative are:

• the Norwegian Industrial and Regional Development Fund (SND) which administers loans and grants schemes for Norwegian businesses;

• the Norwegian Trade Council which provides services and expert knowledge on export and internationalisation to Norwegian businesses and industries;

• the Research Council of Norway which provides basic allocations for institutes and user-driven research programmes and projects as research centres throughout Norway; and

• advisory services from the National Institute of Technology, the Norwegian Industry Attaches and the Euro-Info centres, assisting with technology transfer and international issues.

201

is assumed to be "largely engendered through dialogue and interaction internally within companies and externally in relation to customers, suppliers, competitors, educational and research institutions, public sector programmes and companies and other networks. This means that innovation is linked to training and the sharing of knowledge and experience through a wide variety of learning situations involving many different players."

The Research Council has been issuing a number of papers which relate to and support the Competence Reform and a learning economy. The Council has also, *inter alia* , been funding an innovative programme, BRIDGE, which intends to bridge the gap between industry and research by encouraging more companies to engage in systematic R&D efforts and to collaborate with various R&D centres.

We note that the Ministry of Trade and Industry has initiated a number of programmes which provide a foundation for a much broader set of R&D innovation and learning mechanisms for industry and businesses, supporting the aims of the Competence Reform.

Recommendation:

The Review Team suggests that a register be established for all the initiatives funded under the Competence Reform by the Ministry of Education and the Ministry of Trade and Industry and other funding bodies, and that all initiatives be monitored, evaluated and the evaluation results be disseminated to all stakeholders, in order to facilitate system wide learning.

In the project portfolio of the Ministry of Education, Research and Church Affairs there are also examples of bridging activities, *e.g.* the project that is supposed to pave the way for the start-up of a University of Industry linked with the educational and research activity at Fornebu. NOK 7 million has been allocated to this work in 2000.

Innovation does not happen in isolation. As suggested above, it is facilitated by cross-sectoral, cross-disciplinary, horizontal and vertical discussion and interaction.

The question arises where the locus for innovation should be, or whether there should be a variety of complementary loci for innovation. We believe that schools need to be a locus for innovation, as well as post-secondary and higher education institutions but also the workplace and industry in general. While primary education was regarded highly, there was little evidence that either upper secondary or higher education fostered creativity, teamwork and interpersonal skills though, for example, in Reform 94 the intention to stimulate creativity and innovation was highly profiled.

Indeed, we noted that the social partners had taken initiatives in e-learning and e-commerce and were concerned about the slowness with which educational institutions seemed to respond to this challenge.

In Chapter 3 we note that there is a shift from state initiated policy development towards greater autonomy in the education system, particularly in the higher education institutions. And we endorse this.

This does not mean that there is no role for the State in the promotion of innovation. The Government can promote innovation across the various ministerial portfolios and in collaboration with the private sector. The Government can promote transfer of innovative processes and ideas across the education system and industry by incentive funding, matched by institutions and organisations to ensure that these will become embedded in organisational processes and structures.

Through the Research Council of Norway and SND nationally important agendas can be set, and are set, and competitive funding allocated. In addition, the State in its own agencies can encourage and test new ideas and practices and model innovation for the rest of society.

Recommendations:

We suggest that the Government establish an innovation fund for education, training and learning which would be administered like a research fund, i.e. with peer reviewed applications with objectives and expected outcomes, with timelines and budgets, with an evaluation and dissemination component. The Government has to consider where to locate this fund organisationally.

We suggest that higher education institutions be encouraged to establish innovation funds, e.g. strategic initiatives funds, teaching development or research funds which build on their strengths. Schools, municipalities and counties should also be stimulated to work in this direction.

According to present regulations the higher education institutions would have to finance their innovation funds by setting aside money from their yearly entitlements.

5.4.2. Research

We are convinced that the implementation of the Competence Reform must be based on research, research into the needs of people and organisations, into barriers to participation in education and training, mapping of provisions, and efficacy of those provisions. Indeed, previous reforms in the 1990s of primary, secondary and higher education were all supported by research.

The Ministry of Education, Research and Church Affairs is giving priority to funds used for research and development work in relation to projects within the fields of adult education supporting the reform's areas of focus: evaluation of non-formal learning and documentation schemes, the workplace as an arena for learning, user-adapted training and initiatives designed to provide information, motivation and encouragement. It continues to invest in the research programme "Competence, education and value creation" under the Research Council of Norway.

We note that the three organisations, the Norwegian Institute of Adult Education Research (NVI), the Norwegian State Institute for Distance Education (NFU) and the State Adult Education Centre, have been amalgamated on 1 January 2001 under the name of VOX.

The research conducted by the former NVI has an important place in increasing knowledge about lifelong learning issues, challenges and practices. We trust VOX can strengthen the research base for reforms and recommend that:

- Adult education is not interpreted in a traditional restricted sense.
- Co-operation with other nationally and international researchers is sought and reference is made to the wealth of existing research.
- The findings of research are transferred into practice.

Recommendation:

The Review Team recommends that mechanisms be developed to fund and utilise further research for policy development and implementation.

5.5. Evaluation and dissemination

The Norwegian Government is spending many millions of dollars for projects in support of the Competence Reform. We became aware of dissemination and evaluation procedures in use by the Norwegian Agency for Flexible Learning in Higher Education (SOFF). And we support their approach.

While a greater appreciation for evaluation seems to be spreading, a large variety of grants are distributed in different sectors and to various organisations in Norway where it was unclear how all these initiatives were going to be monitored. SOFF itself, for instance, got a 50% increase in its allocations without any previous evaluation.

A natural requirement is that Government funded projects conduct formative evaluations. The body administering the funds should be responsible for monitoring these processes and guaranteeing the dissemination of results.

But formative evaluation is not enough; there needs also to be summative evaluation and above all dissemination to all the actors and stakeholders of the results of evaluations.

Independent bodies often conduct summative evaluations. In Norway NVI (the Norwegian Institute of Adult Education Research) was earlier responsible for certain evaluations of that kind. One example being its task to evaluate the NOK 5 million project "Motivation, guidance and information" which was co-ordinated by NFU (the State Adult Education Centre). Moreover, the NFU was administrating the even larger Competence Building Programme. This means that it might be difficult for VOX having taken over the functions of both NVI and NFU to combine evaluation and administration of projects (more difficult perhaps than combining research and administration). Other independent evaluators could, of course, be used for the programmes administered by VOX but the evaluation functions of VOX may then risk to become marginalized.

While we were impressed with the range of projects initiated both in the area of formal and informal learning, we were concerned that there seemed to be little learning across the system. No special overarching programme for exchanging of experiences has, for example, been set up while introducing the Competence Reform to ensure that interesting local results become widely known and feed back into the system.

Recommendation:

The Review Team recommends that mechanisms be developed to ensure both institutional and system wide learning from Government funded projects.

5.6. The shift from central steering to market mechanisms

Lifelong learning is future oriented, but steering mechanisms are in the Nor-wegian context predominantly traditional and supply oriented. Norway has steered in the past fifty years via a comprehensive legal framework. Usually com-missions, reports to the *Storting* (Parliament) and hearings followed and accompa-nied by extensive consultation with interest groups result in laws and statutory rights and obligations.

The steering conception was characterised by a dominant public orientation, by focus on central steering, in the education sector by uniformity in curricula, all developed *ex ante* and little feedback into the system.

This steering conception was ideally aligned with the strong equity orienta-tion of the Norwegian Government and people.

Equally suited was the long-established sharing of responsibilities between state, county and municipalities for delivery and funding of education and training on the one hand, and between the publicly funded education system, subsidised voluntary associations, and the social partners on the other.

All of these could be steered via government regulations and via funding. The system was by no means completely inflexible. The reforms of the last decade have led to greater flexibility and autonomy for institutions. Not all institutions

205|

and agencies have as yet exhausted the scope of the autonomy given, nor stretched the boundaries of what they can do.

But the knowledge society needs different knowledge systems and steering mechanisms. Lifelong learning practices are a prerequisite for the realisation of a knowledge society. And in lifelong learning the individual learner is central. This means that the demand for education and training by the individual or groups should shape the education provisions more strongly than is now the case. The use by employers and by individual citizens of private providers is an indication that the supply-orientation has not caught up with the demands by individuals and organisations. Both groups exercise choice and in those areas where the State provisions do not meet the learning needs, private providers have to be seen as part of the overall system.

Recommendation:

We recommend that the Ministry of Education, Research and Church Affairs shift its emphasis from a supply-driven model to a demand-driven model in its shaping of the education system; that it reduce its direct and daily influence by creating a network of interdependent though autonomous institutions; that it create a "level playing field" for all actors in the education system, by giving students choice in all phases of their life.

5.7. Resources and financing

For any major reform or public policy initiative, one of the chief incentives or barriers is funding. We found that the political will expressed through laws and statutory rights and obligations in support of a reform was not always matched by the concomitant obligations for funding, for setting priorities, for implementation and monitoring. We noted that rights are not always accompanied by clear financing mechanisms for the exercise of these rights.

The required contributions by employers, employees and the public to the implementation of the Competence Reform and the implementation of the lifelong learning agenda must be articulated. There needs to be a clear division, and this division needs to be clearly communicated, between public assistance for clearly specified courses or other means of learning, between individuals' contribution, between employer or other labour-market sponsored arrangements.

We found that there is great lack of clarity as to who funds various aspects of lifelong learning – among the State agencies, the providers and students. For instance, it was suggested in relation to the Competence Reform that *Aetet* finance adult education. The Review Team did not find any support in official documents for such an idea. It rather interpreted it as an expression of the confusion existing around the funding of the Competence Reform.

So far the official idea seems to have been that lifelong learning should develop within the existing framework for the financing of education, training provisions and the living costs of students. Certain financial changes have, however, been introduced recently that facilitate lifelong learning:

- A new regulation effective from the 1999 fiscal year provides tax exemption for free education in connection with one's work.

- The State Education Loan Fund was given NOK 90 million more for 2000 to make education more accessible for adults. From the year 2000/2001 the amount one may earn without having one's grant reduced has been raised from NOK 3 550 to NOK 5 000. The level of means testing of the family allowance supplement against the spouse's/partner's income has also been raised from NOK 12 495 to NOK 16 700.

- The State-run institutions of higher education have been given more freedom to establish and terminate courses of study of up to 30 credits. They have also been allowed to charge a fee for more comprehensive courses.

We also understand that much of the funding of the lifelong learning initiatives will occur at county or municipal level. We are aware, from His Majesty's speech on 5 October 2000 at the time of the visit of the Review Team, that local Government will be allocated higher revenues and be given greater freedom to make local decisions in accordance with local needs.

We are also aware of the strong Norwegian tradition of affirming local democracy by giving councils and municipalities freedom to set their own priorities. However, we are concerned that there are few if any incentives for local Government to spend on the implementation of lifelong learning goals when there are other urgent needs. Indeed, block grants, while underlining the autonomy of local Government, can in the poorer municipalities lead to inequitable provision of resources, *i.e.* health may be favoured over education, thus disadvantaging some groups.

We found that altogether these arrangements do not form a comprehensive and consistent financing system of educational provision and living costs:

- Adults, including teachers, can enrol in subjects of a degree programme for free at a university while they would have to pay for continuing education (*i.e.* non-award) in the same subject at state colleges or with private providers.

- Employers could be charged varying amounts for more or less the same course at a public secondary school or resource centre, a state college, a university or with private providers, study associations or distance education institutions; an individual could also register for the course at the uni-

207|

versity for free or in special cases (long-term unemployed over 30 years) have it paid by the *Aetat*.

- A student may have his or her living costs more or less covered by grants and loans from the State Education Loan Fund, Social Security, unemployment benefits or the employer. To what extent these allowances would cover the actual living expenses of the individual of course depends on individual circumstances – older students with family obligations often having higher expenses than younger ones – but also on variations in rules, regulations and practice. Unemployment benefits would normally be higher than study grants but there are, for example, no unemployment benefits while studying in ordinary classes at upper secondary level.

The Review Team found great willingness by the social partners to contribute to the implementation of the Competence Reform. The social partners were more hesitant to commit themselves to its financing at least until the Government has clarified its position as to its own financial engagement. While it was clear that public education is a right of every citizen, the question was raised: where and when should the tuition free level end in post-secondary education – at Bachelor's level in the revised system, Master's, PhD; when studying for the second or third time at the university level, when returning for further education and training? The reforms that will eventually follow the proposals of the newly appointed commission concerning models to finance costs of living while people are on educational leave during working life, can be expected to bring some clarity in this area. However, that will not be enough. Approaches discussed elsewhere include vouchers (essentially portable credits funded by Government) and learning accounts (funded by Government, employers and/or individuals themselves); and loans for which eligibility and/or repayment are income contingent.

For the learner the question of fees and costs will be paramount. While free education is not an incentive in itself, costs can be a deterrent to further study. For a country with a lifelong learning agenda it is essential to clearly delineate the learning rights of its citizens.

Recommendation:

We recommend that the public be informed as soon as feasible what their learning rights are, e.g. free entitlements as students, citizens and workers and who will fund additional education and training – tuition and living costs.

5.8. Information

At the time of the Review Team's visit in October 2000, there was little knowledge in the various ministries, public sector organisations, the private sector and in the public about funding, administrative arrangements for new learning opportunities, timetables for the implementation of actions plans, etc.

We have recommended that the Government communicate its intentions as to lifelong learning and the Competence Reform. However, the actors involved in the reform and the general public also need to be able to find answers to their own questions.

We note that there is as yet no central database for education information nor is there an information plan for the Competence Reform as a whole, as foreshadowed, though we have been assured this is being addressed. We also note that an Information Plan was meant to have been established during 2000 (and indeed were told that the task is being tackled in late 2000) as well as a database for educational information.

We note that the Government acknowledges the need for transparency in the various educational pathways, in the entitlements, in the information about educational programmes.

We agree with the Government that "Good information and communication can help different players to co-operate on common goals so that the information to the user is perceived as being uniform". But we also see provision of good information and consistent communication across ministries and other actors as a requisite for the learner to make an informed choice, or a choice at all.

As with funding, we note a fair amount of confusion among the various actors, providers and "consumers" of education and training as to who is in charge of what, who will provide what and when and for whom.

To use a metaphor of driving: There is a bus and a driver. There are passengers in the bus, *i.e.* actors like schools, colleges, universities, the social partners, teachers, students, etc., who want to know how they will be getting to their destination, in particular they want to have confidence that there is enough fuel to get there.

We note that the Council of Universities and Colleges has established the Norwegian University Network for Lifelong Learning with the aim of providing a database on continuing and further education courses and eventually a marketplace for individuals and companies to access courses and buy places or courses. While this database is a start, it by no means covers the information need for the system as a whole.

We also note that the Competence Reform action plan for 2000 includes the establishment of a common portal with other educational databases on the Internet.

A big reform and an ambition like a comprehensive system of lifelong learning may not have all projects progress on schedule. But we regard it as important that the actors themselves are accurately informed of the progress in achieving the reforms and how they link together. We consider the information need for the system and for the individual as crucial for the realisation and indeed the legitimacy of the various reforms.

Recommendations:

We propose that an instrument be developed which shows the pathways and the funding arrangements for various learning opportunities for the school-age population, adults "catching up" on their educational entitlements (distinguishing between those in employment, those unemployed, those retired), adults in continuing and further education, etc.

We also recommend that an information system easily accessible by the public be created to act as both a central source of location of information about the entire lifelong learning system and a starting point for taking advantage of lifelong learning opportunities.

Chapter 6

Overriding Principles and Conclusions

Norway has gone through a dozen years of reforms affecting all aspects of education. It has been exemplary in ensuring that all young citizens currently in the system have the opportunity to get a full school education, and all those in working life who have missed out on learning opportunities in the past can make up for it now. In addition, there are opportunities for all those in and out of working life who need to keep their skills up to date, who need upskilling or retraining.

His Majesty, the King, in his speech from the Throne on the Occasion of the Opening of the 145th session of the *Storting*, noted the fundamental value the Norwegian welfare society is based on, namely "a shared sense of responsibility for our fellow citizens, solidarity and equitable distribution"; and that the Government would try to strengthen and renew the public sector while at the same time reducing unnecessary red tape and administration. The aim is to provide high quality services and to "secure the basis for economic growth and equitable distribution". The Review Team is most impressed by the ambitions of Norway to become a society where lifelong learning is a reality to the benefit of its citizens and society at large, and by the systematic way it has created the pre-conditions. Indeed, we believe that if lifelong learning is to succeed anywhere, Norway is one of the most likely places in view of its history of reforms, co-operation among bodies, high educational standards and outcomes.

In the following, several themes are further developed where we believe the Government needs to focus in the next phase. These are the tensions between equity for all, quality in all and choice, and the leadership and governance to make these possible.

6.1. Leadership and governance

Any major change or reform needs a champion. Over the past decades and in particularly during the last decade, Norway has positioned itself to become the leading nation in the provision of lifelong learning opportunities for its citizens and residents. As we have noted, reforms have encompassed formal and informal learning, institution-based learning from an early age with no upper age limit and work-based learning. The Competence Reform spelt out a comprehensive agenda, backed by substantial financial resources for a comprehensive training effort.

But a knowledge society where lifelong learning is a reality goes further, and this review was intended to look at the range of lifelong learning policies in Norway and comment on their effectiveness, where possible, and their coherence.

We understand that the Minister for Education, Research and Church Affairs is, and is seen to be, the champion of the current lifelong learning initiatives. While the political responsibility for lifelong learning lies with the Government, the actual responsibility for progressing the agenda is distributed over several ministries, though the Minister for Education has the main carriage.

We are convinced, and were re-enforced in this by the social partners and others with whom we held discussions, that a whole-of-government approach is needed. We believe that the political commitment to lifelong learning and the implementation of the Competence Reform cannot and should not be "owned" by any Minister; they need cabinet solidarity. The Minister can be the champion, harnessing other ministerial colleagues for the common cause. To use a sporting analogy – the Minister is the coxswain steering the boat and ensuring that the team members act in unison.

Indeed, to get the Ministries to work together at an appropriately high level, Ministers themselves will need to be involved. The other ministries more or less often referred to in our discussions were the Ministry of Children and Family Affairs, the Ministry of Labour and Government Administration, the Ministry of Local Government and Regional Development, the Ministry of Trade and Industry, the Ministry of Health and Social Affairs and, of course, also the Ministry of Finance.

Intergovernmental communication is crucial if there is to be a whole-of-government approach. We note that at the time of the Review Team's visit in October 2000 the Forum for Competence Building had not met since the new Government took office earlier that year – although we hear they did meet in spring 2001. The group is made up of representatives from 10 ministries, the social partners and providers of education. While the Reference Group, consisting of representatives from the same institutions, have kept on meeting once a month since the two groups were established, the absence of high level commitment was repeatedly mentioned and created a sense of confusion and lack of ownership.

However the leadership task is approached, leadership is needed. In view of the very great value Norway attaches to the lifelong learning agenda, it would be appropriate for the Prime Minister to delegate explicitly the implementation and co-ordination of the lifelong learning agenda to the Minister of Education.

In Chapter 5 we commented on more detailed operational considerations which need to be addressed and co-ordinated.

Recommendations:

The Review Team suggests that in the further implementation of the lifelong learning agenda a whole-of-government approach be adopted with ministerial level officials involved in driving the implementation.

We further suggest that the Prime Minister ask the Minister for Education, Research and Church Affairs to co-ordinate the implementation of the lifelong learning agenda across the various ministries.

6.2. Equity

We found the commitment to equity for all to be one of the distinguishing features of Norwegian society and public policy. The realisation of equity is an enduring task for governments even in the knowledge society. Formal education and learning in other settings are still of great influence on life chances of citizens. Therefore the Government responsibility to monitor the real possibilities of citizens in the learning society to take part and to be successful will continue to be of major importance. This does not imply that the means that are actually used to reach the goals will stay the same. And, of course, it does not imply that equity is the only criterion that is of importance. In the learning society equity has to be evaluated in relation to choice, diversity and quality.

More than in the past, varied learning opportunities are important, and a kind of competition between different providers is essential for development and innovation. Quality, and therefore evaluation, are much more important than they have been in the recent past. Quality in lifelong learning is not self-evident because of the different needs and capacities of learners. As discussed in Chapter 5, in the knowledge society an adequate evaluation mechanism is as important to citizens as the publication of quality evaluation results so that they can choose between different possibilities on quality grounds. That is an important change, not only in instruments and procedures but even in culture. That will not be easy to accommodate in a society like Norway because of the strong emphasis on equity.

It is, of course, the prerogative of the State to make provisions for the implementation of its political and social agendas. Despite a gradual transfer of responsibilities to individuals and institutions, other values need to influence decisions. Hence the Government should make explicit the value it attaches to lifelong learning for its minority and Indigenous people: for immigrant groups, the Saami population and the Kven people.

The Government should also explicitly refer to the value it attaches to equitable lifelong learning opportunities and attainments in the various regions of Norway and set its priorities accordingly.

Citizens and residents in Norway have been given rights to certain levels of education. They need to be able to exercise these rights, and they need to be empowered and enabled to make informed choices. Quality and equity are connected and the "quality control system" has to deliver the information to the citizens.

Therefore transparency is needed in who provides educational opportunities, when, where, for whom and at what costs. Again, from an individual standpoint, information and consistent communication is crucial for the realisation of the life-long learning reforms.

Informed choice is being exercised above all by those who are already edu-cated and can access information, evaluate information and make choices. The emphasis of the Government's attention and influence should be directed to those with the least chances for taking part in the education system.

Choice is also being exercised primarily by those who can afford to pay. Hence, in order for all citizens to be able to exercise choice, appropriate financial resources need to be made available. These resources should be much more directed immediately to the citizen and not only to the provider of learning opportunities.

Of special concern in a society which values lifelong learning, innovation and knowledge are those groups and individuals who are marginalised because of their ethnic background, their educational level, their social or psychological posi-tion or their physical isolation. Individuals who are lacking in formal education and experience with bureaucracies, individuals who are culturally not attuned like immigrants, individuals who are physically, mentally or personally not in the main-stream of society are all potentially marginalised by lifelong learning reforms unless their access to education and training is appropriately facilitated.

We found that the children of poor immigrants who, one might argue, are among those who need most the opportunities kindergartens provide, are unlikely to attend them, unless there is special project funding for them.

Job seekers without educational qualifications and the self-confidence which grows with successful performance in work or other spheres of life, are more reluc-tant to access educational opportunities unless assistance is given.

We are aware of the great care Aetat takes with its client, but in discussion with other agents, we have come to the conclusion that it is still possible for certain marginal people and groups to "fall between the cracks" of various government providers. The Norwegian welfare state is concerned for all of its citizens. How-ever, with many agencies involved in assisting them, it is easy for individuals not to exercise their right. We recommend that social services in relation to compe-tence development for disadvantaged groups be provided in a one-stop-shop. This would ensure that equitable access is awarded to these marginal groups and communication and information is consistent. We have therefore advocated one-stop-shops to ensure that the process of accessing educational opportunities is as unbureaucratic as possible (see Chapter 4).

Recommendations:

We recommend that the Government as part of its equity and regional agenda make explicit how the learning rights of minority and marginal groups can be realised.

We further recommend that the Government make explicit how regional development agendas will be safeguarded in the move to market-driven educational provisions.

6.3. Quality

The means for achieving lifelong learning goals have, in the main, addressed the equity issue. The emergence of private providers and of for-profit organisations have tested a system which so far has relied on and trusted in the existence of uniform standards and consistent quality. We believe that in a more diverse system, as has emerged in Norway and will increasingly develop, a stronger focus on quality is needed.

It will no longer be possible to assure oneself that good design and processes will lead to good outcomes – *e.g.* the quality of teacher training will have to be assessed not only by the curriculum for teacher training, but also by the effect teachers have on student learning, attitude, motivation, placement and other out-comes.

Similarly, the delegation of responsibility for primary and secondary education to municipalities and counties in itself does not guarantee that local and regional issues are addressed appropriately or adequately to meet the needs of their learners.

The Government's move towards greater decentralisation and greater autonomy for institutions demands greater public accountability and measures to ensure quality and to assure the public that Norwegian education and training provisions are relevant, state-of-the art and internationally competitive.

We note the endeavours to make the public system more flexible and adaptive. With increased autonomy for public institutions, and more private providers, more accountability towards the society and indeed the State is needed.

Accountability exercised properly requires that both those who demonstrate their accountability and those to whom reports are made have adequate information. In order to provide feedback to institutions and to the public, more comprehensive data collection and processing will become necessary. In particular the activities of private providers seem to be unknown and unmonitored.

Accountability is best exercised if an evaluative culture is created where individuals, institutions – and indeed ministries – make decisions based on data and account for the decisions publicly.

Data-free decision-making at any level is perilous. We understand that a fair amount of data on public higher education exists in the system – that some counties collect, evaluate and act on informative data concerning school and adult education. But we were told by a variety of interviewees that data on cost structures of schools, to name but one area, and other statistics are inadequate. System-wide data collection and dissemination and evaluation, in addition to more local data collection, are needed to continually improve the quality of education and learning. Even though since the last OECD review in the eighties there have been considerable efforts to improve the collection and dissemination of statistics at all educational levels, there is still much to be done.

Institution and system-wide learning would also be promoted by the systematic evaluation and learning from innovations and funded projects (see Chapter 5).

Quality assurance and auditing can be achieved in a range of ways, and the experience from various OECD countries as well as international organisations would be helpful in developing a system for Norway which is in tune with its values and accepted modus operandi while fulfilling the aims set for it.

Recommendation:

We recommend that the present system of data collection and dissemination across all educational providers be evaluated and updated, that this complement local data collection and that the data be used for monitoring and evaluation in order to promote organisational learning in all educational establishments.

The Review Team was pleased to read that the Mjøs Commission recommended an independent body, a Centre for Assessment and Accreditation in Higher Education, with the task of assessing courses, disciplines and institutions, serving then as both assessment and accreditation agency. We would take this recommendation a step further and suggest that it or similar bodies be established to assess all learning providers to ensure high quality across the entire lifelong learning spectrum.

In an extensive discussion of quality issues, the Commission makes a host of recommendations, some broad, some quite descriptive; some intended to enhance teaching, others learning; some to support teachers, others to support learners.

In the shift from teacher-centred to student-centred education, such measures are necessary but should be seen as guidance to institutions, not prescriptions. If individual institutions have, as the Mjøs Committee proposes, the main responsibility for quality development, detailed procedural prescriptions are reminiscent of the detailed state rules previously referred to and abandoned in preference for a framework with institutional autonomy and accountability.

While the Review Team would leave many of the details to the Centre, it would go further in relation to quality assurance. We believe that the Centre for Assessment and Accreditation should include in its brief guidance on quality assurance to institutions and the development of a system of benchmarking, preferably for international comparison and for institutional and system wide learning.

The Centre should be the reference agency on quality for the system, providing feedback to institutions and the public on the attainment of agreed outcomes (*i.e.* student achievements, research outcomes).

Recommendation:

We recommend that a Centre for Assessment and Accreditation be established, as proposed in the Mjøs Report, with the following additional broad tasks:

- *give guidance on quality assurance to all providers of lifelong learning;*

- *develop a system of benchmarking for national and international comparison and institutional and system learning; and*

- *provide information and feedback on performance indicator and best practice to providers of lifelong learning, the State, and the public.*

In order to achieve this we do not advocate creating a new bureaucracy. Examples of a higher education system owned agency exist in the Netherlands and New Zealand; there are independent agencies in Denmark, Finland and Australia.

There are already internationally tested questionnaires for students and for graduates to express their satisfaction with various aspects of their educational experience; and there are questionnaires for graduates on their employment since graduation. Likewise, there exist internationally tested processes and methods for collecting these types of information.

6.4. Choice

Over the past decade there has been a deliberate shift from detailed state regulations concerning education to greater autonomy to counties, to municipalities and to higher education institutions.

Counties, since the late 1980s, no longer receive earmarked grants for their delegated responsibilities but receive block grants to cover both education and health expenses, which allows them to set priorities in expenditure within the framework of legal rights to provision set by the State.

217|

Following the restructure of the non-university higher education institutions in the early and mid-90s, a new Universities and Colleges Act became applicable 1 January 1996. Institutions of higher education gained a considerable degree of academic and administrative autonomy. However, the Ministry retained overall responsibility for the sector.

In a much deregulated educational environment, the need of the learners for quality assurance is as high as that of the State. From the learner's perspective, choice in a diverse system should not have to be a gamble with quality. Feedback mechanisms into the public arena should enable learners to make informed choices.

With greater autonomy has come competition within a quasi market. While public education is free, institutions have been encouraged to engage in fee-for-service activities – schools established resource centres; universities offer continuing education courses for free or sell further education courses to employers; Aetat's mandate has been expanded to include fee-for services like temporary staff management, selection of staff, assistance of restructuring and training and training needs analysis.

In a competitive environment the diversity in institutional types and institutions' focus on area of strengths in teaching and research enhance rather than diminish the educational landscape. Indeed they provide real choices for students. But the diversity in institutions and specialities in teaching and research also demand a quality assurance system which satisfies both Government and the public.

Private schools and continuing education providers are increasing and providing much needed learning opportunities at all levels. Various associations, employer organisations, trade unions and agencies respond to either market needs for particular competencies or individual needs for competence development.

As core characteristic of this move from the public education system to a variety of different learning arenas is the equity issue: the learner needs choice so that each individual can develop optimally.

However, providing learners or client organisations with choice also puts pressures on the publicly funded institutions. The social partners as well as the Ministry expressed concern that public education institutions may be somewhat too complacent, detached from society and lacking in flexibility. Increasingly, competition arises between publicly funded institutions as well. Colleges will need to define their own role. All higher education institutions will have to collaborate and compete to provide the optimal learning opportunities for Norwegians and those whom Norway wishes to attract to its education system.

6.5. Summary

Choice, equity and quality are in many cases conflicting: we cannot enjoy them all in the same amount. Many times we have to choose between them. To be aware of that is one of the most important challenges for the Norwegian lifelong learning policy. That policy has to address these matters in an open way. In general terms the equity criterion is the most important in the first phase of educational participation. For the young and especially for minority groups it is the prime focus of the responsibility of the Government. Further on in the educational system the importance of the other criteria increases. There is no exact line to draw. It is a matter of further discussion and deliberation to find out what is the most appropriate in the Norwegian context. Norway is a highly-developed society and it is due to that situation that Norway has to be ahead in the development of new politics regarding the knowledge society. That also implies that there is not a simple example to copy! Norway should be the guide in this completely new area, the exemplar.

We would like to recommend that Norway create or foster arenas for discussing these trade-offs where the various criteria can be weighed by all concerned parties. Furthermore, it will be necessary to examine the processes for making these tradeoffs to ensure that all views are represented.

In conclusion, we would like to re-iterate that the Review Team is most impressed by the ambitions of Norway to become a society where lifelong learning is a reality to the benefit of its citizens and society at large, and by the systematic way it has created the pre-conditions. Indeed, we believe that if lifelong learning is to succeed anywhere, Norway is one of the most likely places in view of its history of reforms, co-operation among bodies, high educational standards and outcomes.

We wish to encourage the Government, the social partners, educational providers, the teachers unions, and indeed the Norwegian citizens in general to continue on this path of progress towards an inclusive lifelong learning society.

With clear policies, with inclusive consultation and communication, with equitable resourcing and with quality assurance mechanisms in place, and indeed with a champion who provides the leadership in steering the reforms, Norway will indeed be a lifelong learning society.

Annex II.A

Summary of Recommendations

Below the recommendations are listed under their section heading where the discussion leading to each recommendation occurred. We are aware that policy developments and actions since our review visit in October 2000 might have made some recommendations redundant.

3.1.1. Early childhood education

The State should work closely with each municipality to ensure that all children have access to appropriate early childhood care and education and to use a bundle of assistance programmes to achieve equitable educational and social outcomes simultaneously.

3.1.2. Primary and secondary education

Career guidance in lower secondary schools particularly for those pupils choosing the vocational stream is seen as needing some improvement.

The Review Team suggests that those upper secondary students who leave the education system before they have used up their statutory allowance be credited for the equivalent costs of the remainder years on a learning account in order to achieve the relevant learning outcomes.

Furthermore, we suggest that these students be given an exit certificate which details their achievements, explicitly describes their entitlement to: a) obtain future upper secondary education; b) have experience outside the school system (work, volunteer activity, etc.) assessed and accredited for the purpose of subsequent entry into education or the workplace (leaving open the possibility of never returning to secondary education); and c) receive whatever financial support might be made available once the financing strategy is in place.

3.1.3. Educational institutions on an intermediate level

With the increase in importance of the intermediate sector and its many private players, a national agency needs to collect data on intermediate institutions and disseminate the data more broadly.

3.1.4. School management

We recommend that school principals be included in the national dialogues on policy development and implementation.

We recommend that the relationships between state, county and municipalities be re-examined to ensure that bureaucratic structures are aligned to current and future practice in management and, particularly, in quality assurance.

221

3.1.5. Teachers

We recommend that the concerns of teachers unions be fully considered in the discussions concerning the future of the education system, its composition, funding and goals, and in the implementation of the Competence Reform.

We recommend that teacher education be reviewed to ensure an adequate supply of appropriately qualified teachers for all schools.

We recommend that the role of teachers be redefined to include, where possible, responsibilities for the education of adults through the school system. At the same time, teacher training, especially for teachers of upper secondary schools, needs an increased emphasis on adult learning.

We further recommend that teachers' bilingual capacity in schools with immigrants be counted as a qualification for salary purposes.

We also recommend that the emphasis on ICT in teacher training be expanded to ensure that all teachers and administrators understand ICT, its appropriate uses, its potential benefits and drawbacks.

3.2.1. Higher education

We suggest that the higher education system be encouraged to implement the Bologna Declaration by introducing Bachelor and Master courses, where appropriate, and to align the degree structure to that of many other OECD countries.

We further suggest that the recommendations of the Mjøs Commission promoting the international orientation of institutions and individuals be adopted.

We recommend that universities and colleges establish governing boards with a majority of members from outside the institution; the exact composition and terms of reference to be negotiated between the Ministry, the Norwegian Council of Universities and Colleges and other organisations, if appropriate.

3.2.5. Seniors

With the increase in average life expectancy it is important that the State address how to engage seniors in life and work and how to provide them with learning opportunities to make the last years of life meaningful, fulfilling, and productive.

4.3.4. The Aetat

To the Review Team the most evident task for the Aetat in the Competence Reform would seem to be to provide:

- *information to the unemployed and job-seekers about the opportunities offered by the Competence Reform. As the target group for the Aetat are individuals with a weak position on the labour market it would appear very natural and valuable for the Competence Reform to use the contacts and networks of the Aetat.*

- *the education and training unemployed individuals will need to get a job, and to get a foothold in working life.*

- *assessments of the qualifications of individuals. Useful experience in this field must have been acquired by the Aetat that could be used in the Competence Reform. Especially its knowledge about assessment of informal qualifications may be helpful.*

We suggest that one-stop shops be established which include in their services information and advice on education and training options for groups outside the public education and labour market system.

4.5.1. Competence or qualifications framework

We recommend that a national framework be developed to ensure transparent national standards of competencies.

4.5.2. Documentation of non-formal learning

We support the recommendation of the Competence Reform that a system for documenting and evaluating non-formal learning be established and disseminated.

We recommend a review of the current process for developing national consistency in the documentation and evaluation of non-formal learning.

4.5.3. Shifting the focus from inputs to outcomes

We recommend that the documentation of competencies focus on assessing the outcomes of learning in a manner that translates both into job qualifications as well as school credits, and that it be capable of recognising these competencies wherever or however they have been acquired.

The learning outcomes should not be expressed in terms of grades, course content, or performance ratings, but rather as descriptions of what an individual knows and is able to do. Taken together this is no simple task; it will certainly require creativity and hard work on the part of willing and committed representatives from both sectors. Again, we suggest that Norway look to international experience in assessing the outcomes of learning to aid its own efforts.

5.1.1. The role of the State

We recommend that high-level communication channels be established or re-established between the different stakeholders in the lifelong learning and Competence Reform agenda.

5.1.2. The role of the social partners

We recommend that the interest of the social partners in lifelong learning be utilised and the demarcation lines between the responsibilities of different actors be clarified.

5.2. The Competence Building Programme

The Review Team recommends that funds continue to be allocated to study and evaluate how ICTs might facilitate learning for different groups and in what instances it should be utilised.

The Review Team recommends that learning institutions and enterprises work toward standards for the development and delivery of ICT facilitated learning that ensure it is of the highest quality possible instead of letting all organisations develop their own manner of ICT-delivered learning.

The Review Team recommends that the Government review the adequacy of the institutional arrangement concerning funding, research, evaluation and dissemination of results of distance education and ICT-based methods.

The Review Team recommends that the Government review access to PCs and broadband.

5.3. Shifting from teacher-centred to learner-centred learning

Previous OECD reports have commented on the state of teaching in tertiary education institutions (see "The design and delivery of the curriculum: teaching and learning" in OECD (1998a), Redefining Tertiary Education, Paris, pp. 55-68). We recommend implementation of their recommendations.

223|

5.4.1. Innovation

The Review Team suggests that a register be established for all the initiatives funded under the Competence Reform by the Ministry of Education and the Ministry of Trade and Industry and other funding bodies, and that all initiatives be monitored, evaluated and the evaluation results be disseminated to all stakeholders, in order to facilitate system wide learning.

We suggest that the Government establish an innovation fund for education, training and learning which would be administered like a research fund, i.e. with peer reviewed applications with objectives and expected outcomes, with timelines and budgets, with an evaluation and dissemination component. The Government has to consider where to locate this fund organisationally.

We suggest that higher education institutions be encouraged to establish innovation funds, e.g. strategic initiatives funds, teaching development or research funds which build on their strengths. Schools, municipalities and counties should also be stimulated to work in this direction.

5.4.2. Research

The Review Team recommends that mechanisms be developed to fund and utilise further research for policy development and implementation.

5.5. Evaluation and dissemination

The Review Team recommends that mechanisms be developed to ensure both institutional and system wide learning from Government funded projects.

5.6. The shift from central steering to market mechanisms

We recommend that the Ministry of Education, Research and Church Affairs shift its emphasis from a supply-driven model to a demand-driven model in its shaping of the education system; that it reduce its direct and daily influence by creating a network of interdependent though autonomous institutions; that it create a "level playing field" for all actors in the education system, by giving students choice in all phases of their life.

5.7. Resources and financing

We recommend that the public be informed as soon as feasible what their learning rights are, e.g. free entitlements as students, citizens and workers and who will fund additional education and training – tuition and living costs.

5.8. Information

We propose that an instrument be developed which shows the pathways and the funding arrangements for various learning opportunities for the school-age population, adults "catching up" on their educational entitlements (distinguishing between those in employment, those unemployed, those retired), adults in continuing and further education, etc.

We also recommend that an information system easily accessible by the public be created to act as both a central source of location of information about the entire lifelong learning system and a starting point for taking advantage of lifelong learning opportunities.

6.1. Leadership and governance

The Review Team suggests that in the further implementation of the lifelong learning agenda a whole-of-government approach be adopted with ministerial level officials involved in driving the implementation.

We further suggest that the Prime Minister ask the Minister for Education, Research and Church Affairs to co-ordinate the implementation of the lifelong learning agenda across the various ministries.

6.2. Equity

We recommend that the Government as part of its equity and regional agenda make explicit how the learning rights of minority and marginal groups can be realised.

We further recommend that the Government make explicit how regional development agendas will be safeguarded in the move to market-driven educational provisions.

6.3. Quality

We recommend that the present system of data collection and dissemination across all educational providers be evaluated and updated, that this complement local data collection and that the data be used for monitoring and evaluation in order to promote organisational learning in all educational establishments.

We recommend that a Centre for Assessment and Accreditation be established, as proposed in the Mjøs Report, with the following additional broad tasks:

- give guidance on quality assurance to all providers of lifelong learning;
- develop a system of benchmarking for national and international comparison and institutional and system learning; and
- provide information and feedback on performance indicator and best practice to providers of lifelong learning, the State, and the public.

Bibliography

EUROSTAT (1997),
  Continuing Vocational Training Survey in Enterprises: Results, Office des publications officielles des Communautés européennes, Luxembourg.

MINISTRY OF EDUCATION, RESEARCH AND CHURCH AFFAIRS (KUF) (1998*a*),
  "Alternative Approaches to Financing Lifelong Learning Country Report: Norway", Oslo.

MINISTRY OF EDUCATION, RESEARCH AND CHURCH AFFAIRS (KUF) (1998*b*),
  The Competence Reform, Report to the *Storting* No. 42 (1997-98), May, Oslo.

MINISTRY OF EDUCATION, RESEARCH AND CHURCH AFFAIRS (KUF) (2000*a*),
  The Competence Reform in Norway: Plan of Action 2000-2003, May, Oslo.

MINISTRY OF EDUCATION, RESEARCH AND CHURCH AFFAIRS (KUF) (2000*b*),
  Freedom with Responsibility: On higher education and research in Norway, Mjøs Commission, Oslo.

MINISTRY OF EDUCATION, RESEARCH AND CHURCH AFFAIRS (KUF) (2000*c*),
  "OECD Education Policy Review: Lifelong Learning in Norway: Draft Background Report", September, Oslo.

MINISTRY OF EDUCATION, RESEARCH AND CHURCH AFFAIRS (KUF) (2001),
  Do Your Duty – Claim Your Right: Quality Reform of Higher Education, Oslo.

NOU (1997),
  New Competence – The Basis for a Comprehensive Policy for Continuing Education, Norwegian Royal Commission Report No. 25, Oslo.

NOU (1999),
  Nyttige lærepenger, Report of the Aamodt Commission, Vol. 33, Oslo.

NOU (2000*a*),
  Frihet med ansvar. Om høgre utdanning og forskning i Norge, Report of the Mjøs Commission, Oslo.

NOU (2000*b*),
  Mellom barken og veden, Report of the Berg-Commission, Vol. 5, Oslo.

OECD (1988),
  Review of National Policies for Education: Norway, Paris.

OECD (1990),
  Review of National Education Policies for Education: Norway, Paris.

OECD (1996),
  Lifelong Learning for All, Paris.

OECD (1997*a*),
  Implementing the OECD Jobs Strategy: Member countries' experience, Paris.

OECD (1997*b*),
"Thematic Review of the First Years of Tertiary Education: Norway", Paris.

OECD (1998*a*),
Redefining Tertiary Education, Paris.

OECD (1998*b*),
"Thematic Review of Early Childhood and Care Policy: Norway", Paris.

OECD (1998*c*),
"Thematic Review of the Transition from Initial Education to Working Life: Norway, Country Note", Paris.

OECD (1999),
OECD *Economic Surveys: Norway*, February, Paris.

OECD (2000*a*),
From Initial Education to Working Life: Making Transitions Work, Paris.

OECD (2000*b*),
Labour Force Statistics 1979-1999, Paris.

OECD (2000*c*),
OECD *Economic Outlook*, No. 68, December, Paris.

OECD (2000*d*),
OECD *Economic Surveys: Norway*, February, Paris.

OECD (2000*e*),
OECD *Employment Outlook*, Paris.

OECD (2000*f*),
"Thematic Review on Adult Learning: Norway", Paris.

OECD (2001),
Education Policy Analysis, Paris.

REKKEDAL, T. and MØYSTAD, E. (1999),
"Recruitment Barriers to Learning on the Internet", NKI.

RESEARCH COUNCIL OF NORWAY (1998),
"The Programme for Bridging the Gap Between Industry and Research: Strategic Platform", Division of Industry and Energy, 17 September.

OECD PUBLICATIONS, 2, rue André-Pascal, 75775 PARIS CEDEX 16
PRINTED IN FRANCE
(91 2002 01 1 P) ISBN 92-64-19722-2 – No. 52409 2002